A
BOOK OF
IRELAND

.

edited by
FRANK O'CONNOR

THE
BLACKSTAFF PRESS
BELFAST

First published in 1959 by
William Collins Sons and Company Limited
This Blackstaff Press edition is a photolithographic facsimile
of the text of the first edition printed by Collins Clear-Type
Press, with a new selection of photographs

This new edition published in 1991 by
The Blackstaff Press Limited
3 Galway Park, Dundonald, Belfast BT16 0AN,
Northern Ireland
with the assistance of
The Arts Council of Northern Ireland

The acknowledgements on pp. 7–8 constitute an extension of
this copyright page

Printed by The Guernsey Press Company Limited

British Library Cataloguing in Publication Data

A Book of Ireland
1. Ireland. English literature
I. O'Connor, Frank *1903–1966*
820.809415

ISBN 0-85640-458-6

In Memoriam
A. E. COPPARD

ACKNOWLEDGEMENTS

Grateful acknowledgement is made to:

BASIL BLACKWELL for permission to quote from *Dublin Days* by L.A.G. Strong

BODLEY HEAD for permission to quote from *Portrait of the Artist as a Young Man* by James Joyce

JONATHAN CAPE for permission to quote from *Fishmonger's Field* by A.E. Coppard; for permission to quote from *Paddy the Cope* by Patrick Gallagher; for permission to quote from *Going Into Exile* by Liam O'Flaherty

THE ESTATE OF PADRAIC COLUM for permission to reprint 'An old woman of the roads', 'A drover', 'I shall not die for thee' (trans.), 'The poor girl's meditation' (trans.) and 'She moved through the fair'

CONSTABLE AND COMPANY for permission to reprint 'Non dolet' from *Collected Poems* by Oliver St John Gogarty

PETER FALLON for permission to reprint 'Inniskeen Road: July evening' from *Ploughman and Other Poems* and 'Memory of Brother Michael' from *A Soul for Sale* by Patrick Kavanagh

JOHN FARQUHARSON for permission to quote from *Experiences of an Irish RM* by E.OE. Somerville and Martin Ross

THE ESTATE OF ROBERT GIBBINGS for permission to quote from *Lovely is the Lee*

A.M. HEATH AND COMPANY for permission to reprint 'Going to the dogs' and 'After hours' by Brian O'Nolan ('Flann O'Brien')

MACMILLAN LONDON for permission to quote from *The Irish Countryman* by Conrad Arensberg; for permission to quote from *The Gap of Brightness* by F.R. Higgins; for permission to quote from *Inishfallen, Fare Thee Well* by Sean O'Casey

MERCIER PRESS for permission to quote from *The Tailor and Ansty* by Eric Cross

JOHN MURRAY for permission to reprint 'Sunday in Ireland' from *Selected Poems* by John Betjeman

OXFORD UNIVERSITY Press for permission to quote from *The Western Isle* by Robin Flower

PETERS FRASER AND DUNLOP for permission to quote from *Irish Miles, The Siege of Howth* (trans.), *The Big Fellow, Leinster, Munster and Connacht, Voyage of Maelduin* (trans.), and *History of Ireland* by Frank O'Connor; for permission to reprint translations by Frank O'Connor of the following poems: 'The Tipperary woodlands', 'Kilcash', 'County Mayo', 'Who'll carve the pig?', 'On Baile's Strand', 'The Viking terror', 'Hugh Maguire', 'Patrick Sarsfield', 'A wild hope', 'Last lines', 'Slievenamon', 'Jealousy', 'A learned mistress', 'To Tomaus Costello at the wars', 'The swimmer', 'Into exile', 'The end of Deidre', 'Grief', 'Irish courtship', 'Scholars', 'The student', 'The scholar and his cat', 'Liadain', 'The old woman of Beare', 'She is my dear', 'Raftery the poet', 'The orphan', 'The lament for yellow-haired Donogh', 'The warrior', 'Generosity', 'Ireland *v.* Rome', 'The priest', 'Thoughts', 'An old flame' and 'To a boy'; and for permission to reprint the Introduction

POOLBEG PRESS for permission to quote from *Call My Brother Back* by Michael McLaverty

ROUTLEDGE for permission to quote from *Stone Mad* by Seumas Murphy

DOUGLAS SEALY for permission to reprint 'My grief on the sea' (trans.) and 'Ringleted youth of my love' (trans.) by Douglas Hyde

THE SOCIETY OF AUTHORS on behalf of the estate of George Bernard Shaw for permission to quote from *Letters to Florence Barr* and *Music in London* by George Bernard Shaw

THE SOCIETY OF AUTHORS on behalf of the copyright holder, Mrs Iris Wise, for permission to quote from *The Charwoman's Daughter, Irish Writing* and *George Moore* (radio broadcast) and for permission to reprint 'Righteous anger' and 'Joy be with us' from *Collected Poems* by James Stephens

THORNTON BUTTERWORTH for permission to quote from *Old Ireland* by A.M. Sullivan

A.P. WATT AND SONS for permission to quote from *An Irish Journey* by Sean O'Faolain

The publishers have made every effort to trace and acknowledge copyright holders. We apologise for any omissions in the above list and we will welcome additions or amendments to it for inclusion in any reprint edition.

CONTENTS

	Page
INTRODUCTION: FRANK O'CONNOR	19
PROLOGUE: The Irish Dancer ANONYMOUS	25

Places

Sunday in Ireland JOHN BETJEMAN *Selected Poems*	27
The Bells of Shandon FRANCIS SYLVESTER MAHONY ("FATHER PROUT")	29
Cork SEAN O'FAOLAIN *An Irish Journey*	31
Londonderry SEAN O'FAOLAIN *An Irish Journey*	33
Coleraine SEAN O'FAOLAIN *An Irish Journey*	34
Belfast MICHAEL MCLAVERTY *Call My Brother Back*	35
Gougane Barra J. J. CALLANAN	37
In Kerry ASENATH NICHOLSON *The Bible in Ireland*	38
Killarney MR. AND MRS. S. C. HALL *Ireland: Its Scenery, Character, etc.*	40
The Splendour Falls ALFRED, LORD TENNYSON *The Princess*	41
The Dingle Peninsula FRANK O'CONNOR *Irish Miles*	42
The Passage at Night—The Blaskets ROBIN FLOWER *The Western Island*	43
The Tipperary Woodlands ANONYMOUS	44
Kilcash ANONYMOUS	45
The Castle GEORGE BORROW *Lavengro*	47
The Dead at Clonmacnoise T. W. ROLLESTON	50
The Grave of Rury T. W. ROLLESTON	51
The County of Mayo THOMAS LAVELLE	52
The Lake Isle of Innisfree W. B. YEATS	53
The Starling Lake SEUMAS O'SULLIVAN	53
County Mayo ANTHONY RAFTERY	54
The Winding Banks of Erne WILLIAM ALLINGHAM	55
Inniskeen Road: July Evening PATRICK KAVANAGH *Ploughman and Other Poems*	59
Meath and Cavan FRANK O'CONNOR *Irish Miles*	59
A Dublin Street SEAN O'CASEY *Inishfallen, Fare Thee Well*	61
Prelude J. M. SYNGE *Poems and Translations*	62
The Oppression of the Hills J. M. SYNGE *In Wicklow and West Kerry*	63

9

History

The Fighting Race J. I. C. CLARKE   65
Who'll Carve The Pig? ANONYMOUS   67
The Death of Mess Gegra ANONYMOUS   *The Siege of Howth*   69
On Baile's Strand ANONYMOUS   71
The Viking Terror ANONYMOUS   74
The Origin of the Battle of Clontarf, A.D. 1014 GEOFFREY KEATING
    History of Ireland   74
The Return From Fingal, A.D. 1014 GEOFFREY KEATING *History
    of Ireland*   76
Kincora Attributed to MAC LIAG   79
The Unforgiven Crime W. B. YEATS *The Dreaming of the Bones*   81
Dark Rosaleen ANONYMOUS   82
Hugh Maguire EOCHY O'HUSSEY   85
The Jacobite War:
    (1) Jacobite: Patrick Sarsfield ANONYMOUS   87
    (2) Williamite: The Boyne Water ANONYMOUS   89
A Wild Hope ANONYMOUS   91
Last Lines EGAN O'RAHILLY   91
The Irish Problem Solved JONATHAN SWIFT *A Modest Proposal*   92
The New Nation JONATHAN SWIFT *The Drapier's Fourth Letter*   94
The Querist, 1735 GEORGE BERKELEY, BISHOP OF CLOYNE   95
The Wearing of The Green   ANONYMOUS   96
The Irish Anthem RUDYARD KIPLING *Humorous Tales*   97
The Shan Van Vocht *Popular Song*   99
The First French Invasion, 1796 THEOBOLD WOLFE TONE
    Journal   100
Slievenamon ANONYMOUS   107
The French Land, 1798 Recorded by RICHARD HAYES *The Last
    Invasion of Ireland*   108
Last Words, 1803 ROBERT EMMET   110
When He Who Adores Thee THOMAS MOORE   111
She is Far From The Land THOMAS MOORE   112
The Famine JOHN MITCHEL   113
The Uncrowned King R. BARRY O'BRIEN *The Life of Charles
    Stewart Parnell*   114
The Dead King JAMES JOYCE *Portrait Of The Artist As A
    Young Man*   115
Parnell W. B. YEATS *Collected Poems*   118
The Englishman in Ireland: Galway Gaol, 1888 WILFRID
    SCAWEN BLUNT *Poems*   118

Poblacht Na H Eireann. The Provisional Government of the
    Irish Republic to the People of Ireland, 1916   119
Easter 1916   W. B. YEATS   *Collected Poems*   121
A Dublin Ballad: 1916 SIR ARNOLD BAX ("DERMOT O'BYRNE")   123
The Death of Collins, 1922 FRANK O'CONNOR *The Big Fellow*   125

Pastoral and Town Life

Irish Hospitality—I LE CHEVALIER DE LA TOCNAYE   128
Irish Hospitality—II ASENATH NICHOLSON *The Bible in Ireland* 129
An Old Woman of the Roads PADRAIC COLUM   131
Boy in Ireland PATRICK GALLEGHER *Paddy the Cope*   132
The Hiring Fair PATRICK GALLEGHER *Paddy the Cope*   134
After the Storm ASENATH NICHOLSON *The Bible in Ireland*   136
A Drover PADRAIC COLUM   137
Four Ducks on a Pond WILLIAM ALLINGHAM   139
Merry Christmas, 1778 SIR JONAH BARRINGTON *Personal
    Sketches*   139
The Tragedy of Sir Kit MARIA EDGEWORTH *Castle Rackrent*   144
At the Show E. Œ. SOMERVILLE and MARTIN ROSS *Experiences
    of an Irish R. M.*   148
Sport E. Œ. SOMERVILLE and MARTIN ROSS *Experiences of an
    Irish R. M.*   150
The Roscarberry Foxhounds Judgment by LORD O'BRIEN OF
    KILFENORA *Irish Law Reports, 1907*   154
The Master of Hounds ANTHONY TROLLOPE *The Land Leaguers* 155
The Deserted Village OLIVER GOLDSMITH *The Deserted Village* 159
But a Bold Peasantry WILFRID SCAWEN BLUNT *The Canon of
    Aughrim*   161
17th Century Dublin RICHARD HEAD   164
Dublin Street Cries JONATHAN SWIFT *An Examination of
    Certain Abuses*   165
Cockles and Mussels ANONYMOUS   167
Going to the Dogs BRIAN O'NOLAN ("FLANN O'BRIEN") *The
    Bell*   168
The Yellow Bittern CATHAL BUIDHE MACELGUN   171
After Hours BRIAN O'NOLAN ("FLANN O'BRIEN") *The Bell*   172

People Great and Small

A Fair People SAMUEL JOHNSON *Boswell's Life of Johnson*   176
These Irish RINUCINNI   176
These Friendly Irish WILLIAM MAKEPEACE THACKERAY *Irish
    Sketch Book*   176

Nice But— ANTHONY TROLLOPE *Autobiography*   177
Decent People ANONYMOUS *Letter, 1825*   178
Temperament ANTHONY TROLLOPE *Autobiography*   178
Carolan OLIVER GOLDSMITH *Prose Works*   180
Oliver Goldsmith WILLIAM MAKEPEACE THACKERAY *English*
   Humorists   182
Sir Boyle Roche SIR JONAH BARRINGTON *Personal Sketches*   183
The Forgetful Poet SYDNEY SMITH *Letter to Thomas Moore*   186
A Loyalist GEORGE BORROW *Lavengro*   186
A Man of the World J. M. SYNGE *In Wicklow and West Kerry*   188
Richard Adams, Limerick County Court Judge A. M. SULLIVAN
   Old Ireland   189
Adams Again MAURICE HEALY *The Old Munster Circuit*   192
A Parson ANTHONY TROLLOPE *The Land Leaguers*   192
Miss Martin of Connemara MARIA EDGEWORTH *Tour in*
   Connemara   193
Miss Makebelieve of Dublin JAMES STEPHENS *The Charwoman's*
   Daughter   196
A Language Enthusiast GEORGE MOORE *Hail and Farewell*   199
A. E., Yeats, Synge and Moore JAMES STEPHENS *The*
   Charwoman's Daughter   201
Yeats MAIRE NIC SHIUBHLAIGH and EDWARD KENNY *The*
   Splendid Years   203
Synge MAIRE NIC SHIUBHLAIGH and EDWARD KENNY *The*
   Splendid Years   205
George Moore JAMES STEPHENS *Radio Broadcast, 1949*   206
George Moore W. B. YEATS *Dramatis Personae*   210
The Great Lady and The Great Man:
   (1) LADY GREGORY *The Journals*   212
   (2) SEAN O'CASEY *Inishfallen, Fare Thee Well*   214
   (3) LADY GREGORY *The Journals*   215
   (4) SEAN O'CASEY *Inishfallen, Fare Thee Well*   216
The Storyteller FRANK O'CONNOR *Leinster, Munster and Connacht*   216
A Telephone Operator ROBERT GIBBINGS *Lovely is the Lee*   220
Epitaphs (1) by JONATHAN SWIFT   221
   (2) George Moore by W. B. YEATS *Dramatis Personæ* 221
   (3) by W. B. YEATS *Under Ben Bulben*   221

Humour, Romance and Sentiment

Righteous Anger JAMES STEPHENS *Collected Poems* 222
The Brewer's Man L. A. G. STRONG *Dublin Days* 222
Smart Boy JAMES STEPHENS *Irish Writing* 223
The Night Before Larry Was Stretched ANONYMOUS 228
The Old Orange Flute ANONYMOUS 230
Eating English Halfpence JONATHAN SWIFT *The Drapier's Fourth Letter* 232
The Tailor on Culture ERIC CROSS *The Tailor and Ansty* 233
The Tailor and Chronology ERIC CROSS *The Tailor and Ansty* 235
Mr. Lightfoot in the Green Isle A. E. COPPARD *Fishmonger's Fiddle* 237
Jealousy ANONYMOUS 241
A Learned Mistress ANONYMOUS 241
To Tomaus Costello at the Wars ANONYMOUS 242
The Swimmer ANONYMOUS 245
Into Exile ANONYMOUS 246
The Heart's A Wonder J. M. SYNGE *The Playboy of the Western World* 246
Legal Aid MAURICE HEALY *The Old Munster Circuit* 249
The End of Deirdre ANONYMOUS 250
Grief ANONYMOUS 252
Tragedy and Triumph LADY GREGORY *The Gaol Gate* 252

Customs and Beliefs

Irish Courtship—I ANONYMOUS 257
Irish Courtship—II BERNARD SHAW *Letters to Florence Farr* 257
Irish Courtship—III W. B. YEATS *Letters to Florence Farr* 258
Country Marriage CONRAD ARENSBERG *The Irish Countryman* 259
Innocent Amusement, 1783 SIR JONAH BARRINGTON *Personal Sketches* 262
A Landlord's Amusement ARTHUR YOUNG *Tour in Ireland* 264
An Irish Election, 18th Century MARIA EDGEWORTH *Castle Rackrent* 265
Carlyle Observes the Savages:
  (1) Catholic THOMAS CARLYLE *Reminiscences of My Irish Journey* 269
  (2) Protestant THOMAS CARLYLE *Reminiscences of My Irish Journey* 271

The Art of Perjury MAURICE HEALY *The Old Munster Circuit* 272
The Perjurer Purged MAURICE HEALY *The Old Munster Circuit* 273
Style MATTHEW ARNOLD *The Study of Celtic Literature* 275
Scholars ANONYMOUS 276
The Student ANONYMOUS 277
Crow Street Theatre SIR JONAH BARRINGTON *Personal Sketches* 278
First Night at the Abbey MAIRE NIC SHIUBHLAIGH and EDWARD
    KENNY *The Splendid Years* 281
The American Wake LIAM O'FLAHERTY *Going Into Exile* 284
Aran Funeral J. M. SYNGE *The Aran Islands* 287
Dublin Funeral—I BERNARD SHAW *Music in London* 289
Dublin Funeral—II SEAN O'CASEY *Inishfallen, Fare Thee Well* 292
Tombstones SEUMAS MURPHY *Stone Mad* 295

Poems, Songs and Ballads

The Scholar and His Cat ANONYMOUS 298
Liadain ANONYMOUS 299
The Old Woman of Beare ANONYMOUS 300
The Sweetness of Earth ANONYMOUS 304
Woodlore ANONYMOUS 305
She Is My Dear ANONYMOUS 307
I Shall Not Die for Thee ANONYMOUS 308
Dear Dark Head ANONYMOUS 309
Raftery the Poet ANTHONY RAFTERY 310
The Orphan ANONYMOUS 310
My Grief on the Sea ANONYMOUS 311
Ringleted Youth of My Love ANONYMOUS 312
The Outlaw of Loch Lene ANONYMOUS 313
Pearl of the White Breast ANONYMOUS 314
The Poor Girl's Meditation ANONYMOUS 316
The Lament for Yellow-Haired Donogh ANONYMOUS 317
Let Us Be Merry Before We Go JOHN PHILPOT CURRAN 318
At The Mid Hour of Night THOMAS MOORE 319
The Nameless One J. C. MANGAN 320
Twenty Golden Years Ago J. C. MANGAN 322
The Song of Wandering Aengus W. B. YEATS *Collected Poems* 324
A Prayer for My Daughter W. B. YEATS *Collected Poems* 325
On Behalf of Some Irishmen Not Followers of Tradition GEORGE
    RUSSELL ("A. E.") *Selected Poems* 327
Non Dolet OLIVER ST. JOHN GOGARTY *Collected Poems* 329
John-John THOMAS MACDONAGH *Poems* 329
Last Lines—1916 PADRAIC PEARSE 313

Padraic O'Conaire, Gaelic Storyteller F. R. HIGGINS *The Gap
   of Brightness*   332
Memory of Brother Michael PATRICK KAVANAGH *A Soul for
   Sale*   334
She Moved Through The Fair PADRAIC COLUM   335
The Maid of the Sweet Brown Knowe ANONYMOUS   335
Ballinderry ANONYMOUS   337
I Know Where I'm Going ANONYMOUS   337
Johnny, I Hardly Knew Ye ANONYMOUS   338
Shule Aroon ANONYMOUS   340

Religious and Philosophical

The Bridge of Glass ANONYMOUS *Voyage of Maelduin*   342
The Fairies—I CONRAD ARENSBERG *The Irish Countryman*   344
The Fairies—II WILLIAM ALLINGHAM   347
The Stolen Child W. B. YEATS *Collected Poems*   349
To the Leanan Sidhe THOMAS BOYD   350
The Warrior ANONYMOUS   352
Generosity ANONYMOUS   354
Gaelic Comes to England THE VENERABLE BEDE   354
Ireland v. Rome—I ANONYMOUS   355
Ireland v. Rome—II THE VENERABLE BEDE   355
Mo Chua and His Three Treasures GEOFFREY KEATING *History
   of Ireland*   361
Irish Missionaries: Seventh Century THE VENERABLE BEDE   362
The Priest ANONYMOUS   363
Thoughts ANONYMOUS   365
An Old Flame ANONYMOUS   366
The Penal Laws SYDNEY SMITH *Selections from the writings of
   the Rev. Sydney Smith*   368
And More Law SYDNEY SMITH *Selections from the writings of
   the Rev. Sydney Smith*   371
To a Boy ANONYMOUS   374
Prayer at Dawn DIARMUID O'SHEA   374

EPILOGUE: Joy Be With Us JAMES STEPHENS *Collected Poems* 376
PRINCIPAL DATES IN IRISH HISTORY   377
INDEX OF AUTHORS, SOURCES, FIRST LINES   379

ILLUSTRATIONS

between pages 32 and 33

CAVEHILL, BELFAST (Northern Ireland Tourist Board)
SLEA HEAD, DINGLE PENINSULA, COUNTY KERRY (Bord Fáilte)
GLEN OF AHERLOW, COUNTY TIPPERARY (Bord Fáilte)
THE WATERGATE, ENNISKILLEN, COUNTY FERMANAGH (Northern
    Ireland Tourist Board)

between pages 96 and 97

HALFPENNY BRIDGE, RIVER LIFFEY, DUBLIN (Bord Fáilte)
CASTLE ESPIE, STRANGFORD LOUGH, COUNTY DOWN (Northern
    Ireland Tourist Board)
THE BURREN, COUNTY CLARE (Bord Fáilte)
SLEMISH MOUNTAIN, COUNTY ANTRIM (Northern Ireland Tourist
    Board)

between pages 160 and 161

SCOTCH STREET, ARMAGH CITY (Northern Ireland Tourist Board)
MARSH'S LIBRARY, DUBLIN (Bord Fáilte)
DERRYCLARE LAKE, CONNEMARA, COUNTY GALWAY (Bord Fáilte)
BEN BULBEN MOUNTAIN, COUNTY SLIGO (Bord Fáilte)

between pages 224 and 225

COBH, COUNTY CORK (Bord Fáilte)
CAHIR CASTLE, COUNTY TIPPERARY (Bord Fáilte)
DERRY CITY (Northern Ireland Tourist Board)
INCH STRAND, COUNTY KERRY (Bord Fáilte)

between pages 288 and 289

POWERSCOURT HOUSE GARDENS, ENNISKERRY, COUNTY WICKLOW
    (Bord Fáilte)
ROCK OF CASHEL, COUNTY TIPPERARY (Bord Fáilte)
THE SKELLIGS, COUNTY KERRY (Bord Fáilte)
NESS COUNTRY PARK, COUNTY DERRY (Northern Ireland Tourist
    Board)

between pages 352 and 353

GLENIFF HORSESHOE, COUNTY SLIGO (Bord Fáilte)
SPERRIN MOUNTAINS, COUNTY TYRONE (Northern Ireland Tourist
    Board)
DUN AENGUS, INISHMORE, ARAN ISLANDS (Bord Fáilte)
LOUGH KEY FOREST PARK, COUNTY ROSCOMMON (Bord Fáilte)

INTRODUCTION

THIS book is one of a series in which the volumes already published are *Scotland*, *Wales* and *England*, and as these books differ each from the other, the present volume differs from them all, for reasons which have to do with historical circumstances rather than with editorial vagaries. Scotland and England have a long tradition in the use of their common tongue and could be adequately presented without recourse to Gaelic or Anglo-Saxon. The Welsh tradition is almost purely vernacular and includes the work of the great poet, Dafydd ap Gwilym, and the editor of the Welsh volume has had to translate a mass of material for which no English equivalent exists. This book differs from the other three, for whereas Ireland has a vernacular tradition as old as that of Wales, and a great part of the contents is in the form of translations, she has also a near contemporary school of major writers like Yeats, Synge, Lady Gregory, Joyce whose work demands representation.

Irish literature began within a century or so after the conversion of the country to Christianity, first by British missionaries in the south and later by St. Patrick's mission which mainly affected the north. The work of the former was the more enduring of the two for the church which St. Patrick founded was a European, diocesan church, but up to the twelfth century the Irish church was of the British type. Even at this time Ireland was a home for lost causes.

During the Dark Ages the country, in spite of the lawlessness of its hundred tiny kingdoms, was a real centre of cultural and religious activity, centred about monasteries of British type; little towns as these appeared to men who had passed through what remained of the great

19

Roman cities; a few streets of wooden huts with tiny churches scattered about them, the whole enclosed by some sort of rampart. Many of the clerics and nobles of Anglo-Saxon England were educated in such institutions, and Armagh had a quarter which was known as "The Third of the Saxons." Regularly burned, they regularly sprang up again. Towards the middle of the Danish period they produced larger churches and tall isolated belfries, and near its end they apparently developed gate-towers in the manner of Danish cities. As on the continent, a number that found themselves on trade routes developed into prosperous communities like Derry, Armagh and Ferns.

In these centres vernacular literature flourished in the form of the pseudo-histories we call sagas; romances, genealogies and a mass of delightful secular verse of which only fragments have come down to us. Apart from occasional poems like *The Scholar and his Cat* or *The Hermit* written by men who were very close to Latin culture, all this vernacular literature suffers from the lack of organisation peculiar to a literature which has no critical apparatus. The result of such a lack is invariably rationalisation. Much medieval literature suffers from it.

Take a simple example from the most famous of the sagas, *The Cattle Raid of Cooley*; this describes how Cu Chulainn single-handed defends Ulster during a Southern Irish invasion, while the men of Ulster are suffering from a peculiar thing called *noinden*. Not more than one in a thousand scribes and scholars knew that *noinden* is simply the Latin word *nundinae*, meaning a festival; they read it *noiden* which means "baby," and assumed it was some sort of illness resembling the illness of childbirth. Scholars of our own time, lacking the same critical apparatus, have turned this into *couvade*, a custom of certain primitive tribes in which the men take on the women's pains. The inability to understand a fairly straightforward Irish word resulted in a proliferation of sagas interpreting the reason for the imaginary illness. One, at least, is very beautiful. To understand the problem of Irish writers of the Dark Ages one has to imagine what the effect on ourselves would be if we had *no* clue to the meaning of an ordinary place name like Belfast. Driven back on rationalisation, we should have had to ask ourselves why it was that the bell was fast.

The monasteries were terribly destroyed during the Danish invasions; I have printed one fragment describing how the monks greeted a stormy night with pleasure because it would keep the Danish ships in harbour, as in the early days of the last war we in London greeted a moonlit night. The rulers moved into the Danish towns, and the style of the sagas and romances degenerated into bombast. It was not, of course, all loss. The story of Clontarf which Keating tells is from some saga about the life of King Brian that was modelled on the Icelandic sagas, with Brian's wife, Gormley, introduced as the Fatal Woman whom Scandinavian writers loved.

This was the Ireland the Normans invaded in the late twelfth century and on which they tried to impose their own genius for organisation. The process was largely a failure. The Norman-Irish aristocracy is represented here by a few of its delightful love poems, but apart from these it produced little in the way of literature. The link with the English crown which dragged Ireland into each English quarrel and made the country a battleground between great lords and kings, Protestants and Catholics, Williamites and Jacobites, condemned it to provincialism.

Modern Irish nationalism derives mainly from Swift. Swift is a strange character. He may, as most of his biographers believe, have regarded himself merely as an Englishman in exile; but English or Irish, he was determined that he should enjoy the same liberties as a native-born Englishman, and as a result the leaders of most of our subsequent revolutions, Emmett, Tone, Parnell and Collins are Irish *sans phrase*, Irish by birth and choice and not by race or religion. The temper of these revolutionary movements is all in *The Wearin' o' the Green*, the Irish Marseillaise. This little song, written in pseudo-Irish dialect, probably by an Ulster Presbyterian and set to what seems to be an adaptation of a Scottish pibroch, is our real national anthem. It gave a whole people of mixed race and religion a working conception of national identity, and made that idea seem as simple as the growing of the grass or the leaves. For what it meant to subsequent generations I refer the reader to Kipling. There is a whole world of pathos in Scawen Blunt's story of the nun who had written innocuous words to the tune so that the school-children could sing it without giving offence to the anti-Irish clergy. Imagine French school-children during the German occupation singing something like *Nuts in May* to the tune of the Marseillaise!

At the same time in a way that is not unfamiliar to historians, a contrary process was at work. By the time *The Wearin' o' the Green* was written, the Irish language and Irish cultural tradition were almost dead. But, having adopted a new allegiance, the very people whose ancestors had destroyed both were growing curious about them. It was the period of the Enlightenment and of the revival of folk-lore, and not only was there a considerable interest in Irish music, of which we can see the beginnings in Goldsmith's essay on Carolan, but, by way of Ossian, there was also a tentative groping backward to the saga culture. This received a tremendous impetus from two things: Arnold's mighty essay *On the Study of Celtic Literature* and the work of the German philologists who at last discovered what even the surviving Gaelic speakers did not know—how to read Old Irish. The study of Old Irish and of the Ulster Sagas is behind not only Yeats, Synge and Lady Gregory, but also behind Patrick Pearse and the Revolution of 1916 which culminated in the establishment of the Irish Free State.

That period, too, is over, and the theatre of Yeats, Synge and Lady Gregory has descended to pantomimes which parody the great sagas, and to Gaelic versions of American jazz songs. But tradition rarely dies, and while I write there are young men like James Plunkett, Benedict Kiely and Mervyn Wall who are seeking for a new ideal of national conduct.

In general I have used many of my own translations because they enabled me to emphasise what it was that impressed me in the originals. Where translations done by true poets have become part of English literature, I have not intruded my own efforts on the reader.

FRANK O'CONNOR

New York, 1959

PROLOGUE

The Irish Dancer

I am of Ireland,
And of the holy land
  Of Ireland.
Good Sir, pray I thee,
For of *saint charité*
Come and dance with me
  In Ireland.

ANONYMOUS (14th cent.)

Places

SUNDAY IN IRELAND

Bells are booming down the bohreens,
   White the mist along the grass.
Now the Julias, Maeves and Maureens
   Move between the fields to Mass.
Twisted trees of small green apple
Guard the decent whitewashed chapel,
Gilded gates and doorways grained,
Pointed windows richly stained
   With many-coloured Munich glass.

See the black-shawled congregations
   On the broidered vestment gaze,
Murmur past the painted stations
   As Thy Sacred Heart displays
Lush Kildare of scented meadows,
Roscommon, thin in ash-tree shadows,
And Westmeath the lake-reflected,
Spreading Leix the hill-protected,
   Kneeling all in silver haze?

In yews and woodbine, walls and guelder,
   Nettle-deep the faithful rest,
Winding leagues of flowering elder,
   Sycamore with ivy dressed,
Ruins in demesnes deserted,
Bog-surrounded, bramble-skirted—
Townlands rich or townlands mean as
These, oh, counties of them screen us
   In the Kingdom of the West.

27

Stony seaboard, far and foreign,
    Stony hills poured over space,
Stony outcrop of the Burren,
    Stones in every fertile place,
Little fields with boulders dotted,
Grey-stone shoulders saffron-spotted,
Stone-walled cabins thatched with reeds,
Where a Stone Age people breeds
    The last of Europe's stone age race.

Has it held, the warm June weather?
    Draining shallow sea-pools dry,
Where we bicycled together
    Down the bohreens fuchsia-high.
Till there rose, abrupt and lonely,
A ruined abbey, chancel only,
Lichen-crusted, time-befriended,
Soared the arches, splayed and splendid,
    Romanesque against the sky.

There in pinnacled protection
    One extinguished family waits
A Church of Ireland resurrection
    By the broken, rusty gates.
Sheepswool, straw and droppings cover
Graves of spinster, rake and lover,
Whose fantastic mausoleum
Sings its own seablown Te Deum
    In and out the slipping slates.

JOHN BETJEMAN (b. 1906)
Selected Poems

THE BELLS OF SHANDON

With deep affection,
And recollection,
I often think of
  Those Shandon bells,
Whose sounds so wild would,
In the days of childhood,
Fling around my cradle
  Their magic spells.
On this I ponder
Where'er I wander,
  And thus grow fonder,
Sweet Cork, of thee;
With thy bells of Shandon,
That sound so grand on
  The pleasant waters of the River Lee.

I've heard bells chiming
Full many a clime in,
Tolling sublime in
  Cathedral shrine,
While at a glib rate
Brass tongues would vibrate—
But all their music
  Spoke naught like thine;
For memory, dwelling
On each proud swelling
Of the belfry knelling
  Its bold notes free,
Made the bells of Shandon
Sound far more grand on
The pleasant waters
  Of the River Lee.

I've heard bells tolling
Old Adrian's Mole in,
Their thunder rolling
   From the Vatican,
And cymbals glorious
Swinging uproarious
In the gorgeous turrets
   Of Notre Dame;
But thy sounds were sweeter
Than the dome of Peter
Flings o'er the Tiber,
   Pealing solemnly—
O, the bells of Shandon
Sound far more grand on
The pleasant waters
   Of the River Lee.

There's a bell in Moscow,
While on tower and kiosk O!
In Saint Sophia
   The Turkman gets,
And loud in air
Calls men to prayer
From the tapering summits
   Of tall minarets.
Such empty phantom
I freely grant them;
But there's an anthem
   More dear to me,—
'Tis the bells of Shandon,
That sound so grand on
The pleasant waters
   Of the River Lee.

FRANCIS SYLVESTER MAHONY
("Father Prout") (1804-66)

CORK

As for the pocket of the town itself, what the natives call "the flat of the city," or, really, in their own flat accent, "the flaat o' deh city," having lived in it all through my youth I know that there must be many corners in it that my homesick ghost will haunt. There is the whole length of the quays, especially the pleasant bits where there are a few trees, such as the North Mall, or the Sand Quay, or the bit near the Opera House, though there only at particular hours, such as at about five o'clock on a summer afternoon, or perhaps a little later than that, when the fishermen are drying their nets, or tarring their nets, and the angelus will soon be ringing in various tones and at various speeds all over the city, whose humming then slowly drops away into silence as the day ends. At such an hour Cork becomes without pretension the Lilliput it is. It offers no obstacle to the quiet tasting of quiet love. One season above all will haunt me, I know, and that for any corner of Cork—the time of the equinoctial gales: reminding us that Cork is a seaport and the sea at our door. Then the floods rise, the streets are sometimes submerged, and the winds from the ocean tear into the cup of the valley of the town. Then the age of the place, so well hidden under its rouge of paint (like a French seaport), is shamelessly exposed in the rattling and shaking and shivering and banging of all its poor decrepit parts. In these gales it flies in slivers through the air and, on mornings after gales, the streets where there are such houses are likely to be strewn with slates. The winters are hard here, and lashing rains, gutters spilling, pavements rippled with flood-water, hoardings flapping, and the news, passing from mouth to mouth like the gossip

in a Dutch town, that the river is rising, all give a great
sense of nearness to the elements. Cork, in its old
meaning of *marsh*, is never far from its origins in that
way—sleepy in summer, wet in winter. So that you soon
find out that the city is not merely built on a marsh but
on islands in the marsh, and that the streets are, often,
covered canals or rivers. Patrick Street is winding merely
because the river under it winds—one winter the river
burst the wood-paving and we saw it underneath; and
if you lean over the parapet near Patrick's Bridge you
will (or used to) see it emerge there into the Lee. The
South Mall was water—hence the name Morrison's
Island behind it. Drawbridge Street indicates that water
was near; it came up as a quay into Emmet Place. The
Coal Quay is not a quay now, but it was. Oh, but any
winter evening, stand on Montenotte, in the bay of some
cosy bourgeois house, and look down through the
battered, wind-rattling window at the rain-washed town,
and the spars of the ships on the quay shining in arc-
light, and you can recapture easily the maritime quality
of Cork. My father-in-law who lived away at the
farthest, western end of the city, in Sunday's Well, an
old sailor, used to hurl it all back on me when, as he lay
bedridden in the heel of his days, he would suddenly cock
an ear and say—"There's a ship coming up the river."
And I would lift my head, and ever so faint and far away,
out of the little, poky, stuffy sick-room, down the valley
of the city, down the river between its mudflats or on
its first loch, I would hear the gentle hoot of a siren, a
cock-crow of triumph for safe entry from the sea. The
arms of Cork record that endless adventure—a ship
entering between two castles. *Statio Bene Fida Carinis.*

SEAN O'FAOLAIN (*b.* 1900)
An Irish Journey

CAVEHILL, BELFAST
(Northern Ireland Tourist Board)

SLEA HEAD, DINGLE PENINSULA, COUNTY KERRY
(Bord Fáilte)

GLEN OF AHERLOW, COUNTY TIPPERARY
(Bord Fáilte)

THE WATERGATE, ENNISKILLEN, COUNTY FERMANAGH
(Northern Ireland Tourist Board)

LONDONDERRY

I landed in Derry the next night in the pitchy darkness of a coalhole black-out, which was unfortunate; for the journey up the river is a very pleasant one, and Derry is, to my mind, the loveliest of all Northern cities, and in normal times looks lovely at night from the fortifications, with all the little lights of the valley below you to the west, and shining across the river below you to the east. As, for Connaught, I would willingly live only in Ballina, for the North I would willingly live only in Londonderry. Its river is noble. The town has antiquity and dignity. It has some very fine houses—such as the Deanery. Its main shopping-district is bright and busy. Its size is about right, fifty thousand people—a little on the small side, perhaps, for a city but perfect for a large town.

I think that what makes me so fond of Derry is that it reproduces the pictorial effect of Cork—river, quays, hills, deep valley, and it has behind it the hinterland of the lovely Inishowen peninsula and all Donegal, just as Cork has the mountains to its west. If one took Cork, and bent it up in the middle, like the fallen-in cone of a volcano, or a great sombrero, that would be Derry. And when I got up in the morning and strolled around the ramparts, the Walls as they call them, wide enough to let forty men march abreast, and looked down over Bogside, towards the Clay Pits of Templemore and to the cathedral at Brooke Park, and saw all the little threads of morning smoke rising from the thousands and thousands of little houses far below, it was just like being up on Patrick's Hill in Cork, and seeing the smoke rising from the little homes of Blackpool and Barrack Street. The Walls are hemmed in by houses and streets, so that one could drop a pebble from the gravel at one's feet down a Bigside chimney, and see into the top-floor windows. . . .

Across the river, Waterside looked equally charming —the river pale, smooth, and motionless, reflecting the houses rising up Fountain Hill, or fading out into greenery beyond the barracks to the North. I climbed the cathedral tower, over the Ferry bastion, and got a glorious view over the whole width and stretch of Lough Foyle with the hills of Inishowen shining faintly beyond.

SEAN O'FAOLAIN (*b.* 1900)
An Irish Journey

COLERAINE

Apart from two songs—one about Kitty of Coleraine, and the other about Coleraine whisky—I could remember nothing about the town until I entered it. Then I realised that it was on the River Bann and I began to remember a little more than that. Swift stayed here. Lever, the author of those fine novels *Harry Lorrequer*, and *Charles O'Malley*, lived here. The MacDonnells of Antrim got a good lump of land here after the Flight of the Earls. In the Town Hall, in the square (which, as in Derry, is for some reason called the Diamond), is a window to commemorate the London Companies who originally took over the whole district from James I. Four miles to the west is the cyclopean fortress of Dun Ceithern, where the legendary Heroes of the Red Branch —the second to fourth century fighting men of Ulster— are reputed to have lived when not at Emain (now called Navan Fort) near Armagh. King Conor Mac Nessa (the Conchubar of the great Deirdre story) is said to have come down the river to stay at the fort now called Mount Sandel.

Coleraine is one of the cleanest market-towns in these

islands, solid and bright and comfortable. If a Norfolk man or a Kentish man were dropped into it he would feel so much at home that not until he noted such names as McClusky or McKimmins, would he see anything at all unusual enough for wonder. And that is what this really is—a British market-town, in a fine farming centre, with a lovely setting of wood and river. . . .

My new friend had the afternoon free and we motored up the Bann to see the country—of which any resident might well be as fond and proud as she was—and to see the salmon-falls and the eel-fisheries at Castleroe. If a Kentish man could feel at home in the town, he would not here: but I did. It could have been Castleconnel in Limerick, or a reach of the Nore, or a bend of the upper Lee. There is some alchemy of climate in Ireland that bedews the country-side with an unmistakable personality: it is in the softness of colour, the mobility of the light, the gentleness with which sound caresses the ear. There is a benevolence about Castleroe that is like the dreams of youth and the resignation of age; it has a lyrical quality, a smooth tempo, a friendly touch.

SEAN O'FAOLAIN (*b.* 1900)
An Irish Journey

BELFAST

At the top of the mountain they lay in the heather and gazed at Belfast spread out in the flat hollow below them, its lean mill chimneys stretched above the haze of smoke. Rows of red-bricked houses radiated on all sides and above them rose blocks of factories with many of their windows catching the sunlight.

They saw their own street and could make out the splash of white-wash on the wall that Alec had daubed there as a mark for his pigeons; it was all very far away like a street scene through the wrong end of a telescope. . . .

Their eyes ranged over the whole city to the low ridge of the Castlereagh Hills, netted with lovely fields and skimming cloud-shadows, to the blue U-shaped lough covered with yachts as small as paper boats, and steamers moving up towards the docks where the gantries stood like poised aeroplanes.

They shouted out to each other the names of all the churches that they knew: there were the green spires of Ardoyne where the sinners brought their great sins to the Passionists, there was the stumpy spire of the Monastery, and farther along in the heart of the city, sticking high above the smoke, were the sharp spires of St. Peter's—the church that was always crowded with shawled factory workers saying their beads. Near their own street was the Dominican Convent, its field very green and its hockey posts very white. And when Jamesy asked was it true that the nuns dug a bit of their graves each day and slept in their coffins at night Alec laughed: "It'd be a quare deep grave some of them ladies would have for they're as ould as the hills."

The numerous spires of the Protestant churches were everywhere. Then there was the Falls Park and they could see people walking about in it, and below it Celtic Football ground with its oval field and one grand stand, and farther to the right Linfield Ground with its tin advertisements for cigarettes. . . . The noise of the city came up to them; they heard a train whistle and saw its white fluttering scarf of smoke above the houses, burrowing through trees, rush past the Bog Meadows smashed with pools of water, and out into the quietude of the open fields.

MICHAEL McLAVERTY (*b.* 1907)
Call My Brother Back

GOUGANE BARRA

There is a green island in lone Gougane Barra,
Whence Allua of songs rushes forth like an arrow;
In deep Valley Desmond a thousand wild fountains
Come down to that lake, from their home in the
  mountains.
There grows the wild ash; and a time-stricken willow
Looks chidingly down on the mirth of the billow,
As, like some gay child that sad monitor scorning,
It lightly laughs back to the laugh of the morning.

And its zone of dark hills—oh! to see them all bright-
  'ning,
When the tempest flings out its red banner of lightning,
And the waters come down, 'mid the thunder's deep
  rattle,
Like clans from their hills at the voice of the battle;
And brightly the fire-crested billows are gleaming,
And wildly from Malloc the eagles are screaming:
Oh, where is the dwelling, in valley or highland,
So meet for the bard as this lone little island?

How oft, when the summer sun rested on Clara,
And lit the blue headland of sullen Ivera,
Have I sought thee, sweet spot, from my home by the
  ocean,
And trod all thy wilds with a minstrel's devotion,
And thought on the bards who, oft gathering together,
In the cleft of thy rocks, and the depth of thy heather,
Dwelt far from the Saxon's dark bondage and slaughter,
As they raised their last song by the rush of thy water!

High sons of the lyre! oh, how proud was the feeling
To dream while alone through that solitude stealing;

Though loftier minstrels green Erin can number,
I alone waked the strain of her harp from its slumber,
And gleaned the gray legend that long had been sleeping,
Where oblivion's dull mist o'er its beauty was creeping,
From the love which I felt for my country's sad story,
When to love her was shame, to revile her was glory!

Least bard of the free! were it mine to inherit
The fire of thy harp and the wing of thy spirit,
With the wrongs which, like thee, to my own land have
    bound me,
Did your mantle of song throw its radiance around me;
Yet, yet on those bold cliffs might Liberty rally,
And abroad send her cry o'er the sleep of each valley.
But rouse thee, vain dreamer! no fond fancy cherish,
Thy vision of Freedom in bloodshed must perish.

I soon shall be gone—though my name may be spoken
When Erin awakes and her fetters are broken—
Some minstrel will come in the summer eve's gleaming,
When Freedom's young light on his spirit is beaming,
To bend o'er my grave with a tear of emotion,
Where calm Avonbuee seeks the kisses of ocean,
And a wild wreath to plant from the banks of that river
O'er the heart and the harp that are silent forever.

                              J. J. CALLANAN (1795-1829)

IN KERRY

The sun had sunk behind a black mountain, twilight was
letting down her soft curtain upon the heathy landscape,
and not the buzz of an insect fell upon my ear. Not the
smoke of a cabin curled in the air, and neither man nor
beast met my admiring eye. From a far distant mountain,

a mournful sound fell on my ear. It was the wail for the dead. It swelled in heavy tones, and then died away, as they who chanted it descended a valley; thus alternately rising and falling, for five long miles, did this lamentation float on the air. The solitude, the lateness of the hour, my distance from the land of my fathers, among so primitive a people, whose Bible customs have been retained since the mourning for Jacob in the "threshing-floor of Atad," made this lamentation a pleasant mournful accompaniment over the barren waste I was walking. The rustics afterwards told me it was a lone old woman who had died in her cabin on the mountain, and she must be brought "to lie with her kin in the valley."

The shadows of night were now heavy on the outstretched bog before me. The road, long and dreary, was covered with coarse gravel, without the smoke of a cabin to tell me that I was not alone in the world. The stillness of death reigned; and not a sound broke upon my ear. Suddenly the barking of a dog from a far-distant mountain told me that I was in the precincts of man's abode. The Irish peasant dogs, like their masters, are patient and kind; many a one has met me at the door of a cabin, and instead of barking as a surly dog would, by the wagging of his tail and inviting look of the eye, said, "Walk in, walk in; my master will make ye welcome to our fire and our potato."

The next morning was beautiful. I soon found myself in something like a vast amphitheatre, with mountains piled on mountains, covered with heath, without a tree, the sun-rays streaming athwart from behind me to the top of the mountains before. I sat down to enjoy it upon a moss-hillock, and commenced singing, for the Kerry mountains are the best conductors of sound of any I have ever met. I had sung but a passage, when, from over a wide-stretched valley, a mountain boy, with a herd of cattle, struck up a lively piper's song, so clear and shrill that I gladly exchanged my psalmody for morning notes like these. I listened till a pause ensued, and again commenced; instantly he responded, and though the distance was a mile at least, yet alternately we kept up the song till his was lost in the distance.

Romantic as I was, the spot was more so; and as I sat upon a rock, eating a deliciously sweet and dry crust, with my bonnet and parasol by my side on this fairy spot, had youth and beauty been mine, some artist's pencil might have made a landscape of no small interest.

ASENATH NICHOLSON (*c.* 1800)
The Bible in Ireland

KILLARNEY

We put into a little creek on the opposite side of the river; but remained in our boat, having been recommended to do so. Our expectations of the coming treat had been highly raised, and we were in breathless anxiety to enjoy it. The bugle-player, Spillane—to whose skill and attention we gladly add our testimony to that of every traveller who had preceded us—landed, advanced a few steps, and placed the instrument to his lips—the effect was MAGICAL—the word conveys a poor idea of its effect. First he played a single note—it was caught up and repeated, loudly, softly, again loudly, again softly, and then as if by a hundred instruments, each a thousand times more musical than that which gave its rivals birth, twirling and twisting around the mountain, running up from its foot to its summit, then rolling above it, and at length dying away in the distance until it was heard as a mere whisper, barely audible, far away. Then Spillane blew a few notes—ti-ra-la-ti-ra-la: a multitude of voices, seemingly from a multitude of hills, at once sent forth a reply; sometimes pausing for a second, as if waiting for some tardy comrade to join in the marvellous chorus, then mingling together in a strain of sublime grandeur, and delicate sweetness, utterly indescribable. Again Spillane sent forth his summons to the mountains, and blew, for perhaps a minute, a variety of sounds; the effect was indeed that of "enchanting ravishment" giving

"resounding grace to all Heaven's harmonies."

It is impossible for language to convey even a remote idea of the exceeding delight communicated by this development of a most wonderful property of Nature; sure we are that we shall be guilty of no exaggeration if we say that this single incident, among so many of vast attraction, will be sufficient recompense to the tourist who may visit these beautiful lakes.

MR. AND MRS. S. C. HALL (1800-81)
Ireland: Its Scenery, Character, etc.

THE SPLENDOUR FALLS

The splendour falls on castle walls
    And snowy summits old in story:
The long light shakes across the lakes,
    And the wild cataract leaps in glory.
Blow, bugle, blow, set the wild echoes flying,
Blow bugle; answer, echoes, dying, dying, dying.

O hark, O hear! how thin and clear,
    And thinner, clearer, farther going!
O sweet and far from cliff and scar
    The horns of Elfland faintly blowing!
Blow, let us hear the purple glens replying:
Blow, bugle; answer, echoes, dying, dying, dying.

O love, they die in yon rich sky,
    They faint on hill or field or river:
Our echoes roll from soul to soul,
    And grow for ever and for ever.

Blow, bugle, blow, set the wild echoes flying,
And answer, echoes, answer, dying, dying, dying.

ALFRED, LORD TENNYSON (1809-92)
The Princess

THE DINGLE PENINSULA

We started out from Dingle against the same fierce west
wind which contested every inch of the road with us,
and a spattering rain that chased us frequently to the
uneasy shelter of a bush, but by the time we reached the
brow of the hill, the wind had rent the awning of cloud,
and little coloured rags of light fluttered through. We
climbed a wall, battered by the wind. The view was
magnificent. The sea was far away below; at the mouth
of the bay were Sybil Head and the Three Sisters, with
the snout of Teeracht, black and vicious like something
out of an El Greco background, showing round a headland to our left. Down the grey elephant pelt of the hills
behind streamed the long lines of the fences, caught in
the rush of the land as in a waterfall, wriggling and
twisting and jumping in sudden cascades that dragged
the little fields awry like faces drawn in pain, into cubes
and triangles, each with its own pale, bright, almost
hectic colour.

Brightest of all were the little chessboards of the corn-
fields where the stooks stood up in rows like golden
chessmen. The white-washed houses, poker-faced like
the figures of playing cards, were caught up in the rush
too, and stood not in the usual way of seaside houses,
looking all in one direction like a crowd at the races,
but staring stiffly in every direction out of the wind as
if they had been halted in some fantastic drill. By the
edge of the bay, where fields and fences grew bluer and
paler, was a black spit of rock with a fountain of foam
above it, and beyond it, the golden strand, with its silver

waves foamed into phosphorescent mist, was filling the hollow of the hills with its distant booming. Above them the great low, ragged rain-clouds trundled eastward out of the Atlantic, searching the fields with the misty rays of their sun-lanterns as if for something they had lost.

This was the Munster Thebaiad where the old monks, inspired by the stories of the desert fathers, flocked in thousands, putting off humanity and building themselves little beehive huts and Eskimo oratories fitter for seagulls than men. The remains of these are scattered everywhere about the stony hills, and in the middle of them the little twelfth-century church, its front bleached snow-white by the terrible winds, its high gable soaring to the heart-shaped finial which in Irish churches took the place of a cross, seemed a strange lost outpost of European civilisation. The carved doorway had a tympanum—plain but still an unusual feature in an Irish church; the north wall was panelled in half-columns which formed a frame for the windows, and there was a handsome little chancel arch much in the style of Cormac's Chapel. This is Cormac's country, and the church may even be another of his attempts to provide Ireland with a contemporary culture—poor man!

FRANK O'CONNOR (1903-1966)
Irish Miles

THE PASSAGE AT NIGHT—THE BLASKETS

The dark cliff towered up to the stars that flickered
And seemed no more than lights upon its brow,
And on the slippery quay
Men talked—a rush of Gaelic never-ending.
I stepped down to the boat,

A frail skin rocking on the unquiet water,
And at a touch she trembled
And skimmed out lightly to the moonlit seaway.
I lying in the stern
Felt all the tremble of water slipping under,
As wave on wave lifted and let us down.
The water from the oars dripped fiery; burning
With a dull glow great globes
Followed the travelling blades. A voice rose singing
To the tune of the running water and loud oars:
"I met a maiden in the misty morning,
And she was barefooted under rippling tresses.
I asked her was she Helen, was she Deirdre?
She answered: 'I am none of these but Ireland.
Men have died for me, men have still to die.'"
The voice died then, and, growing in the darkness,
The shape of the Great Island
Rose up out of the water hugely glooming,
And wearing lights like stars upon its brow.

ROBIN FLOWER (b. 1881)
The Western Island

THE TIPPERARY WOODLANDS

To the Irish, the English clearance of woodland represented the loss
of their old hunting grounds. This beautiful song deals with the
felling of the woods in the Dwyer country round Aherlow.

When once I rose at morning
The summer sun was shining,
I heard the horn awinding
    And birds' merry songs;
There were coney and beaver,
Woodcock and plover
And echo repeating
    The music of the guns;

The winded fox was flying,
Horsemen followed shouting,
Counting geese on the highway
  Some woman's heart was sore;
But now the woods are falling,
We must go over the water:
Shaun O'Dwyer of the Valley
  Your pleasure is no more.

Cause enough for grieving,
My shelter a-felling,
The north wind freezing
  And death in the sky;
My merry hound tied tightly
From sporting and chasing
That would lift a child's sorrow
  In noondays gone by.
The stag is on the mountain,
Swift and proud as ever;
He will come up the heather
  When our day is o'er.
All the woods are falling,
So we'll to the ships at Galway;
Shaun O'Dwyer of the Valley,
  Your pleasure is no more.

ANONYMOUS (17th cent.)
translated from the Irish by
FRANK O'CONNOR

KILCASH

What shall we do for timber?
  The last of the woods is down,
Kilcash and the house of its glory
  And the bell of the house are gone;

The spot where that lady waited
 Who shamed all women for grace,
When earls came sailing to greet her
 And Mass was said in the place.

My grief and my affliction
 Your gates are taken away,
Your avenue needs attention;
 Goats in the garden stray;
The courtyard's filled with water
 And the great earls where are they?
The earls, the lady, the people
 Beaten into the clay.

No sound of duck or geese there,
 Hawk's cry or eagle's call,
No humming of the bees there
 That brought honey and wax for all,
Nor even the song of the birds there
 When the sun has gone down in the west,
Nor a cuckoo on top of the boughs there,
 Singing the world to rest.

There's mist there tumbling from branches
 Unstirred by night and by day,
And a darkness falling from heaven,
 And our fortunes have ebbed away;
There's no holly nor hazel nor ash there;
 The pasture is rock and stone,
The crown of the forest is withered
 And the last of its game is gone.

I beseech of Mary and Jesus
 That the great come home again,
With long dances danced in the garden,
 Fiddle music and mirth among men,

That Kilcash, the home of our fathers,
  Be lifted on high again,
And from that to the deluge of waters
  In bounty and peace remain.

ANONYMOUS (18th cent.)
translated from the Irish by
FRANK O'CONNOR

THE CASTLE

One of the most peculiar features of this part of Ireland is the ruined castles, which are so thick and numerous that the face of the country appears studded with them, it being difficult to choose any situation from which one, at least, may not be descried. They are of various ages and styles of architecture, some of great antiquity, like the stately remains which crown the Crag of Cashel; others built by the early English conquerors; others, and probably the greater part, erections of the times of Elizabeth and Cromwell. The whole speaking monuments of the troubled and insecure state of the country, from the most remote periods to a comparatively modern time.

From the windows of the room where I slept I had a view of one of these old places—an indistinct one, it is true, the distance being too great to permit me to distinguish more than the general outline. I had an anxious desire to explore it. It stood to the south-east; in which direction, however, a black bog intervened, which had more than once baffled all my attempts to cross it. One morning, however, when the sun shone brightly upon the old building, it appeared so near, that I felt ashamed at not being able to accomplish a feat seemingly so easy; I determined, therefore, upon another trial. I reached the bog, and was about to venture upon its black surface, and to pick my way among its innumerable holes, yawning horribly, and half-filled with water

black as soot, when it suddenly occurred to me that there
was a road to the south, by following which I might find
a more convenient route to the object of my wishes. The
event justified my expectations, for, after following the
road for some three miles, seemingly in the direction of
the Devil's Mountain, I suddenly beheld the castle on
my left.

I diverged from the road, and, crossing two or three
fields, came to a small grassy plain, in the midst of which
stood the castle. About a gun-shot to the south was a
small village, which had, probably, in ancient days,
sprung up beneath its protection. A kind of awe came
over me as I approached the old building. The sun no
longer shone upon it, and it looked so grim, so desolate
and solitary; and here was I, in that wild country, alone
with that grim building before me. The village was
within sight, it is true; but it might be a village of the
dead for what I knew; no sound issued from it, no
smoke was rising from its roofs, neither man nor beast
was visible, no life, no motion—it looked as desolate as
the castle itself. Yet I was bent on the adventure, and
moved on towards the castle across the green plain,
occasionally casting a startled glance around me; and
now I was close to it.

It was surrounded by a quadrangular wall, about ten
feet in height, with a square tower at each corner. At
first I could discover no entrance; walking round, however, to the northern side, I found a wide and lofty
gateway with a tower above it, similar to those at the
angle of the wall; on this side the ground sloped gently
down towards the bog, which was here skirted by an
abundant growth of copse-wood, and a few evergreen
oaks. I passed through the gateway, and found myself
within a square enclosure of about two acres. On one
side rose a round and lofty keep, or donjon, with a
conical roof, part of which had fallen down, strewing
the square with its ruins. Close to the keep, on the other

side, stood the remains of an oblong house, built something in the modern style, with various window-holes; nothing remained but the bare walls and a few projecting stumps of beams, which seemed to have been half-burnt. The interior of the walls was blackened, as if by fire; fire also appeared at one time to have raged out of the window-holes, for the outside about them was black, portentously so.

"I wonder what has been going on here!" I exclaimed.

There were echoes along the walls as I walked about the court. I entered the keep by a low and frowning doorway: the lower floor consisted of a large dungeon-like room, with a vaulted roof; on the left hand was a winding stair-case in the thickness of the wall; it looked anything but inviting; yet I stole softly up, my heart beating. On the top of the first flight of stairs was an arched doorway, to the left was a dark passage, to the right, stairs leading still higher. I stepped under the arch, and found myself in an apartment somewhat similar to the one below, but higher. There was an object at the farther end.

An old woman, at least eighty, was seated on a stone, cowering over a few sticks burning feebly on what had once been a right noble and cheerful hearth; her side-glance was towards the doorway as I entered, for she had heard my footsteps. I stood suddenly still, and her haggard glance rested on my face.

"Is this your house, mother?" I at length demanded, in the language which I thought she would best understand.

"Yes, my house, my own house; the house of the broken-hearted."

"Any other person's house?" I demanded.

"My own house, the beggar's house—the accursed house of Cromwell!"

GEORGE BORROW (1803-81)
Lavengro

THE DEAD AT CLONMACNOISE

Nominally "from the Irish of Angus O'Gillan"; actually a highly
original poem.

In a quiet water'd land, a land of roses,
   Stands Saint Kieran's city fair;
And the warriors of Erin in their famous generations
   Slumber there.

There beneath the dewy hillside sleep the noblest
   Of the clan of Conn,
Each below his stone with name in branching Ogham
   And the sacred knot thereon.

There they laid to rest the seven kings of Tara,
   There the sons of Cairbre sleep—
Battle-banners of the Gael that in Kieran's plain of crosses
   Now their final hosting keep.

And in Clonmacnois they laid the men of Teffia,
   And right many a lord of Breagh;
Deep the sod above Clan Creide and Clan Conaill,
   Kind in hall and fierce in fray.

Many and many a son of Conn the Hundred-fighter
   In the red earth lies at rest;
Many a blue eye of Clan Colman the turf covers,
   Many a swan-white breast.

                      T. W. ROLLESTON (1857-1920)

THE GRAVE OF RURY

As a matter of historical accuracy, Rory O'Connor, last king of
Ireland, is buried in Clonmacnoise, not in Cong.

Clear as air, the western waters
Evermore their sweet, unchanging song
Murmur in their stony channels
Round O'Connor's sepulchre in Cong.

Crownless, hopeless, here he lingered;
Year on year went by him like a dream,
While the far-off roar of conquest
Murmured faintly like the singing stream.

Here he died and here they tombed him
Men of Fechin chanting round his grave.
Did they know, ah! did they know it,
What they buried by the babbling wave.

Now above the sleep of Rury
Holy things and great have passed away;
Stone by stone the stately abbey
Falls and fades in passionless decay.

Darkly grows the quiet ivy,
Pale the broken arches glimmer through;
Dark upon the cloister-garden
Dreams the shadow of the ancient yew.

Through the leafless aisles the verdure
Flows, the meadow-sweet and fox-glove bloom
Earth, the mother and consoler,
Winds soft arms about the lonely tomb.

Peace and holy gloom possess him,
Last of Gaelic monarchs of the Gael,
Slumbering by the young, eternal
River voices of the western vale.

T. W. ROLLESTON (1857-1920)

THE COUNTY OF MAYO

On the deck of Patrick Lynch's boat I sit in woeful plight,
Through my sighing all the weary day, and weeping all
the night,
Were it not that full of sorrow from my people forth I go,
By the blessed sun! 'tis royally I'd sing thy praise, Mayo!

When I dwelt at home in plenty, and my gold did much
abound,
In the company of fair young maids the Spanish ale went
round—
'Tis a bitter change from those gay days that now I'm
forced to go,
And must leave my bones in Santa Cruz, far from my
own Mayo.

They are altered girls in Irrul now; 'tis proud they're
grown and high,
With their hair-bags and their top-knots—for I pass their
buckles by;
But it's little now I heed their airs, for God will have
it so,
That I must depart for foreign lands, and leave my sweet
Mayo.

'Tis my grief that Patrick Loughlin is not Earl in Irrul
still,
And that Brian Duff no longer rules as lord upon the hill,

And that Colonel Hugh MacGrady should be lying cold
and low,
And I sailing, sailing swiftly, from the County of Mayo.

THOMAS LAVELLE (17th cent.)
translated from the Irish by
GEORGE FOX

THE LAKE ISLE OF INNISFREE

I will arise and go now, and go to Innisfree,
And a small cabin build there, of clay and wattles made:
Nine bean-rows will I have there, a hive for the honeybee,
And live alone in the bee-loud glade.

And I shall have some peace there, for peace comes
dropping slow,
Dropping from the veils of the morning to where the
cricket sings;
There midnight's all a glimmer, and noon a purple glow,
And evening full of the linnet's wings.

I will arise and go now, for always night and day
I hear lake water lapping with low sounds by the shore;
While I stand on the roadway, or on the pavements gray,
I hear it in the deep heart's core.

W. B. YEATS (1865-1939)

THE STARLING LAKE

My sorrow that I am not by the little dun
By the lake of the starlings at Rosses under the hill,
And the larks there, singing over the fields of dew,
Or evening there and the sedges still.

For plain I see now the length of the yellow sand,
And Lissadell far off and its leafy ways,
And the holy mountain whose mighty heart
Gathers into it all the coloured days.
My sorrow that I am not by the little dun
By the lake of the starlings at evening when all is still,
And still in whispering sedges the herons stand.
'Tis there I would nestle at rest till the quivering moon
Uprose in the golden quiet over the hill.

SEUMAS O'SULLIVAN (*b.* 1879)

COUNTY MAYO

Now with the springtime the days will grow longer
    And after St. Bride's Day my sail I'll let go;
I put my mind to it and I never will linger
    Till I find myself back in the County Mayo;
It is in Claremorris I'll stop the first evening
    And at Balla beneath it I'll first take the floor,
I'll go to Kiltimagh and have a month's peace there,
    And that's not two miles from Ballinamore.

I give you my word that the heart in me rises
    As when the wind rises and all the mists go,
Thinking of Carra and Gallen beneath it,
    Scahaveela and all the wide plains of Mayo;
Killeadan's the village where everything pleases,
    Of berries and all sorts of fruit there's no lack,
And if I could but stand in the heart of my people
    Old age would drop from me and youth would come
        back.

ANTHONY RAFTERY (*c.* 1784-1835)
translated from the Irish by
FRANK O'CONNOR

THE WINDING BANKS OF ERNE

Adieu to Belashanny, where I was bred and born;
Go where I may I'll think of you, as sure as night and
  morn:
The kindly spot, the friendly town, where every one is
  known,
And not a face in all the place but partly seems my own;
There's not a house or window, there's not a field or hill,
But east or west, in foreign lands, I'll recollect them
  still;
I leave my warm heart with you, though my back I'm
  forced to turn—
Adieu to Belashanny and the winding banks of Erne.

No more on pleasant evenings we'll saunter down the
  Mall,
When the trout is rising to the fly, the salmon to the fall.
The boat comes straining on her net, and heavily she
  creeps,
Cast off, cast off—she feels the oars, and to her berth she
  sweeps;
Now fore and aft keep hauling, and gathering up the
  clew,
Till a wave of silver salmon rolls in among the crew
Then they may sit with pipes alit, and many a joke and
  yarn;
Adieu to Belashanny, and the winding banks of Erne!

The music of the waterfall, the mirror of the tide,
When all the green-hill'd harbour is full from side to side,
From Portnasun to Bulliebawns, and round the Abbey
  bay,
From rocky Inis Saimer to Coolnargit sandhills grey;

While far upon the southern line, to guard it like a
    wall,
The Leitrim mountains clothed in blue gaze calmly over
    all,
And watch the ship sail up or down, the red flag at her
    stern—
Adieu to these, adieu to all the winding banks of Erne!

Farewell to you, Kildoney lads, and them that pull
    an oar,
A lugsail set, or haul a net, from the point of Mullagh-
    more;
From Killybegs to bold Slieve-League, that ocean moun-
    tain steep,
Six hundred yards in air aloft, six hundred in the
    deep;
From Dooran to the Fairy Bridge, and round by Tullen
    Strand,
Level and long, and white with waves, where gull and
    curlew stand;
Head out to sea, when on your lee the breakers you
    discern—
Adieu to all the billowy coast and the winding banks of
    Erne!

Farewell, Coolmore, Bundoran! and your summer
    crowds that run
From inland homes to see with joy the Atlantic setting
    sun;
To breathe the buoyant salted air, and sport among the
    waves;
To gather shells on sandy beach, and tempt the gloomy
    caves;
To watch the flowing, ebbing tide, the boats, the crabs,
    the fish;
Young men and maids to meet and smile, and form a
    tender wish;

The sick and old in search of health, for all things have
their turn
And I must quit my native shore and the winding banks
of Erne!

Farewell to every white cascade from the Harbour to
Belleek,
And every pool where fins may rest, and ivy-shaded
creek;
The sloping fields, the lofty rocks, where ash and holly
grow,
The one split yew-tree gazing on the curving flood below;
The Lough that winds through islands under Turaw
mountain green
And Castle Caldwell's stretching woods, with tranquil
bays between;
And Breesie Hill, and many a pond among the heath and
fern—
For I must say adieu—adieu to the winding banks of
Erne!

The thrush will call through Camlin groves the live-long
summer day;
The waters run by mossy cliff, and banks with wild
flowers gay;
The girls will bring their work and sing beneath a twisted
thorn,
Or stray with sweethearts down the path among the
growing corn;
Along the riverside they go, where I have often been—
Oh, never shall I see again the days that I have seen!
A thousand chances are to one I never may return—
Adieu to Belashanny, and the winding banks of Erne!

Adieu to evening dances, where merry neighbours meet,
And the fiddle says to boys and girls " get up and shake
your feet!"

To shanachies and wise old talk of Erin's days gone by
Who trenched the rath on such a hill, and where the
          bones may lie
Of saint, or king, or warrior chief; with tales of fairy
          power,
And tender ditties sweetly sung to pass the twilight hour.
The mournful song of exile is now for me to learn—
Adieu, my dear companions on the winding banks of
          Erne!

Now measure from the Commons down to each end of
          the Purt,
Round the Abbey, Moy and Knather,—I wish no one any
          hurt;
The Main Street, Back Street, College Lane, the Mall and
          Portnasun
If any foes of mine are there, I pardon every one.
I hope that man and womankind will do the same by me;
For my heart is sore and heavy at voyaging the sea.
My loving friends I'll bear in mind, and often fondly turn
To think of Belashanny and the winding banks of Erne!

If ever I'm a money'd man, I mean, please God, to cast
My golden anchor in the place where youthful years
          were past:
Though heads that now are black and brown must mean-
          while gather grey,
New faces rise by every breath, and old ones drop away—
Yet dearer still that Irish hill than all the world beside;
It's home, sweet home, where'er I roam, through lands
          and waters wide;
And if the Lord allows me, I surely will return
To my native Belashanny, and the winding banks of
          Erne!

                              WILLIAM ALLINGHAM (1824-1889)

INNISKEEN ROAD: JULY EVENING

The bicycles go by in twos and threes—
There's a dance in Billy Brennan's barn to-night,
And there's the half-talk code of mysteries
And the wink-and-elbow language of delight,
Half-past eight and there is not a spot
Upon a mile of road, no shadow thrown
That might turn out a man or woman, not
A footfall tapping secrecies of stone.

I have what every poet hates in spite
Of all the solemn talk of contemplation.
Oh, Alexander Selkirk knew the plight
Of being king and government and nation.
A road, a mile of kingdom, I am king
Of banks and stones and every blooming thing.

PATRICK KAVANAGH (*b.* 1905)
Ploughman and Other Poems

MEATH AND CAVAN

Yellow, broken-backed, heavy with history, the dese-
crated market cross of Kells filled the opening of the
clean, pale, decorous Georgian street like a lifted finger.
Tradition says it was used by the English as a gallows,
but its ninth- or tenth-century sculpture is still remote
enough. About its base a procession of horsemen hunted
a procession of stags, and above were Christ crowned and
crucified. Within the graveyard with its fatty green, the
yellow, thickly-set crosses seemed like trees, as though
they had been there so long that they had taken root and
drawn their yellow colour from the earth. One had

snapped under the stone-cutter's chisel, for he had left it
so, with the panels merely sketched out, and in one of
them the five or six strokes which were the basis of his
simple composition. Behind it, under the Round Tower,
was another cross with another mysterious procession of
huntsmen and stags, and near it a beautifully carved shaft
broken off a few feet from the ground.

As we cycled north from the rich Boyne country the
land began to rise; the grass lost its enamel, and the bare
earth its burnish. In Cavan they still build lovers' seats
by the roadside, and a very pleasant custom it seemed
when the three of us, Geronte, Célimène and I, sat down
to lunch. We were only a mile or so inside the Cavan
boundary, and already there was a blue lake at the foot
of the field, and the little hills, continuous and rolling
like a grey wintry sea, began to tumble on top of one
another, with the dark curves of the fences echoing the
folds in the land; while here and there some roller,
pinched at the top into a narrow spine like the crown of
a soft hat, broke into a thin dark foam of rock.

It was beautiful country, crabbed and stunted and grey,
like an orchard full of old apple trees; country for a
draughtsman, not for a painter, for nothing interrupted
that continuous subtle variation of pattern except where
some fool from a Government office had planted a belt
of pines: nothing cloyed as in Kerry or Connemara; the
country moved with us; the roads, climbing and dropping and insinuating themselves between the scooped-out
troughs of the grey rollers, produced a constant sense of
gentle animation; and it was only at the top of a hill
where two screens of rock-crested hillside drew back from
the road that we could sit down to tea, and watch
through the gap the immense distance of bumpy Tuscan
hills among which the sunlight fell in long shafts, pale
as the ghosts of primroses.

FRANK O'CONNOR (1903-1966)
Irish Miles

A DUBLIN STREET

He could see the street stretching along outside, its roughly cobbled roadway beset with empty match-boxes, tattered straws, tattered papers, scattered mounds of horse-dung, and sprinkled deep with slumbering dust waiting for an idle wind to come and raise it to irritating life again. Lean-looking gas-lamps stood at regular intervals on the footpaths, many of them deformed from the play of swinging children, bending over like old men standing to gasp, and wait for a pain in the back to go. The melancholy pathway meandered along by the side of the tall houses, leading everywhere to tarnishing labour, to consumption's cough, to the writhings of fever, to bitter mutterings against life, and frantic calls on St. Anthony, the Little Flower, and Bernadette of Missabielle to be absent helps in time of trouble. Upon these stones, I will build my church.

There were the houses, too—a long, lurching row of discontented incurables, smirched with the age-long marks of ague, fevers, cancer, and consumption, the soured tears of little children, and the sighs of disappointed newly-married girls. The doors were scarred with time's spit and anger's hasty knocking; the pillars by their sides were shaky, their stuccoed bloom long since peeled away, and they looked like crutches keeping the trembling doors standing on their palsied feet. The gummy-eyed windows blinked dimly out, lacquered by a year's tired dust from the troubled street below. Dirt and disease were the big sacraments here—outward and visible signs of an inward and spiritual disgrace. The people bought the cheapest things in food they could find in order to live, to work, to worship; the cheapest spuds, the cheapest tea, the cheapest meat, the cheapest fat; and waited for unsold bread to grow stale that they might buy that cheaper, too. Here they gathered up the fragments so that nothing would be lost. The streets were long haggard corridors of rottenness and ruin. What wonderful mind of memory could link this shrinking wretchedness with the flaunting gorgeousness of silk and satin; with bloom of rose and scent of lavender? A thousand years must have passed since the last lavender lady was carried out feet first from the last surviving one of them. Even the sun shudders now when she touches a roof, for she feels some evil has chilled the glow of her garment. The flower that here once bloomed is dead forever. No wallflower here has crept into a favoured cranny; sight and sigh of the primrose were far away; no room here for a dance of daffodils; no swallow twittering under a shady eave; and it was sad to see an odd sparrow seeking a yellow grain from the mocking dust; not even a spiky-headed thistle, purple mitred, could find a corner here for a sturdy life.

SEAN O'CASEY (1880–1964)
Inishfallen, Fare Thee Well

PRELUDE

Still south I went and west and south again,
Through Wicklow from the morning till the night,
And far from cities, and the sights of men,
Lived with the sunshine, and the moon's delight.

I knew the stars, the flowers, and the birds,
The grey and wintry sides of many glens,
And did but half remember human words,
In converse with the mountains, moors, and fens.

J. M. SYNGE (1871–1909)
Poems and Translations

THE OPPRESSION OF THE HILLS

Among the cottages that are scattered through the hills of County Wicklow I have met with many people who show in a singular way the influence of a particular locality. These people live for the most part beside old roads and pathways where hardly one man passes in the day, and look out all the year on unbroken barriers of heath. At every season heavy rains fall for often a week at a time, till the thatch drips with water stained to a dull chestnut, and the floor in the cottages seems to be going back to the condition of the bogs near it. Then the clouds break, and there is a night of terrific storm from the south-west—all the larches that survive in these places are bowed and twisted towards the point where the sun rises in June—when the winds come down through the narrow glens with the congested whirl and roar of a torrent, breaking at times for sudden moments of silence that keep up the tension of the mind. At such times the people crouch all night over a few sods of turf, and the dogs howl in the lanes.

When the sun rises there is a morning of almost supernatural radiance, and even the oldest men and women come out into the air with the joy of children who have recovered from a fever. In the evening it is raining again. This peculiar climate, acting on a population that is already lonely and dwindling, has caused or increased a tendency to nervous depression among the people, and every degree of sadness, from that of the man who is merely mournful to that of the man who has spent half his life in the madhouse, is common among these hills.

Not long ago in a desolate glen in the south of the country I met two policemen driving an ass-cart with a coffin on it, and a little farther on I stopped an old man and asked him what had happened.

"This night three weeks," he said, "there was a poor fellow below reaping in the glen, and in the evening he had two glasses of whisky with some other lads. Then some excitement took him, and he threw off his clothes and ran away into the hills. There was great rain that night, and I suppose the poor creature lost his way, and was the whole night perishing in the rain and darkness. In the morning they found his naked footmarks on some mud half a mile above the road, and again where you go up by a big stone. Then there was nothing known of him till last night, when they found his body on the mountain, and it near eaten by the crows."

J. M. SYNGE (1871-1909)
In Wicklow and West Kerry

History

THE FIGHTING RACE

"Read out the names!" and Burke sat back.
  And Kelly drooped his head.
While Shea—they call him Scholar Jack—
  Went down the list of the dead.
Officers, seamen, gunners, marines,
  The crews of the gig and yawl,
The bearded man and the lad in his teens,
  Carpenters, coal passers—all.
Then, knocking the ashes from out his pipe,
  Said Burke in an offhand way:
"We're all in that dead man's list, by Cripe!
  Kelly and Burke and Shea."
"Well, here's to the Maine, and I'm sorry for Spain."
  Said Kelly and Burke and Shea.

"Wherever there's Kellys there's trouble," said Burke.
  "Wherever fighting's the game,
Or a spice of danger in grown man's work,"
  Said Kelly, "you'll find my name."
"And do we fall short," said Burke, getting mad,
  "When it's touch and go for life?"
Said Shea, "It's thirty-odd years, bedad,
  Since I charged to drum and fife
Up Marye's Heights, and my old canteen
  Stopped a rebel ball on its way.
There were blossoms of blood on our sprigs of green—
  Kelly and Burke and Shea—
And the dead didn't brag." "Well, here's to the flag!"
  Said Kelly and Burke and Shea.

"I wish 'twas in Ireland, for there's the place,"
  Said Burke, "that we'd die by right,
In the cradle of our soldier race,
  After one good stand-up fight.
My grandfather fell on Vinegar Hill,
  And fighting was not his trade;
But his rusty pike's in the cabin still,
  With Hessian blood on the blade."
"Aye, aye," said Kelly, "the pikes were great
  When the word was ' clear the way! '
We were thick on the roll in ninety-eight—
  Kelly and Burke and Shea."
"Well, here's to the pike and the sword and the like!"
Said Kelly and Burke and Shea.

And Shea, the scholar, with rising joy,
  Said, "We were at Ramillies;
We left our bones at Fontenoy
  And up in the Pyrenees;
Before Dunkirk, on Landen's plain,
  Cremona, Lille, and Ghent.
We're all over Austria, France, and Spain,
  Wherever they pitched a tent.
We've died for England from Waterloo
  To Egypt and Dargai;
And still there's enough for a corps or crew,
  Kelly and Burke and Shea."
"Well, here's to good honest fighting blood!"
Said Kelly and Burke and Shea.

"Oh, the fighting races don't die out,
  If they seldom die in bed,
For love is first in their hearts, no doubt,"
  Said Burke; then Kelly said:
"When Michael, the Irish Archangel, stands,
  The angel with the sword,
And the battle-dead from a hundred lands
  Are ranged in one big horde,

Our line, that for Gabriel's trumpet waits,
Will stretch three deep that day,
    From Jehoshaphat to the Golden Gates—
    Kelly and Burke and Shea."
"Well, here's thank God for the race and the sod!"
    Said Kelly and Burke and Shea.

J. I. C. CLARKE (1846-1925)

WHO'LL CARVE THE PIG?

"Keep up the contest," said Cet, "or let me carve the pig."

"You're not the right man to carve it," said a big fair-haired warrior of the Ulstermen.

"Who's this?" asked Cet.

"Eogan mac Durtacht," said all, "king of Farney."

"I saw him before," said Cet.

"Where did you see me?" asked Eogan.

"In the doorway of your house when I was taking a spoil of cattle from you. The alarm was raised. You came at the cry. You threw a spear at me and it stuck in my shield. I threw it back at you and it went through your head and took out the eye. The men of Ireland see you with one eye. I cut the other eye out of your head." So *he* sat down.

"Keep up the contest, Ulstermen," said Cet.

"You won't carve it yet," said Muinremor mac Gerginn.

"And is this Muinremor?" said Cet. "You were the last I wiped my spears in, Muinremor," said Cet. "It isn't three days since I took three warriors' heads off you and the head of your eldest son." So *he* sat down.

"More contest," said Cet.

"Here you are," said Menn mac Salchada.

"Who's this?" asked Cet.

"Menn," said they all.

"And what do herdsmen's sons with nicknames mean by competing with me? Because I was the priest that baptised your father; I cut his heel off with my sword so that he went off from me a cripple. What's the cripple's son doing, challenging me?" So *he* sat down. . . .

But when he took the knife in his hand and approached the pig they saw Conall Cernach come in. He gave a jump into the middle of the house. The Ulstermen gave Conall a great welcome. Conchobar tossed the helmet from his head and exulted. . . .

"I'm glad the food is ready," said Conall. "Who's carving for you?"

"It went to the man who is carving," said Conchobar. "Cet mac Magach."

"Is it true that you are carving the pig, Cet?" asked Conall. . . . "Get up from the pig now."

"What will get it for you?" asked Cet.

"I have the right to challenge," said Conall. "I give contest to you, Cet. I swear by my people's gods since I took a spear in my hand I was never a day without killing a Connachtman, or a night without raiding one, and I never slept without a Connachtman's head under my knee."

"True," said Cet. "You're a better hero than I am. But if Anluan[1] were here he would give you contest. It is hard luck on us that he isn't here."

"Oh, but he is," said Conall, taking Anluan's head from his belt; and he hit Cet in the chest with it and blood burst from his lips. So he went from the pig and Conall sat down at it.

ANONYMOUS (8th-9th cent.)
translated from the Irish by
FRANK O'CONNOR

[1] His brother.

THE DEATH OF MESS GEGRA

Conall Cernach went alone in pursuit of the Leinstermen to avenge his two brothers who had been killed in the battle: Mess Dead and Loegaire. He went by Dublin, past Drimnagh by Hy-Gavla in Forcharthain, past Oughterard and past Naas to Clane.

When the Leinstermen reached their country, they scattered, each to his own place. Mess Gegra, however, remained alone by Clane pathway with his charioteer after the hosting.

"I want to sleep for a while," said the charioteer to Mess Gegra, "and then you sleep."

"That suits me," said the King.

As Mess Gegra watched the water, he saw a nut coming towards him on the river. It was the size of a man's head. He climbed down, caught it and split it with his knife; and left half of the kernel for the boy. Then he saw how the boy raised himself from the ground in his sleep and he waked him.

"What ails you, boy?" said the King.

"A bad dream I had," said the boy.

" Harness the horses, boy," said the King.

The boy harnessed the horses.

"Did you eat the nut?" said the boy.

"I did," said the King.

"Did you leave half for me?" said the boy.

"I ate a little of it first," said the King.

"Who ate a little on me, ate a lot," said the boy. And as the King reached out his hand with the kernel in it the boy struck it with his sword and cut off his hand.

"That is wrong, boy," said the King. "Open my fist; half the kernel is inside it."

When the boy saw that he turned the sword against himself and it pierced his back.

" Alas, boy!" said the King. Then he hitched the horses to the chariot and laid his hand in front of him. As he left the ford going west, Conall reached it, coming east.

"Aha, is this Mess Gegra?" said Conall.

"I am he," said the other.

" Well?" asked Conall.

"What more can you ask for, but as the saying goes: The man who owes you anything, catch him where you can."

"You have my brothers with you," said Conall.

"I haven't them in my belt."

"You will pay for it," said Conall.

"That is no honourable fight; I have only one hand."

"I shall look after that," said Conall. "I shall have my hand tied to my side."

His hand was bound three times over to his side. They fought one another till the river was red with them. But Conall won the game.

"That is enough, Conall!" said Mess Gegra. "I know you will not leave without my head; so add my head to your head, and my glory to your glory. . . ."

Then Conall went in his own chariot, and his charioteer in Mess Gegra's chariot, and they went through Uachtar Fine. There fifty women met him; they were Buan, Mess Gegra's wife, and her followers, coming south from the border.

"Whose wife are you, woman?" said Conall.

"The wife of Mess Gegra, the King of Leinster."

"You are ordered to come with me," said Conall.

"Who ordered it?"

"Mess Gegra."

"Have you brought a sign?" asked the woman.

"These are his chariots and his horses."

"He gives treasures to many," said the woman.

"And here is his head."

"This time I am lost to him," said the woman.

The head blushed and paled, turn by turn.

"What ails the head, woman?" said Conall.

"I know," said the woman. "A dispute he had with Athirne. He said no Ulsterman would ever carry me away single-handed. Breaking his word is what ails his head."

"Come into the chariot with me," said Conall.

"Wait for me till I lament my husband," she said.

Then she raised her cry till it was heard in Tara and Allen, threw herself backwards and was dead. Her grave is on the road, Coll Buana; a blackthorn tree grew through her grave.

The Siege of Howth (12th cent.)
translated from the Irish by
FRANK O'CONNOR

ON BAILE'S STRAND

What was the reason Cu Chulainn killed his son? Not difficult. Cu Chulainn went to learn arms with Scathach daughter of Airdgeimm in Letha and mastered the trade of arms with her, and Aife daughter of Airdgeimm went to him and he left her pregnant and told her she would bear a son. "Keep this gold thumb-ring," he said, "till it fits the boy. When it fits him let him come and find me in Ireland, and let no man put him from his path and let him refuse single combat to none, and let him tell his name to no man."

After seven years the boy went to look for his father. The Ulstermen were gathered at Tracht Eisi before him, and they saw the boy coming to them over the sea and a bronze skiff under him and gilt oars in his hand. He had a heap of stones in the skiff. He would put a stone in his sling and let a stunning shot at the birds, and take their senses from them, and they alive, and then let them off in the air again. He would do his jawtrick between his two hands so that the eye could not perceive it. He would tune his voice to the birds so that they came down for a second time. Then he would wake them again.

"Well," said Conchobar, "I'm sorry for the country that lad comes to. Since a young lad does that trick, if grown men came from the island he comes from, they would crush us into dust. Some one go to meet him. Let him not land at all." "Who will go against him?" "Who but Condere mac Echach?" said Conchobar. "Why should Condere go?" asked all. "Not difficult," said Conchobar. "If he has sense and reason, Condere is the right man." "I will go meet him," said Condere.

Condere went just as the boy was landing. "You have come far enough, lad," said Condere, "till we know where you are going and who your family is." "I give my name to no man," said the boy, "and I avoid none." "You will not land," said Condere, "till you tell your name." "I shall go to the place I set out for," said the boy.

The boy turned away. Then Condere said: "Come back, my boy. You are a mighty fellow. You are the stuff of a fighting man. The chief of the Ulster warriors are before you. Conchobar will protect you." (Here, Condere, the master of flowery speech, breaks into rhetorical kennings.)

"You have met me well," said the boy. "So you will have your speech. (The boy replies in kind.) Go back again," said the boy, "because if you had the strength of a hundred, you are not able to halt me."

"Very well," said Condere, "let someone else come to debate with you." Condere then went to the Ulstermen and told them.

"It is not right," said Conall Cernach, "the honour of Ulster to be snatched away while I live." So he went to meet the boy.

"Your style is pretty," said Conall.

"It will not be the uglier for you," said the boy.

The boy put a stone in his sling. He shot it in the air

—a stunning shot—so that its din and roar reached Conall as it ascended. It threw Conall on his back. Before he rose, the boy tied his hands with the strap of his shield.

"Someone else to meet him," said Conall. The boy made a joke of the whole host in this way.

Cu Chulainn at the time was going to meet the boy, and the hand of Forgall's daughter, Emer, round his neck.

"Do not go down," she said. "It is a son of yours that is below." (She also breaks into a speech of kennings, which Cu Chulainn, rejecting her advice, replies to in the same style).

Then he went down himself.

"Your style is good, boy," he said.

"Your style is bad to begin with," said the little fellow, "that two of you did not come to ask my name."

"You think I should have had a baby with me?" asked Cu Chulainn. "You will die unless you tell your name."

"Let it be so," said the boy.

The boy attacked him. He cut a bald patch through his hair with his sword, i.e. with a measured stroke.

"The joke is over," said Cu Chulainn. "Let us wrestle."

"I cannot reach to your belt," said the boy. The boy stood on two pillar stones, and three times he thrust Cu Chulainn between the stones, and the boy did not move his feet from the stones till they went into the stones up to the ankles. The track of his two feet are there still. That is why it is called the Strand of the Track. Then they went into the sea to duck one another and the boy ducked Cu Chulainn twice. Then Cu Chulainn attacked him from the water and showed him foul play with the belly spear, because Scathach had taught no one but Cu Chulainn that skill. He shot it at the boy through the water, till his guts fell about his feet.

"That is what Scathach never taught me," said the boy. "My grief that you wounded me."

"True," said Cu Chulainn. He lifted the boy then in his two arms, and carried him and brought him to where the Ulstermen were.

"Ulstermen," he said, "here is my son."

ANONYMOUS (9th-10th cent.)
translated from the Irish by
FRANK O'CONNOR

THE VIKING TERROR

Since tonight the wind is high,
The sea's white mane a fury,
I need not fear the hordes of hell
Coursing the Irish Channel.

ANONYMOUS (9th cent.)
translated from the Irish by
FRANK O'CONNOR

THE ORIGIN OF THE BATTLE
OF CLONTARF

A.D. 1014

When Brian Boru was living in Kincora, without war or dissension, he asked the King of Leinster—Maol Mórdha son of Murrough, to send him three masts of fine wood from Feegile. The King of Leinster cut the masts, and went with them to Kincora where Brian then was, and ordered the Ui Failghe to carry one mast, the Ui Faolain to carry another and the Ui Muireadhaigh the third; and they squabbled going up Sliabh an Bhogaigh. Then the King of Leinster himself gave a hand with the Ui Faolain's mast while he was wearing a satin tunic Brian had given him previously with a gold fringe around it and a silver button, and with the effort he made under the mast, the button broke. And when they reached Kincora, the King of Leinster took off his tunic, and gave it to his sister, Gormley daughter of Murrough, Brian's wife, to sew a button in. The queen took the tunic and tossed it into the fire before her and began abusing her brother for being in subjection or slavery to anyone in the world. "The thing," she said, "your father or grandfather never agreed to." And she said Brian's son would demand the same thing from Maol Mórdha's son.

Maol Mórdha remembered the queen's words. And it happened next day that Murrough son of Brian and Conaing son of Donn Chuan were playing chess next day—or according to some, it was the Abbot of Glendalough who was playing with Murrough. Maol Mórdha began to advise Murrough in his play and advised one move that lost him the game.

"You gave the Danes the advice that defeated them in the battle of Glen Mama," said Murrough.

"If I gave them advice that defeated them then," said Maol Mórdha, "I shall give them other advice that will make them defeat you another day."

"I should like to see them," said Murrough.

That made Maol Mórdha furious, and he went to his quarters, and couldn't be induced to go to the drinking house that night, and left early next morning without taking leave of Brian.

When Brian heard that the King of Leinster had left the fort without taking leave of him, he sent a favourite serving man to detain him till he received wages and gifts. The serving man caught up on him at the end of the plank bridge of Killaloe on the eastern bank of the Shannon, while he was mounting his horse, and the serving man revealed his message from Brian. Maol Mórdha turned on the serving man and struck him three blows with the yew-stick he carried in his hand, and broke the bones of his skull, so that he had to be carried back to Brian. Cogaran was the man's name, and it is from him the Ui Chogarain of Munster are descended. Some of the Kincora household wished to follow the King of Leinster and not let him back to Leinster till he submitted to Brian. But Brian said he would not permit treachery against him in his own house. "All the same," he said, "it is from the doorpost of his own house that satisfaction will be asked of him."

GEOFFREY KEATING (1570-1646)
History of Ireland

THE RETURN FROM FINGAL

A.D. 1014

After the battle of Clontarf and the slaying of Brian and Murrough and many of the Irish with them, and after the defeat of the Danes and the Leinstermen and the slaying of a great many of them in the battle, when the Dal gCais and the South Munstermen—those of them who were alive after the battle—returned to Mullaghmast, the South Munstermen made themselves a group apart and separated from the Dal gCais, and agreed that as the Dal gCais were short of men, they would send messages to Donough, Brian's son, and ask hostages, and explain to him that his father and his father's brother had had hostages of them, and they said that the kingship of Munster in alternation was theirs by right.

"You were not hostages to my father or brother of your own free will," said Donough, "but they won your obedience in your own despite, and the men of Ireland along with you."

And Donough said he would not give hostages or pledges to them nor to any man, and said if only he had men enough for battle with him that he would not let them go without hostages that they might be subject to him as they were to his father.

When the South Munstermen heard this they promptly rose and took their arms and came to give battle to the Dal gCais. Then Donough Brian's son ordered his people to put their wounded in the fort of Mullagh- mast with a third of the army to guard them. "And," said he, "let the other two-thirds give battle to that crowd."

All the same, the Dal gCais at that time were only a thousand survivors, and the South Munstermen were three thousand strong. When the wounded men heard Donough's order they rapidly rose and stuffed moss in their wounds, and took arms in their hands, and they advised that the battle should be given. When the South Munstermen saw the courage with which the Dal gCais, sick and well, were animated they said no more about giving battle and departed to their homes without getting hostages from the Dal gCais.

Regarding the Dal gCais, they went on to Athy on the bank of the Barrow, and began to drink there. Donn- chadh Mac Giolla Padraic, king of Ossory was awaiting them there with the full of his troops and hosting— Leinster and Ossory—of Magh Clann Ceallaigh, keeping a watch on the Dal gCais to see which way they went, being inimical to them. Because it was Brian who tied and imprisoned his father, Donnchadh, and kept him a year in prison and plundered and wasted Ossory entire and killed a great many of his people. Because of that Mac Giolla Padraic was hostile to the Dal gCais, and sent messengers to them at Athy, asking them to send him hostages before he let them pass. Even so Donough, son of Brian, replied to them that he would give them no hostages.

"If that is so," said the messengers, "you must give battle to Mac Giolla Patrick."

"I shall give him battle," said Donough, "and it is a

pity that I did not die as my father died before I had the misfortune to have them ask hostages of me."

The messengers told him not to be angry, and that he had not sufficient men to give battle to Mac Giolla Padraic.

"But if it were customary to blame messengers for the impudence of their messages I would have your tongues plucked out," said Donough. "Because if I were only a one-man army I would not refuse fight to Mac Giolla Padraic and the Ossory men."

Then Donough ordered a third of the army to protect the wounded and the other two-thirds to fight the battle. When the wounded heard this they rose up hastily; their wounds broke out and they filled them with moss, took their spears and swords and joined with the rest, and they told Brian's son to send to the wood and bring strong stakes and stick them in the ground. "And let us be tied to them," they said, "and put arms in our hands and put our sons and brothers with us—two hale men at either side of the wounded man—so that our strength may be re-inforced by it. Because shame will not let the hale man run till the tied and wounded man run as well."

They did this, and it was a great wonder of courage and a great astonishment the order the Dal gCais adopted.

When the Leinstermen and the Ossorymen saw the great courage rising in the Dal gCais, they were horrified and afraid, and they said: "It is no flight, nor scattering nor terror the Dal gCais look like making, but to make a hard strong body of themselves. For that reason let us not fight them, for they are equally ready for death or life."

Mac Giolla Padraic said: "It's cowardly of you to say that for there are enough of you there to eat them, if they were cooked food."

"True," they said, "but true or not, none of them

will be killed without five or six falling at his hands. And what advantage is our common slaughter with them?"

"Since you do not wish to fight," said Mac Giolla Padraic, "follow them up. They are heavily wounded, and they are not in a position to skirmish with you."

They did so, and it was worse for the Dal gCais than to have given them battle. The Dal gCais proceeded to their own country in want and hardship, and there came to the township together with Brian's son only eight hundred and fifty of them, because they had lost one hundred and fifty in skirmishes with the Ossory men when these refused battle.

GEOFFREY KEATING (1570-1646)
History of Ireland

KINCORA

Oh, where, Kincora! is Brian the Great?
And where is the beauty that once was thine?
Oh, where are the princes and nobles that sate
At the feast in thy halls, and drank the red wine?
Where, oh, Kincora?

Oh, where, Kincora! are thy valorous lords?
Oh, whither, thou Hospitable! are they gone?
Oh, where are the Dalcassians of the Golden Swords?
And where are the warriors Brian led on?
Where, oh, Kincora?

And where is Murrough, the descendant of kings—
The defeater of a hundred—the daringly brave—
Who set but slight store by jewels and rings—
Who swam down the torrent and laughed at its wave?
Where, oh, Kincora?

And where is Donogh, King Brian's worthy son?
And where is Conaing, the Beautiful Chief?
And Kian, and Corc? Alas! they are gone—
They have left me this night alone with my grief,
                    Left me, Kincora!

And where are the chiefs with whom Brian went forth,
The ne'er vanquished sons of Erin the Brave,
The great King of Onaght, renowned for his worth,
And the hosts of Baskinn, from the western wave?
                    Where, oh, Kincora?

Oh, where is Duvlann of the swift-footed Steeds?
And where is Kian, who was son of Molloy?
And where is King Lonergan, the fame of whose deeds
In the red battle-field no time can destroy?
                    Where, oh, Kincora?

And where is that youth of majestic height,
The faith-keeping Prince of the Scots?—Even he,
As wide as his fame was, as great as his might,
Was tributary, oh, Kincora, to thee!
                    Thee, oh, Kincora!

They are gone, those heroes of royal birth,
Who plundered no churches, and broke no trust,
'Tis weary for me to be living on earth
While they, oh, Kincora, lie low in the dust!
                    Low, oh, Kincora!

Oh, never again will Princes appear,
To rival the Dalcassians of the Cleaving Swords!
I can never dream of meeting afar or anear,
In the east or the west, such heroes and lords!
                    Never, Kincora!

Oh, dear are the images my memory calls up
Of Brian Boru!—how he never would miss
To give me at the banquet the first bright cup!
Ah, why did he heap on me honour like this?

> Why, oh, Kincora?

I am Mac Liag, and my home is on the Lake;
Thither often, to that palace whose beauty is fled
Came Brian to ask me, and I went for his sake.
Oh, my grief! that I should live, and Brian be dead!

> Dead, oh, Kincora!

> Attributed to MAC LIAG (*c.* 1015)
> translated from the Irish by
> JAMES CLARENCE MANGAN (1803-49)

THE UNFORGIVEN CRIME

YOUNG MAN: You speak of Dermot and of Dervorgilla
Who brought the Norman in?
YOUNG GIRL: Yes, yes, I spoke
Of that most miserable, most accursed pair
Who sold their country into slavery, and yet
They were not wholly miserable and accursed
If somebody of their race at last would say:
"I have forgiven them."
YOUNG MAN: Oh, never, never
Shall Dermot and Dervorgilla be forgiven.
YOUNG GIRL: If someone of their race forgave at last
Lip would be pressed on lip.
YOUNG MAN: Oh, never, never
Shall Dermot and Dervorgilla be forgiven. . . .
So here we're on the summit. I can see
The Aran Islands, Connemara Hills,
And Galway in the breaking light; there too
The enemy has toppled roof and gable;
And torn the panelling from ancient rooms;

What generations of old men had known
Like their own hands, and children wondered at,
Has boiled a trooper's porridge. That town had lain,
But for the pair that you would have me pardon,
Amid its gables and its battlements
Like any old admired Italian town;
For though we have neither coal, nor iron ore,
To make us wealthy and corrupt the air,
Our country, if that crime were uncommitted,
Had been most beautiful.

W. B. YEATS (1865-1939)
The Dreaming of the Bones

DARK ROSALEEN

O my dark Rosaleen,
   Do not sigh, do not weep!
The priests are on the ocean green,
   They march along the deep.
There's wine from the royal Pope,
   Upon the ocean green;
And Spanish ale shall give you hope,
   My Dark Rosaleen!
   My own Rosaleen!
Shall glad your heart, shall give you hope,
Shall give you health, and help, and hope.
   My Dark Rosaleen!

Over hills, and thro' dales,
   Have I roam'd for your sake;
All yesterday I sail'd with sails
   On river and on lake.
The Erne, at its highest flood,
   I dash'd across unseen,
For there was lightning in my blood,
   My Dark Rosaleen!

My own Rosaleen!
O, there was lightning in my blood,
Red lightning lighten'd thro' my blood.
   My Dark Rosaleen!

All day long, in unrest,
   To and fro, do I move.
The very soul within my breast
   Is wasted for you, love!
The heart in my bosom faints
   To think of you, my Queen,
My life of life, my saint of saints,
   My Dark Rosaleen!
   My own Rosaleen!
To hear your sweet and sad complaints,
My life, my love, my saint of saints,
   My Dark Rosaleen!

Woe and pain, pain and woe,
   Are my lot, night and noon,
To see your bright face clouded so,
   Like to the mournful moon.
But yet will I rear your throne
   Again in golden sheen;
'Tis you shall reign, shall reign alone,
   My Dark Rosaleen!
   My own Rosaleen!
'Tis you shall have the golden throne,
'Tis you shall reign, and reign alone,
   My Dark Rosaleen!

Over dews, over sands,
   Will I fly, for your weal:
Your holy delicate white hands
   Shall girdle me with steel.

At home, in your emerald bowers,
  From morning's dawn till e'en,
You'll pray for me, my flower of flowers,
  My Dark Rosaleen!
  My fond Rosaleen!
You'll think of me through daylight hours,
My virgin flower, my flower of flowers,
  My Dark Rosaleen!

I could scale the blue air,
  I could plough the high hills,
Oh, I could kneel all night in prayer,
  To heal your many ills!
And one beamy smile from you
  Would float like light between
My toils and me, my own, my true,
  My Dark Rosaleen!
  My fond Rosaleen!
Would give me life and soul anew,
A second life, a soul anew,
  My Dark Rosaleen!

O, the Erne shall run red,
  With redundance of blood,
The earth shall rock beneath our tread,
  And flames wrap hill and wood,
And gun-peal and slogan-cry
  Wake many a glen serene,
Ere you shall fade, ere you shall die,
  My Dark Rosaleen!
  My own Rosaleen!
The Judgement Hour must first be nigh,
Ere you can fade, ere you can die,
  My Dark Rosaleen!

From the Irish (16th cent.)
translated by
JAMES CLARENCE MANGAN (1803-49)

HUGH MAGUIRE

Too cold this night for Hugh Maguire;
I tremble at the pounding rain;
  Alas, that venomous cold
  Is my companion's lot!

It brings an anguish to my heart
To see the fiery torrents fall;
  He and the spiky frost—
  A horror to the mind!

The floodgates of the heavens yawn
Above the bosom of the clouds,
  And every pool a sea
  And murder in the air.

One thinks of the hare that haunts the wood,
And of the salmon in the bay;
  Even the wild bird: one grieves
  To think they are abroad.

Then one remembers Hugh Maguire
Abroad in a strange land tonight,
  Under the lightning's glare,
  And clouds with fury filled.

He in West Munster braves his doom,
And without shelter strides between
  The drenched and shivering grass
  And the impetuous sky.

Cold on that tender blushing cheek
The fury of the springtime gales
  That toss the stormy rays
  Of stars about his head.

I can scarce bear to conjure up
The contour of his body, crushed
  This rough and gloomy night
  In its cold iron suit.

The gentle and war-mastering hand
To the slim shaft of his sharp spear
  By icy weather pinned—
  Cold is the night for Hugh.

The low banks of the swollen streams
Are covered where the soldiers pass;
  The meadows stiff with ice;
  The horses cannot feed.

And yet as though to bring him warmth
And call back brightness to his face
  Each wall that he attacks
  Sinks in a wave of fire.

The fury of the fire dissolves
The frost that sheaths the tranquil eye,
  And from his wrists the flame
  Thaws manacles of ice.

EOCHY O'HUSSEY (*c.* 1600)
translated from the Irish by
FRANK O'CONNOR

THE JACOBITE WAR

1. *Jacobite*

PATRICK SARSFIELD

Farewell, Patrick Sarsfield, wherever you may roam,
You crossed the seas to France and left empty camps at
  home,
To plead our cause before many a foreign throne
Though you left ourselves and poor Ireland overthrown.

Farewell, Patrick Sarsfield, you were sent to us by God,
And holy forever is the earth that you trod;
May the sun and the white moon light your way,
For you trounced King Billy and won the day.

With you, Patrick Sarsfield, goes the prayer of everyone,
My own prayer too and the prayer of Mary's Son;
As you passed through Birr the Narrow Ford you won,
You beat them off at Cullen and took Limerick town.

I'll climb the mountain, a lonely man,
And I'll go east again if I can,
'Twas there I saw the Irish ready for the fight,
The lousy crowd that wouldn't unite.

Who's that I see now yonder on Howth Head?
"One of Jamie's soldiers, sir, now the King has fled;
Last year with gun and knapsack I marched with joyous
  tread,
But this year, sir, I'm begging my bread."

And God, when I think of how Diarmuid was attacked,
His limbs wrenched asunder, his standard cracked,

And Christ himself couldn't fight a way through
As they chopped off his head and held it in our view.

The ears tumbled fast as the scythes went on,
The first we lost were the twelve Kilkennymen,
My two brothers followed—my very breath—
But the death that broke me was Diarmuid's death.

At the Boyne Bridge we took our first beating,
From the bridge at Slane there was great retreating,
And then we were beaten at Aughrim too—
Ah, fragrant Ireland, that was goodbye to you!

The fumes were choking at the house went alight,
And Black Billy's bastards were warming to the fight,
And every shell that came, wherever it lit,
Colonel Mitchell asked was Lord Lucan hit.

Farewell to you, Limerick, and your houses so fair,
And all the good company that was quartered with us
    there;
We played cards at night by the watchfires' glare,
And often the priests called us in to prayer.

But on you, Londonderry, may misfortune come
Like the smoke that lit with every bursting gun,
For all the fine soldiers you gathered together
By your walls without shelter from wind or weather.

Many and many a soldier, all proud and gay,
Seven weeks ago they passed this way,
With guns and swords and pikes on show,
And now in Aughrim they're lying low.

Kelly's Aughrim has manure that's neither lime nor sand
But sturdy young soldiers stretched over the land,
The lads were left behind on the battlefield that day,
Torn like horsemeat by the dogs where they lay.

Oversea they all are, Ireland's best,
The Dukes and the Burkes, Prince Charlie and the rest,
And Captain Talbot their ranks adorning,
And Patrick Sarsfield, Ireland's darling.

ANONYMOUS (*c.* 1690)
translated from the Irish by
FRANK O'CONNOR

THE JACOBITE WAR

2. *Williamite*

THE BOYNE WATER

July the First, of a morning clear one thousand six
    hundred and ninety,
King William did his men prepare—of thousands he had
    thirty—
To fight King James and all his foes, encamped near the
    Boyne Water
He little feared, though two to one, their multitudes to
    scatter.

King William called his officers, saying: "Gentlemen,
    mind your station,
And let your valour here be shown before this Irish
    nation;
My brazen walls let no man break, and your subtle foes
    you'll scatter,
Be sure you show them good English play as you go over
    the water."

*   *   *

Within four yards of our fore-front, before a shot was
    fired,
A sudden snuff they got that day, which little they
    desired;
For horse and man fell to the ground, and some hung in
    their saddle:
Others turned up their forked ends, which we call *coup
de ladle*.

Prince Eugene's regiment was the next, on our right
    hand advanced,
Into a field of standing wheat, where Irish horses
    pranced—
But the brandy ran so in their heads, their senses all did
    scatter,
They little thought to leave their bones that day at the
    Boyne Water.

*   *   *

Now, praise God, all true Protestants, and heaven's and
    earth's Creator,
For the deliverance that He sent our enemies to scatter . . .
The Church's foes will pine away, like churlish-hearted
    Nabal.
For our deliverer came this day like the great Zorobabel.

So praise God, all true Protestants, and I will say no
    further,
But had the Papists gained the day, there would have
    been open murder,
Although King James and many more were ne'er that
    way inclined,
It was not in their power to stop what the rabble they
    designed.

ANONYMOUS (*c.* 1690)

A WILD HOPE

Life has conquered: the wind has blown away
Alexander, Caesar and all their power and sway;
Tara and Troy have made no longer stay;
Maybe the English too will have their day.

ANONYMOUS (18th cent.)
translated from the Irish by
FRANK O'CONNOR

LAST LINES

I shall not call for help until they coffin me,
What good for me to call when hope of help is gone?
Princes of Munster that would have heard my cry
Will not rise from the dead because I am alone.

Mind shudders like a wave in this tempestuous mood,
My bowels and my heart are pierced and filled with pain
To see our lands, our hills, our gentle neighbourhood
A plot where any English upstart stakes his claim.

The Shannon and the Liffey and the tuneful Lee,
The Boyne and the Blackwater a sad music sing,
The waters of the west run red into the sea—
No matter what be trumps their knave will beat our king.

And I have never ceased weeping these useless tears,
I am a man, oppressed, afflicted, and undone,
Who where he wanders mourning no companion hears
Only some waterfall that has no cause to mourn.

Now I shall cease, death comes and I must not delay
By Laune and Lane and Lee diminished of their pride,
I shall go after the heroes, ay, into the clay,
My fathers followed theirs before Christ was crucified.

EGAN O'RAHILLY (1665-1726)
translated from the Irish by
FRANK O'CONNOR

THE IRISH PROBLEM SOLVED

I have been assured by a very knowing American of my
acquaintance in London, that a young healthy child well
nursed is at a year old a most delicious, nourishing and
wholesome food, whether stewed, roasted, baked, or
boiled, and I make no doubt that it will equally serve
in a *fricassée* or a *ragoût*.

I do therefore humbly offer it to public consideration,
that of the hundred and twenty thousand children,
already computed, twenty thousand may be reserved for
breed, whereof only one-fourth part to be males, which
is more than we allow to sheep, black cattle, or swine,
and my reason is that these children are seldom the fruits
of marriage, a circumstance not much regarded by our
savages, therefore one male will be sufficient to serve
four females. That the remaining hundred thousand
may at a year old be offered in sale to the persons of
quality, and fortune, through the kingdom, always
advising the mother to let them suck plentifully in
the last month, so as to render them plump and fat
for a good table. A child will make two dishes at an
entertainment for friends, and when the family dines
alone, the fore or hind quarter will make a reasonable
dish, and seasoned with a little pepper or salt will
be very good boiled on the fourth day, especially in
winter.

I have reckoned upon a medium, that a child just born will weigh twelve pounds, and in a solar year if tolerably nursed increaseth to twenty-eight pounds.

I grant this food will be somewhat dear, and therefore very proper for landlords, who, as they have already devoured most of the parents, seem to have the best title to the children.

Infant's flesh will be in season throughout the year, but more plentiful in March, and a little before and after, for we are told by a grave author, an eminent French physician, that fish being a prolific diet, there are more children born in Roman Catholic countries about nine months after Lent, than at any other season: therefore reckoning a year after Lent, the markets will be more glutted than usual, because the number of popish infants is at least three to one in this kingdom, and therefore it will have one other collateral advantage by lessening the number of papists among us.

I have already computed the charge of nursing a beggar's child (in which list I reckon all cottagers, labourers and four-fifths of the farmers) to be about two shillings *per annum*, rags included, and I believe no gentleman would repine to give ten shillings for the carcase of a good fat child, which, as I have said will make four dishes of excellent nutritive meat, when he hath only some particular friend, or his own family to dine with him. Thus the squire will learn to be a good landlord, and grow popular among his tenants, the mother will have eight shillings net profit, and be fit for work till she produces another child.

Those who are more thrifty (as I must confess the times require) may flay the carcase; the skin of which, artificially dressed, will make admirable gloves for ladies, and summer boots for fine gentlemen.

As to our City of Dublin, shambles may be appointed for this purpose, in the most convenient parts of it, and butchers we may be assured will not be wanting, although I rather recommend buying the children alive, and dressing them hot from the knife, as we do roasting pigs.

JONATHAN SWIFT (1667-1745)
A Modest Proposal

THE NEW NATION

Let whoever think otherwise, I M. B. Drapier, desire to be excepted, for I declare next under God I depend only on the King, my sovereign, and on the laws of my own country; and I am so far from depending upon the people of England that if they should ever rebel against my sovereign (which God forbid) I would be ready at the first command from his Majesty to take arms against them as some of my countrymen did against theirs at Preston. And if such a rebellion should prove so successful as to fix the Pretender on the throne of England, I would venture to transgress that statute so far as to lose every drop of my blood to hinder him from being King of Ireland.

'Tis true indeed that within the memory of man the parliaments of England have sometimes assumed the power of binding this kingdom by laws enacted there, wherein they were at first openly opposed (as far as truth, reason and justice are capable of opposing) by the famous Mr. Molyneux, an English gentleman born here, as well as by several of the greatest patriots and best Whigs in England. But the love and torrent of power prevailed. Indeed the arguments on both sides were invincible; for in reason, all government without the consent of the governed is the very definition of slavery; but in fact eleven men well armed will certainly subdue one single man in his shirt. But I have done. For those who have used power to cramp liberty have gone so far as to resent even the liberty of complaining, although a man upon the rack was never known to be refused the liberty of roaring as loud as he thought fit.

And as we are apt to sink too much under unreasonable fears, so we are too soon inclined to be raised by groundless hopes (according to the nature of all consumptive bodies like ours). Thus it hath been given about for several days past that somebody in England empowered a second somebody to write to a third somebody here to assure us that we should no more be troubled with those half-pence. And this is reported to have been done by the same person who was said to have sworn some months ago that he would "ram them down our throats" (though I doubt they would stick in our stomachs); but whichever of these reports is true or false, it is no concern of ours. For in this point we have nothing to do with English ministers, and I should be sorry it lay in their power to redress this grievance or to enforce it; for the report of the Committee hath given me a surfeit. The remedy is wholly in your own hands, and therefore I have digressed a little in order to refresh and continue that spirit so seasonably raised amongst you, and to let you see that, by the laws of God, of Nature, of Nations and of your own country, you are and ought to be as free a people as your brethren in England.

JONATHAN SWIFT (1667-1745)
The Drapier's Fourth Letter

THE QUERIST—1735

Some queries proposed to the consideration of the public:

Whether there be upon earth any Christian or civilised people so beggardly wretched and destitute, as the common Irish?

Whether, nevertheless, there is any other people whose wants may be more easily supplied from home?

Whether, if there was a wall of brass a thousand cubits high round their kingdom, our natives might not nevertheless live cleanly and comfortably, till the land, and reap the fruits of it?

Whether an Irish lady, set out with French silks and Flanders lace, may not be said to consume more beef and butter than fifty of our labouring peasants?

Whether there be any country in Christiandom more capable of improvement than Ireland?

Whether the maxim, "What is everybody's business is nobody's business," prevails in any country under the sun more than in Ireland?

Whether we are the only people who starve in the market of plenty?

Whether there be not every year more cash circulated at the card-tables of Dublin than at all the fairs of Ireland?

Whose fault is it if poor Ireland continues poor?

GEORGE BERKELEY, BISHOP OF CLOYNE (1685-1753)

THE WEARING OF THE GREEN

"O Paddy dear, and did ye hear the news that's goin' round?
The shamrock is by law forbid to grow on Irish ground!
No more Saint Patrick's Day we'll keep, his colour can't be seen,
For there's a cruel law ag'in the Wearin' o' the Green.
I met with Napper Tandy, and he took me by the hand,
And he said, ' How's poor ould Ireland, and how does she stand? '
' She's the most distressful country that ever yet was seen,
For they're hanging men and women there for the Wearin' o' the Green.'

HALFPENNY BRIDGE, RIVER LIFFEY, DUBLIN
(Bord Fáilte)

CASTLE ESPIE, STRANGFORD LOUGH, COUNTY DOWN
(Northern Ireland Tourist Board)

THE BURREN, COUNTY CLARE
(Bord Fáilte)

SLEMISH MOUNTAIN, COUNTY ANTRIM
(Northern Ireland Tourist Board)

"So if the colour we must wear be England's cruel red
Let it remind us of the blood that Irishmen have shed;
And pull the shamrock from your hat, and throw it on
  the sod,
But never fear, 'twill take root there, though underfoot
  'tis trod.
When laws can stop the blades of grass from growin' as
  they grow,
And when the leaves in summer-time their colour dare
  not show,
Then I will change the colour too I wear in my caubeen;
But till that day, please God, I'll stick to the Wearin' o'
  the Green."

ANONYMOUS (18th cent.)

THE IRISH ANTHEM

The door was thrown open and I entered the smoky
interior of a Thibetan hut crammed with children. And
every child had flaming red hair. A raw cow's-tail lay
on the floor, and by its side two pieces of black velvet—
my black velvet—rudely hacked into the semblance of
masks.

"And what is this shame, Namgay Doola?" said I.

He grinned more willingly than ever. "There was no
shame," said he. "I did but cut off the tail of that man's
cow. He betrayed me. I was minded to shoot him,
Sahib. But not to death. Indeed not to death. Only in
the legs."

"And why at all, since it is the custom to pay revenue
to the King? Why at all?"

"By the God of my father I cannot tell," said Namgay
Doola.

"And who was thy father?"

"The same that had this gun." He showed me his

4

weapon—a Tower musket bearing date 1832 and the stamp of the Honourable East India Company.

"And thy father's name?" said I.

"Timlay Doola," said he. "At the first, I being then a little child, it is in my mind that he wore a red coat."

"Of that I have no doubt. But repeat the name of thy father thrice or four times."

He obeyed, and I understood whence the puzzling accent in his speech came. "Thimlay Doola," said he excitedly. "To this hour I worship his God."

"May I see that God?"

"In a little while—at twilight time."

"Rememberest thou aught of thy father's speech?"

"It is long ago. But there is one word which he said often. Thus ' Shun.' Then I and my brethren stood upon our feet, our hands at our sides. Thus."

"Even so. And what was thy mother?"

"A woman of the hills. We be Lepchas of Darjeeling, but me they call an outlander because my hair is as thou seest."

The Thibetan woman, his wife, touched him on the arm gently. The long parley outside the fort had lasted far into the day. It was now close upon twilight—the hour of the Angelus. Very solemnly, the red-headed brats rose from the floor and formed a semi-circle. Namgay Doola laid his gun against the wall, lighted a little oil lamp, and set it before a recess in the wall. Pulling aside a curtain of dirty cloth, he revealed a worn brass crucifix leaning against the helmet-badge of a long-forgotten East India regiment. "Thus did my father," he said, crossing himself clumsily. The wife and children followed suit. Then all together they struck up the wailing chant that I had heard on the hillside—

> *Dir hane mard-i-yemen dir*
> *To weeree ala gee*

I was puzzled no longer. Again and again they

crooned, as if their hearts would break, their version of
the chorus of the *Wearing of the Green*—

> They're hanging men and women too
> For the wearing of the green.

RUDYARD KIPLING (1865-1936)
Humorous Tales

THE SHAN VAN VOCHT

Oh! the French are on the sea,
    Says the Shan Van Vocht;
The French are on the sea,
    Says the Shan Van Vocht:
Oh! the French are in the Bay,
They'll be here without delay,
And the Orange will decay,
    Says the Shan Van Vocht.

And where will they have their camp?
    Says the Shan Van Vocht;
Where will they have their camp?
    Says the Shan Van Vocht;
On the Curragh of Kildare;
The boys they will be there,
With their pikes in good repair,
    Says the Shan Van Vocht.

Then what will the yeomen do?
    Says the Shan Van Vocht;
What will the yeomen do?
    Says the Shan Van Vocht.
What should the yeomen do
But throw off the Red and Blue,
And swear that they'll be true
    To the Shan Van Vocht?

And what colour will they wear?
   Says the Shan Van Vocht;
What colour will they wear
   Says the Shan Van Vocht;
What colour should be seen
Where our fathers' homes have been
But our own immortal Green?
   Says the Shan Van Vocht.

And will Ireland then be free?
   Says the Shan Van Vocht;
Will Ireland then be free?
   Says the Shan Van Vocht;
Yes, Ireland shall be free,
From the centre to the sea;
Then hurrah for Liberty!
   Says the Shan Van Vocht.

              Popular song (18th cent.)

THE FIRST FRENCH INVASION, 1796

December 23. Last night it blew a heavy gale from the eastward with snow, so that the mountains are covered this morning, which will render our bivouacs extremely amusing. It is to be observed that of the thirty-two points of the compass, the east is precisely the most unfavourable to us. In consequence, we are this morning separated for the fourth time; sixteen sail, including nine or ten of the line, with Bouvet and Grouchy, are at anchor with us, and about twenty are blown to sea; luckily the gale set from the shore, so I am in hopes no mischief will ensue. The wind is still high, and as usual, right ahead; and I dread a visit from the English; and altogether I am in great uneasiness. Oh, that we were once ashore, let what might ensue after; I am sick to the very soul of this suspense. It is curious to see how things are managed in this best of all possible worlds. We are here, sixteen sail, great and small, scattered up and down in a noble bay, and so dispersed that there are not two together in any spot save one, and there they are now so close, that if it blows to-night as it did last night they will inevitably run foul of each other, unless one of them prefers driving on shore. . . .

December 24. This morning the whole état-major has been miraculously converted, and it was agreed, in full council, that general Cherin, colonel Waudre, chef d'état-major of the artillery, and myself, should go aboard the *Immortalité*, and press General Grouchy in the strongest manner, to proceed on the expedition with the ruins of our scattered army. Accordingly we made a signal to speak with the admiral, and in about an hour we were aboard. I must do Grouchy the justice to say, that the moment we gave our opinion in favour of proceeding, he took his part decidedly, and like a man of spirit; he instantly set about preparing the *ordre de bataille*, and we finished it without delay. We are not more than 6,500 strong, but they are tried soldiers who have seen fire, and I have the strongest hopes that, after all, we shall bring our enterprise to a glorious termination. It is a bold attempt and truly original. All the time we were preparing the *ordre de bataille*, we were laughing most immoderately at the poverty of our means; and I believe, under the circumstances, it was the merriest council of war that was ever held; but, " *Des chevaliers Francais tel est le caractère.*" Grouchy, the commander-in-chief, never had so few men under his orders since he was adjutant-general; Waudre, who is lieutenant colonel, finds himself now at the head of the artillery, which is a furious park, consisting of one piece of eight, one of four, and two six-inch howitzers; when he was a captain, he never commanded fewer than ten pieces, but now that he is in fact general of the artillery, he prefers taking the field with four. He is a gallant fellow, and offered, on my proposal last night, to remain with me and command his company, in case General Grouchy had agreed to the proposal I made to Cherin. It is altogether an enterprise truly *unique*; we have not one guinea; we have not a tent; we have not a horse to draw our four pieces of artillery; the general-in-chief marches on foot; we leave all our baggage behind us; we have nothing but the arms in our hands, the clothes on our backs, and a good courage, but that is sufficient. With all these original circumstances, such as I believe never were· found united in an expedition of such magnitude as that we are about to attempt, we are all as gay as larks. I never saw the French character better exemplified than in this morning's business. Well, at last I believe we are about to disembark; God knows how I long for it. My enemy, the wind, seems just now, at eight o'clock to relent a little, so we may reach Bantry by to-morrow. The enemy has now had four days to recover from his panic, and prepare to receive us; so much the worse, but I do not mind it. We purpose to make a race for Cork, as if the devil were in our bodies; and when we are there we will stop for a day or two to take breath, and look about us. From Bantry to Cork is about forty-five miles, which, with all our efforts, will take us three days, I suppose we may have a brush by the way; but I think we are able to deal with any force that can, at a week's notice, be brought against us. . . .

December 25. Last night I had the strongest expectations that to-day we should debark, but at two this morning I was awakened by the wind. I rose immediately, and wrapping myself in my great coat, walked for an hour in the gallery, devoured by the most gloomy reflections. The wind continues right ahead, so that it is absolutely impossible to work up to the landing place, and God knows when it will change. The same wind is exactly favourable to bring the English upon us, and these cruel delays give the enemy time to assemble his entire force in this neighbourhood; and perhaps (it is, unfortunately, more than perhaps) by his superiority in numbers, in cavalry, in artillery, in money, in provisions, in short in everything we want, to crush us, supposing we are even able to effectuate a landing at last; at the same time that the fleet will be caught as in a trap. Had we been able to land the first day and march directly to Cork, we should have infallibly carried it by a coup de main; and then we should have a footing in the country, but as it is—if we are taken, my fate will not be a mild one; the best I can expect is to be shot as an *emigré rentré*, unless I have the good fortune to be killed in action; for most assuredly if the enemy will have us, he must fight for us. Perhaps I may be reserved for a trial, for the sake of striking terror into others, in which case I shall be hanged as a traitor and embowelled, etc. As to the embowelling, "*je m'en fiche*," if ever they hang me, they are welcome to embowel me if they please. These are pleasant prospects! Nothing on earth could sustain me now, but the consciousness that I am engaged in a just and righteous cause. For my family, I have, by a desperate effort, surmounted my natural feelings so far, that I do not think of them at this moment. This day, at twelve, the wind blows a gale, still from the east; and our situation is now as critical as possible, for it is morally certain that this day or to-morrow on the morning, the English fleet will be in the harbour's mouth, and then adieu to every thing. In this desperate state of affairs, I proposed to Cherin to sally out with all our forces, to mount to the Shannon, and disembarking the troops, make a forced march to Limerick, which is probably unguarded; the garrison being, I am pretty certain, on its march to oppose us here; to pass the river at Limerick, and by forced marches, push to the north.

December 26. Last night, at half after six o'clock, in a heavy gale of wind still from the east, we were surprised by the admiral's frigate running under our quarter, and hailing the *Indomptable*, with orders to cut our cable and put to sea instantly; the frigate then pursued her course, leaving us all in the utmost astonishment. Our first idea was that it might be an English frigate lurking in the bottom of the bay, which took advantage of the storm and darkness of the night to make her escape, and wished to separate our squadron by this stratagem; for it seems utterly incredible that an admiral should cut and run in this manner, without any previous signal of any kind to warn the fleet; and that the first notice we should have of his intention, should be his hailing us in this extraordinary manner, with such unexpected and peremptory orders. After a short consultation with his officers (considering the storm, the darkness of the night, that we have two anchors out, and only one spare one in the hold), Captain Bedout resolved to wait, at all events, till to-morrow morning, in order to ascertain whether it was really the admiral who hailed us. The morning is now come, the gale continues, and the fog is so thick that we cannot see a ship's length ahead; so here we lie in the utmost uncertainty and anxiety. In all probability we are now left without admiral or general; if so Cherin will command the troops, and Bedout the fleet, but, at all events, there is an end of the expedition. Certainly we have been persecuted by a strange fatality from the very night of our departure at this hour. We have lost two commanders-in-chief; of four admirals not one remains; we have lost one ship of the line that we know of, and probably many others of which we know nothing; we have been now six days in Bantry Bay, within five hundred yards of the shore, without being able to effectuate a landing; we have been dispersed four times in four days; and at this moment, of forty-three sail, of which the expedition consisted, we can muster of all sizes but fourteen. There only wants our falling in with the English to complete our destruction; and to judge of the future by the past, there is every probability that that will not be wanting. . . . This infernal wind continues without intermission, and now that all is lost, I am as eager to get back to France as I was to come to Ireland.

December 27. Yesterday several vessels, including the *Indomptable*, dragged their anchors several times, and it was with great difficulty they rode out the gale. At two o'clock, the *Revolution*, a seventy-four, made signal that she could hold no longer, and in consequence of the commodore's permission who now commands our little squadron, cut her only cable and put to sea. In the night, the *Patriote* and *Pluton*, of seventy-four each, were forced to put to sea with the Nicomede flute, so that this morning we are reduced to seven sail of the line and one frigate. Any attempt here is now desperate; but I think still, if we were debarked at the mouth of the Shannon, we might yet recover all. At ten o'clock the commodore made signal to get under way, which was delayed by one of the ships, which required an hour to get ready. This hour we availed ourselves of to hold a council of war, at which were present, generals Cherin, and Harty, and Humbert, who came from their ships for that purpose; adjutant-generals Simon, Chasseloup, and myself; lieutenant-colonel Waudre, commanding the artillery, and Favory, captain of engineers, together with commodore Bedout, who was invited to assist; general Harty, as senior officer being president. It was agreed that our force being now reduced to 4,168 men, our artillery to two four-pounders, our ammunition to 1,500,000 cartridges and 500 rounds for the artillery, with 500 pounds of powder—this part of the country being utterly wild and savage, furnishing neither provisions nor horses, and especially as the enemy, having seven days' notice, together with three more which it would require to reach Cork, supposing we even met with no obstacle, had time more than sufficient to assemble his forces in numbers sufficient to crush our little army; considering, moreover, that this province is the only one of the four which has testified no disposition to revolt; that it is the most remote from the party which is ready for insurrection; and finally, captain Bedout having communicated his instructions, which are, to mount as high as the Shannon and cruise there five days; it was unanimously agreed to quit Bantry Bay directly, and proceed for the mouth of the Shannon, in hopes to rejoin some of our scattered companions; and when we are there we will determine, according to the means in our hands, what part we shall take. I am the more content with this determination, as it is substantially the same with the paper which I read to general Cherin, and the rest, the day before yesterday. The wind, at last, has come round to the southward, and the signal is now flying to get under way. At half after four, there being every appearance of a stormy night, three vessels cut their cables and put to sea. The *Indomptable*, having with great difficulty weighed anchor, we were forced, at length, to cut the cable of the other, and make the best of our way out of the bay, being followed by the whole of our little squadron, now reduced to ten sail, of which seven are of the line, one frigate, and two corvettes or luggers.

December 28. Last night it blew a perfect hurricane. At one this morning a dreadful sea took the ship in the quarter, stove in the quarter gallery, and one of the dead-lights in the great cabin, which was instantly filled with water to the depth of three feet. The cots of the officers were almost all torn down, and themselves and their trunks floated about the cabin. For my part, I had just fallen asleep when awakened by the shock, of which I at first did not comprehend the meaning; but hearing the water distinctly rolling in the cabin beneath me, and two or three of the officers mounting in their shirts as wet as if they had risen from the bottom of the sea, I concluded instantly that the ship had struck and was filling with water, and that she would sink directly. . . . Immediately after this blow, the wind abated, and at daylight, having run nine knots an hour under one jib only, during the hurricane, we found ourselves at the rendezvous, having parted company with three ships of the line, and the frigate, which makes our *sixth* separation. The frigate *Coquille* joined us in the course of the day, which we spent standing off and on the shore, without being joined by any of our missing companions.

December 29. At four this morning, the commodore made the signal to steer for France; so there is an end of our expedition for the present; perhaps for ever.

THEOBALD WOLFE TONE (1763-98)
Journal

SLIEVENAMON

It is my sorrow that this day's troubles
   Poor Irishmen so sore did strike,
Because our tyrants are laughing at us
   And say they fear neither fork nor pike;
Our major never came to lead us;
   We had no orders, and drifted on.
As you'd send a drover with a cow to the fair
   On the sunny side of Slievenamon.

The sturdy Frenchman with ships in order
   Beneath sharp masts is long at sea;
They are always saying they will come to Ireland,
   And they will set the Irish free.

Light as a blackbird on a green bough swinging
  Would be my heart if the French would come—
O the broken ranks and the trumpets ringing
  On the sunny side of Slievenamon!

ANONYMOUS (18th cent.)
translated from the Irish by
FRANK O'CONNOR

THE FRENCH LAND

1798

The French and the Irish that were with them came the mountain road from Crossmolina. They had little light cannon that they dragged with them. 'Twas midnight when they got here to Lahardane, and they stopped for an hour at the Fair Green beyond. They came to free Ireland, but a lot of people at the time were afraid and didn't rightly understand. The people gathered about them in the Green but they couldn't understand the French language. The French were going by another road, but Father Conroy, the parish priest, told them to take the way by the Windy Gap. They took it and they drove in all the cattle about the Gap. They went on then to Castlebar and they won a big battle there. The Irish fought well with them there, but they'd fight better if they were trained. . . .

There was a lot from here joined the French. There was a poor labouring man—"Paidin a' choga" he was called—went from here to Killala when he heard they were landed. He lived over in Rawkell. He fought well with them through all the battles and came back after the troubles were over. And when he was dying long after, he sent for Liam Pleimionn, whose own father was with the French, and he told Pleimionn that he had sixteen shillings left in his pocket and to get a piper to play *The White Cockade* over his grave when he was dead.

A man named Gaughan that lived here joined them. He was caught and was in the jail at Castlebar. The prisoners made a hole in the wall, and Gaughan got through with two others, though he was a big man. They stripped themselves of their clothes first, and when they got out they made for Nephin. There was another man too joined them—he was from Carrowfluffy. In the battle at Castlebar a French officer and an English officer were at the corner of the square firing at each other with pistols. The man from Carrowfluffy came up behind the Englishman and knocked him dead with a pike. And the French officer and himself were good friends after that. There was a man from this neighbourhood, Larry Gillespie, that followed Humbert too. He was in the fighting at Ballinamuck and in the scattering made his way home. But he was arrested and taken in to Ballina. After being tried he was sentenced to be hanged. He was only a short time married and his wife went to the jail. She took a bottle of poteen with her that she gave to the guards, and they let her in to see him. The two of them exchanged clothes and Larry got out. He faced for Erris and was never taken. Next morning Larry was missed, and they brought the wife before the same judges that ordered Larry to be hanged —Ormsby, Jackson and Lord Portarlington. "Well," says Lord Portarlington, "since Larry can't be hanged now, there's nothing for it but to give a reprieve to his wife." Larry got away to France and stayed there for seventeen years, and when he came back he found his wife married.

recorded by RICHARD HAYES
The Last Invasion of Ireland

LAST WORDS, 1803

I have been charged with that importance in the emancipation of my country as to be considered the keystone of the combination of Irishmen; or, as your lordship expressed it, " the life and blood of the conspiracy." You do me honour overmuch; you have given to the subaltern all the credit of a superior. There are men engaged in this conspiracy who are not only superior to me, but even to your own conceptions of yourself, my lord—men before the splendour of whose genius and virtues I should bow with respectful deference, and who would think themselves disgraced by shaking your blood-stained hand.

What, my lord, shall you tell me, on the passage to the scaffold, which that tyranny (of which you are only the intermediary executioner) has erected for my murder, that I am accountable for all the blood that has and will be shed in this struggle of the oppressed against the oppressor—shall you tell me this, and must I be so very a slave as not to repel it? I do not fear to approach the Omnipotent Judge to answer for the conduct of my whole life; and am I to be appalled and falsified by a mere remnant of mortality here? By you, too, although if it were possible to collect all the innocent blood that you have shed in your unhallowed ministry in one great reservoir, your lordship might swim in it. . . .

Here Lord Norbury told Mr. Emmet that his sentiments and language disgraced his family and his education, but more particularly his father, Dr. Emmet, who was a man, if alive, that would not countenance such opinions. To which Mr. Emmet replied:

If the spirits of the illustrious dead participate in the concerns and cares of those who were dear to them in this transitory life, oh! ever dear and venerated shade of my departed father, look down with scrutiny upon the conduct of your suffering son, and see if I have even for a moment deviated from those principles of morality and patriotism which it was your care to instil into my youthful mind, and for which I am now about to offer up my life. My lords, you are impatient for the sacrifice. The blood which you seek is not congealed by the artificial terrors which surround your victim—it circulates warmly and unruffled through the channels which God created for noble purposes, but which you are now bent to destroy, for purposes so grievous that they cry to heaven. Be yet patient! I have but a few more words to say—I am going to my cold and silent grave—my lamp of life is nearly extinguished—my race is run—the grave opens to receive me, and I sink into its bosom. I have but one request to make at my departure from this world, it is—the charity of its silence. Let no man write my epitaph; for as no man, who knows my motives, dare now vindicate them, let not prejudice or ignorance asperse them. Let them rest in obscurity and peace! Let my memory be left in oblivion, and my tomb remain uninscribed, until other times and other men can do justice to my character. When my country takes her place among the nations of the earth, *then*, and *not till then*, let my epitaph be written. I have done.

ROBERT EMMET (1778-1803)

WHEN HE WHO ADORES THEE

Robert Emmet

When he who adores thee has left but the name
    Of his fault and his sorrows behind,
O, say wilt thou weep, when they darken the fame
    Of a life that for thee was resigned!

Yes, weep, and however my foes may condemn,
    Thy tears shall efface their decree;
For Heaven can witness, though guilty to them,
    I have been but too faithful to thee.

With thee were the dreams of my earliest love;
    Every thought of my reason was thine:
In my last humble prayer to the Spirit above
    Thy name shall be mingled with mine!
O, blest are the lovers and friends who shall live
    The days of thy glory to see;
But the next dearest blessing that Heaven can give
    Is the pride of thus dying for thee.

                 THOMAS MOORE (1780-1852)

SHE IS FAR FROM THE LAND

This poem refers to Sarah Curran who was engaged to Robert Emmet.
After his death she became the wife of an officer who took her to
Sicily hoping that travel would restore her spirits, but her grief for
Emmet was so great she died of a broken heart.

She is far from the land where her young hero sleeps,
    And lovers are round her sighing;
But coldly she turns from their gaze, and weeps,
    For her heart in his grave is lying!

She sings the wild songs of her dear native plains,
    Every note which he loved awaking:
Ah! little they think who delight in her strains,
    How the heart of the minstrel is breaking!

He had lived for his love, for his country he died,
    They were all that to life had entwined him;
Nor soon shall the tears of his country be dried,
    Nor long will his love stay behind him.

O, make her a grave where the sunbeams rest
  When they promise a glorious morrow;
They'll shine o'er her sleep, like a smile from the west,
  From her own loved island of sorrow!

THOMAS MOORE (1780-1852)

THE FAMINE

A calm, still horror was over all the land. Go where you would, in the heart of the town or in the church, on the mountain side or on the level plain, there was the stillness and heavy pall-like feeling of the chamber of death. You stood in the presence of a dread, silent, vast dissolution. An unseen ruin was creeping round you. You saw no war of classes, no open Janissary war of foreigners, no human agency of destruction. You could weep, but the rising curse died unspoken within your heart, like a profanity. Human passion there was none, but inhuman and unearthly quiet. Children met you, toiling heavily on stone-heaps, but their burning eyes were senseless, and their faces cramped and weasened like stunted old men. Gangs worked, but without a murmur, or a whistle, or a laugh, ghostly, like voiceless shadows to the eye. Even womanhood had ceased to be womanly. The birds of the air carolled no more, and the crow and raven dropped dead upon the wing. The very dogs, hairless, with the hair down, and the vertebrae of the back protruding like the saw of a bone, glared at you from the ditchside with a wolfish avid eye, and then slunk away scowling and cowardly. Nay, the sky of heaven, the blue mountains, the still lake stretching far away westward, looked not as their wont. Between them and you rose up a steaming agony, a film of suffering, impervious and dim. It seemed as if the *anima mundi*, the soul of the land, was faint and dying, and that the faintness and the death had crept into all things of earth and heaven. You stood there, too, in the presence of something unseen and terrible.

JOHN MITCHEL (1818-75)

THE UNCROWNED KING

On September 19, Parnell attended a mass meeting at Ennis. There, in a speech which rang through the land, he struck the keynote of the agitation; he laid down the lines on which the League should work. Slowly, calmly, deliberately, without a quiver of passion, a note of rhetoric, or an exclamation of anger, but in a tone that penetrated his audience like the touch of cold steel, he proclaimed war against all who should resist the mandates of the League.

"Depend upon it that the measure of the Land Bill next session will be the measure of your activity and energy this winter. It will be the measure of your determination not to pay unjust rents; it will be the measure of your determination to keep a firm grip on your homesteads. It will be the measure of your determination not to bid for farms from which others have been evicted, and to use the strong force of public opinion to deter any unjust men amongst yourselves—and there are many such—from bidding for such farms. Now what are you to do to a tenant who bids for a farm from which his neighbour has been evicted?"

Here there was much excitement, and cries of "Kill him!" "Shoot him!" Parnell waited, with his hands clasped behind his back, looking quietly out upon the crowd until the tumult subsided, and then softly resumed: "Now I think I heard somebody say 'Shoot him!'—(a voice: 'Yes, quite right')—but I wish to point out to you a very much better way—a more

Christian and a more charitable way, which will give the lost sinner an opportunity of repenting."

Here there were inquiring glances, and a lull, and a silence, which was scarcely broken until Parnell finished the next sentence—a long sentence, but every word of which was heard, as the voice of the speaker hardened and his face wore an expression of remorseless determination. "When a man takes a farm from which another has been evicted, you must show him on the roadside when you meet him, you must show him in the streets of the town—(a voice: ' Shun him! ')—you must show him at the shop counter, you must show him in the fair, and in the market-place, and even in the house of worship, by leaving him severely alone, by putting him into a moral Coventry, by isolating him from his kind as if he was a leper of old—you must show him your detestation of the crime he has committed, and you may depend upon it that there will be no man so full of avarice, so lost to shame, as to dare the public opinion of all right-thinking men and to transgress your unwritten code of law."

R. BARRY O'BRIEN (*b.* 1874)
The Life of Charles Stewart Parnell

THE DEAD KING

He was for Ireland and Parnell and so was his father: and so was Dante too for one night at the band on the esplanade she had hit a gentleman on the head with her umbrella because he had taken off his hat when the band played *God save the Queen* at the end.

Mr. Dedalus gave a snort of contempt.

— Ah, John, he said. It is true for them. We are an unfortunate priestridden race and always were and always will be till the end of the chapter.

Uncle Charles shook his head, saying:

— A bad business! A bad business!

Mr. Dedalus repeated:

— A priestridden Godforsaken race!

He pointed to the portrait of his grandfather on the wall to his right.

— Do you see that old chap up there, John? he said. He was a good Irishman when there was no money in the job. He was condemned to death as a whiteboy. But he had a saying about our clerical friends, that he would never let one of them put his two feet under his mahogany.

Dante broke in angrily:

— If we are a priestridden race we ought to be proud of it! They are the apple of God's eye. *Touch them not*, says Christ, *for they are the apple of My eye.*

— And can we not love our country then? asked Mr. Casey. Are we not to follow the man that was born to lead us?

— A traitor to his country! replied Dante. A traitor, an adulterer! The priests were right to abandon him. The priests were always the true friends of Ireland.

— Were they, faith! said Mr. Casey.

He threw his fist on the table and, frowning angrily, protruded one finger after another.

— Didn't the bishops of Ireland betray us in the time of the union when Bishop Lanigan presented an address of loyalty to the Marquess Cornwallis? Didn't the bishops and priests sell the aspirations of their country in 1829 in return for catholic emancipation? Didn't they denounce the fenian movement from the pulpit and in the confession box? And didn't they dishonour the ashes of Terence Bellew MacManus?

His face was glowing with anger and Stephen felt the glow rise to his own cheek as the spoken words thrilled him. Mr. Dedalus uttered a guffaw of coarse scorn.

— O, by God—he cried—I forgot little old Paul Cullen. Another apple of God's eye!

Dante bent across the table and cried to Mr. Casey:

— Right! Right! They were always right! God and morality and religion come first.

Mrs. Dedalus, seeing her excitement, said to her:

— Mrs. Riordan, don't excite yourself answering them.

— God and religion before everything! Dante cried. God and religion before the world!

Mr. Casey raised his clenched fist and brought it down on the table with a crash.

— Very well, then, he shouted hoarsely, if it comes to that, no God for Ireland!

— John! John ! cried Mr. Dedalus, seizing his guest by the coat sleeve.

Dante stared across the table, her cheeks shaking. Mr. Casey struggled up from his chair and bent across the table towards her, scraping the air from before his eyes with one hand as though he were tearing aside a cobweb.

— No God for Ireland! he cried. We have had too much God in Ireland. Away with God!

— Blasphemer! Devil! screamed Dante, starting to her feet and almost spitting in his face.

Uncle Charles and Mr. Dedalus pulled Mr. Casey back into his chair again, talking to him from both sides reasonably. He stared before him out of his dark flaming eyes, repeating:

— Away with God, I say!

Dante shoved her chair violently aside and left the table, upsetting her napkinring which rolled slowly along the carpet and came to rest against the foot of an easy chair. Mrs. Dedalus rose quickly and followed her towards the door. At the door Dante turned round violently and shouted down the room, her cheeks flushed and quivering with rage:

— Devil out of hell! We won! We crushed him to death! Fiend!

The door slammed behind her.

Mr. Casey, freeing his arms from his holders, suddenly bowed his head on his hands with a sob of pain.

— Poor Parnell! he cried loudly. My dead king!

He sobbed loudly and bitterly.

Stephen raising his terrorstricken face, saw that his father's eyes were full of tears.

JAMES JOYCE (1882-1941)
Portrait Of The Artist As A Young Man

PARNELL

The rest I pass, one sentence I unsay.
Had de Valera eaten Parnell's heart
No loose-lipped demagogue had won the day,
No civil rancour torn the land apart.

Had Cosgrave eaten Parnell's heart, the land's
Imagination had been satisfied,
Or lacking that, government in such hands,
O'Higgins its sole statesman had not died.

Had even O'Duffy—but I name no more—
Their school a crowd, his master solitude;
Through Jonathan Swift's dark grove he passed, and
    there
Plucked bitter wisdom that enriched his blood.

W. B. YEATS (1865-1939)
Collected Poems of W. B. Yeats

THE ENGLISHMAN IN IRELAND
GALWAY GAOL 1888

Honoured I lived e'erwhile with honoured men
    In opulent state. My table nightly spread
Found guests of worth, peer, priest and citizen,
    And poet crowned, and beauty garlanded.

Nor these alone, for hunger too I fed,
And many a lean tramp and sad Magdalen
  Passed from my doors less hard for sake of bread.
Whom grudged I ever purse or hand or pen?

To-night, unwelcomed at these gates of woe
  I stand with churls, and there is none to greet
My weariness with smile or courtly show
  Nor, though I hunger long, to bring me meat.
God! what a little accident of gold
Fences our weakness from the wolves of old!

WILFRID SCAWEN BLUNT (1840-1922)
Poems

POBLACHT NA H EIREANN

THE PROVISIONAL GOVERNMENT
OF THE
IRISH REPUBLIC
TO THE PEOPLE OF IRELAND
1916

Irishmen and Irishwomen: In the name of God and
of the dead generations from which she receives her old
tradition of nationhood, Ireland, through us, summons
her children to her flag and strikes for her freedom.

Having organised and trained her manhood through
her secret revolutionary organisation, the Irish Repub-
lican Brotherhood, and through her open military
organisations, the Irish Volunteers and the Irish Citizen
Army, having patiently perfected her discipline, having
resolutely waited for the right moment to reveal itself,
she now seizes that moment, and, supported by her
exiled children in America and by gallant allies in
Europe, but relying in the first on her own strength, she
strikes in full confidence of victory.

We declare the right of the people of Ireland to the ownership of Ireland, and to the unfettered control of Irish destinies, to be sovereign and indefeasible. The long usurpation of that right by a foreign people and government has not extinguished the right, nor can it ever be extinguished except by the destruction of the Irish people. In every generation the Irish people have asserted their right to national freedom and sovereignty; six times during the past three hundred years they have asserted it in arms. Standing on that fundamental right and again asserting it in arms in the face of the world, we hereby proclaim the Irish Republic as a Sovereign Independent State, and we pledge our lives and the lives of our comrades-in-arms to the cause of its freedom, of its welfare, and of its exaltation among the nations.

The Irish Republic is entitled to, and hereby claims, the allegiance of every Irishman and Irishwoman. The Republic guarantees religious and civil liberty, equal rights and equal opportunities to all its citizens, and declares its resolve to pursue the happiness and prosperity of the whole nation and of all its parts, cherishing all the children of the nation equally, and oblivious of the differences carefully fostered by an alien government, which have divided a minority from the majority in the past.

Until our arms have brought the opportune moment for the establishment of a permanent National Government, representative of the whole people of Ireland and elected by the suffrages of all men and women, the Provisional Government, hereby constituted, will administer the civil and military affairs of the Republic in trust for the people.

We place the cause of the Irish Republic under the protection of the Most High God, Whose blessing we invoke upon our arms, and we pray that no one who serves that cause will dishonour it by cowardice, inhumanity, or rapine. In this supreme hour the Irish nation must, by its valour and discipline and by the readiness of its children to sacrifice themselves for the common good, prove itself worthy of the august destiny to which it is called.

Signed on Behalf of the Provisional Government

Thomas J. Clarke

Sean Mac Diarmada   *Thomas Mac Donagh*
P. H. Pearse   *Eamonn Ceannt*
James Connolly   *Joseph Plunkett*

EASTER 1916

I have met them at close of day
Coming with vivid faces
From counter or desk among grey
Eighteenth-century houses.
I have passed with a nod of the head
Or polite meaningless words,
Or have lingered awhile and said
Polite meaningless words,
And thought before I had done
Of a mocking tale or a gibe
To please a companion
Around the fire at the club,
Being certain that they and I
But lived where motley is worn:
All changed, changed utterly:
A terrible beauty is born.

That woman's days were spent
In ignorant good-will,
Her nights in argument
Until her voice grew shrill.

What voice more sweet than hers
When, young and beautiful,
She rode to harriers?
This man had kept a school
And rode our wingéd horse;
This other his helper and friend
Was coming into his force;
He might have won fame in the end,
So sensitive his nature seemed,
So daring and sweet his thought.
This other man I had dreamed
A drunken, vainglorious lout.
He had done most bitter wrong
To some who are near my heart,
Yet I number him in the song;
He, too, has resigned his part
In the casual comedy;
He, too, has been changed in his turn,
Transformed utterly:
A terrible beauty is born.

Hearts with one purpose alone
Through summer and winter seem
Enchanted to a stone
To trouble the living stream
The horse that comes from the road,
The rider, the birds that range
From cloud to tumbling cloud,
Minute by minute they change;
A shadow of cloud on the stream
Changes minute by minute;
A horse-hoof slides on the brim,
And a horse plashes within it;
The long-legged moor-hens dive,
And hens to moor-cocks call;
Minute by minute they live:
The stone's in the midst of all.

Too long a sacrifice
Can make a stone of the heart.
O when may it suffice?
That is Heaven's part, our part
To murmur name upon name,
As a mother names her child
When sleep at last has come
On limbs that had run wild.
What is it but nightfall?
No, no, not night but death;
Was it needless death after all?
For England may keep faith
For all that is done and said.
We know their dream; enough
To know they dreamed and are dead;
And what if excess of love
Bewildered them till they died?
I write it out in a verse—
MacDonagh and MacBride
And Connolly and Pearse
Now and in time to be,
Wherever green is worn,
Are changed, changed utterly:
A terrible beauty is born.

W. B. YEATS (1865-1939)
Collected Poems of W. B. Yeats

A DUBLIN BALLAD: 1916

O write it up above your hearth
And troll it out to sun and moon,
To all true Irishmen on earth
Arrest and death come late or soon.

Some boyo whistled *ninety-eight*
One Sunday night in College Green,

And such a broth of love and hate
Was stirred ere Monday morn was late
As Dublin town had never seen.

And god-like forces shocked and shook
Through Irish hearts that lively day,
And hope it seemed no ill could brook.
Christ! for that liberty they took
There was the ancient deuce to pay!

The deuce in all his bravery,
His girth and gall grown no whit less,
He swarmed in from the fatal sea
With pomp of huge artillery
And brass and copper haughtiness.

He cracked up all the town with guns
That roared loud psalms to fire and death,
And houses hailed down granite tons
To smash our wounded underneath.

And when at last the golden bell
Of liberty was silenced—then
He learned to shoot extremely well
At unarmed Irish gentlemen!

Ah, where was Michael and gold Moll
And Seumas and my drowsy self?
Why did fate blot us from the scroll?
Why were we left upon the shelf,

Fooling with trifles in the dark
When the light struck us wild and hard?
Sure our hearts were as good a mark
For Tommies up before the dark
At rifle practice in the yard!

Well, the last fire is trodden down,
Our dead are rotting fast in lime,
We all can sneak back into town,
Stravague about as in old time,

And stare at gaps of grey and blue
Where Lower Mount Street used to be,
And where flies hum round muck we knew
As Abbey Street and Eden Quay.

And when the devil made us wise
Each in his own peculiar hell,
With desert hearts and drunken eyes
We're free to sentimentalize
By corners where the martyrs fell.

SIR ARNOLD BAX ("DERMOT O'BYRNE") (1883-1953)

THE DEATH OF COLLINS

1922

Next morning as he stood in the lounge of the Imperial
Hotel chatting with Dalton, the hero of the Mountjoy
attempt, he saw another old friend, Pat MacCrea, his
driver, pass through the hall.   MacCrea had been
ambushed and wounded in Wicklow.

"Ah, Pat," he said, "your fellow-countrymen nearly
did for you."

It is the same theme repeated in various forms. The
shadow of the end is on him, yet he cannot believe it
will reach him here, in his beloved Cork among the
familiar houses and fields where nature itself should rise
and shelter him.

He set out with a party under Dalton. They passed

through Macroom, Bandon, Clonakilty, Rosscarberry, Skibbereen, and Sam's Cross, where years before he had recited "The lisht" for the neighbours. They crowded in again to shake his hand as Head of the Irish Government.

It was evening before they struck the back road from Bandon to Macroom.   An ambush party had been waiting there since morning. Now, with the failing light, they scattered to their billets, and as Collins' convoy tore up the narrow road through the glen there was only a handful of men to dispute the way with it. They opened fire. Dalton shouted to the driver to go like hell. Collins countermanded the order: the cars screamed to a halt, and he leaped out with his rifle in his hand. For close on half an hour the fight went on. Collins continued to fire until the little group of ambushers took to flight. He followed them with his rifle. All at once Dalton and the others noticed that he had ceased to fire. They thought they heard him call. When they rushed to where he was lying they found him, his head resting on his arms, a great wound in his skull. Afterwards they thought it might have been one of the old gestures, that lightning turn of the head which brought the wound where it was.

O'Connell whispered the Act of Contrition into his ear, and dragged him across the road into shelter while Dalton continued to fight. Dalton then came and bandaged the wound. He had scarcely completed the task when he saw that Collins was dead. Darkness was coming on. O'Connell was weeping. Dalton still supported the heavy, bleeding head upon his knee.

The glen was quiet again, only the wind stirred in the bushes. Over all a wild and lovely county night fell; the men came in from the fields, gathered at the crossroads for a smoke, sat about the fire where soon they would say

the rosary; clearer in the darkness sounded the wheels
of the little country cart thumping over a ledge of stone,
a cart such as Collins had seen and thrilled at in the
Shepherd's Bush Road. But he would hear it no longer.
The countryside he had seen in dreams, the people he
had loved, the tradition which had been his inspira-
tion—they had risen in the falling light and struck
him dead.

FRANK O'CONNOR (1903-1966)
The Big Fellow

Pastoral and Town Life

IRISH HOSPITALITY—I

Half a dozen children, almost naked were sleeping on a little straw, with a pig, a dog, a cat, two chickens and a duck: I never before saw such a sight. The poor woman told me her husband was a sailor, that he had gone to sea three years ago, and that she had never heard from him since. She spread a mat on a chest, the only piece of furniture in the house, and invited me to lie there. . . . It rained very hard, and I knew not where to go, so I lay down on this bed of thorns. The animals saluted the first rays of the sun by their cries, and began to look about for something to eat. The novelty of my situation amused me for a moment; I transported myself in imagination into the Ark, and fancied myself Noah. It would seem that I appeared as odd to these animals as they did to me, the dog came to smell me, at the same time showing his teeth and barking; the pig also put up her snout to me, and began to grunt, the chickens and the duck began to eat my powder-bag, and the children began to laugh: I got up very soon for fear of being devoured myself. I should add that I had no small difficulty in making my hostess accept a shilling.

LE CHEVALIER DE LA TOCNAYE (1796)

IRISH HOSPITALITY—II

The habits of cabin life and cabin hospitality have so much sameness, that the specimen which follows may answer for the whole.

About seven one evening I reached the cabin of a woman whose daughter had been a servant in my house in New York. In a corner, where a bed might have stood, was a huge bank of turf, and a pile of straw for the pigs. There was but one room beside, and the family consisted of some five or six individuals. The cabin door being open, the pigs, geese, ducks, hens, and dogs walked in and out at option.

After the usual warm greeting, the girl was bidden to go out and dig some potatoes; the pot was hung over the fire, the potatoes boiled, the table was removed into the adjoining room, and a touch from the finger of the matron was the signal for me to follow her into supper. On a naked deal table stood a plate of potatoes and a mug of milk. The potatoes must be eaten from the hand, without knife, fork, or plate; and the milk taken in sups from the mug. I applied my nails to divesting the potato of its coat, and my hostess urged the frequent use of the milk, saying, "It was provided on purpose for you, and you must take it." It must be remembered that a sup of sweet milk among the poor in Ireland, is as much a rarity and a luxury as a slice of plum-pudding in a farmhouse in America. After supper we returned to the kitchen.

The good man of the house soon entered, and gave me as hearty a welcome as an Irishman could give; and the neighbouring women and children gathered in, till the pile of turf and every stool was occupied. A cheerful peat fire was burning upon the hearth; the children

5

were snugly cowered in each corner; two large pigs
walked in, and adjusted their nest upon the straw; two
or three straggling hens were about the room, which
the woman caught, and raising the broken lid of a chest
in one end of the apartment, she put them in; the dog
was bidden to drive out the geese; the door was shut,
and the man then turning to me, said, "You see how
these pigs know their place, and when it's a little cowld
not a ha'p'orth of 'em will stay out of doors; and we
always keep a handful of straw in that corner for their
bed." The company seemed quite inclined to stay; but
the good woman, looking well to my comfort called me
at an early hour to the next room, and pointing to a bed
which had been erected for my accommodation said,
"This troop here would be talking all night; ye must
be tired, and see what I've got for ye." This was a
bed fixed upon chairs, and made so wide that two
could occupy it; and she assured me that so glad
was she to see me, that she would sleep in a part of it
by my side. It was certainly an extra extension of
civility to leave the good man, who, by the way, had
two daughters and a son of sixteen to sleep under
the same covering, and in the same room with us.
His bed was made of a bundle or two of straw spread
upon rough sticks, and a decent woollen covering put
over it.

In my own native land I had slept under rich canopies,
in stately mansions of the rich, in the plain, wholesome
dwelling of the thrifty farmer, the log-cabin of the poor,
and under tents on the hunting-ground of the Indian,
but never where poverty, novelty, and kindness were so
happily blended. I fell asleep, nor did the barking of a
dog, the squealing of a pig, or the breathing of man,
woman, or child arouse me till I heard, at sun-rising,
"Well, Maggie, how are ye this morning? D'ye know,
I was lonesome without ye." "God be praised," responded
the good woman, "and I hope ye are well, Johnny." I

thought of the Castle at Windsor, where Prince Albert, Victoria, and the young princes were reclining, and I very much queried whether their feelings were more kindly or more happy this morning, than were those of these unsophisticated peasants.

ASENATH NICHOLSON (*c.* 1840)
The Bible in Ireland

AN OLD WOMAN OF THE ROADS

Oh, to have a little house!
To own the hearth and stool and all!
The heaped-up sods upon the fire,
The pile of turf against the wall!

To have a clock with weights and chains
And pendulum swinging up and down,
A dresser filled with shining delph,
Speckled and white and blue and brown!

I could be busy all the day
Clearing and sweeping hearth and floor.
And fixing on their shelf again
My white and blue and speckled store!

I could be quiet there at night
Beside the fire and by myself,
Sure of a bed and loath to leave
The ticking clock and the shining delph!

Och! but I'm weary of mist and dark,
And roads where there's never a house nor bush,
And tired I am of bog and road,
And the crying wind and the lonesome hush!

And I am praying to God on high,
And I am praying him night and day,
For a little house, a house of my own-
Out of the wind and the rain's way.

PADRAIC COLUM (b. 1881)

BOY IN IRELAND

Our house was like the other Cleendra houses; one room, thatched with straw, a small window of one pane. Even if people could improve their cottages they had to be careful about doing it, for as like as not the landlord would raise the rent.

We owned one cow, an old muelen. She had a calf every year. If it was a heifer we reared it and sold it when it was two years. If it was a bull we killed it, kept one quarter for ourselves and divided the remainder among the neighbours. The cow went dry every year for three months, but I think we never drank black tea, for the neighbours brought in bottles of milk every morning. To be sure we did likewise when our cow was milking and some other family was short. There were a couple of families who owned two cows and they were scarcely ever done helping somebody. There never was a pennyworth of milk sold in the townland of Cleendra and I hope there never will be.

We grew potatoes, oats and cabbage. We threshed the oats with flails, and the threshing was a great day. Two men keeping time with flails is a grand thing to hear. When the grain was cleaned we took it over to the local kiln to be dried. Then the miller took it and ground it into meal. We got back the husk of the grain, too, and put it to good use. What you do is put some of it in a clean tub or an old churn and steep it in hot water. After a time the water becomes a sort of whey, and when cow's milk is scarce you can use it instead with your porridge. If you wanted to ask for it in any house in Cleendra you just asked for "Bull's milk." We never used Bull's milk with potatoes.

The main seasoning with potatoes was "dippity," a drop of milk in a saucer with a good pinch of salt in it. We dipped the potato for each bite. If there was no milk we used water. At very odd times we had red herring; there was no herring fishing around the coast when I was a child. We ate potatoes for breakfast as well as dinner and supper.

Tea was already popular in my young days although my mother remembered when it first came in. Flour bread was rare. We had oat bread and boxty instead. Boxty was looked on as a rare feast, probably because there was white flour in it. There were no shop graters to grate the potatoes on then. Every house made its own grater by ripping a canister and punching holes in it. We had great feeds of boxty on turf cutting days and on the days of scouring flannel.

My mother made all our clothes. She scoured the wool, carded and spun it herself and then took the thread to the weaver. After the weaving came the scouring. For this job Cleendra had bought itself a great pot, every family having a share in it. The pot was set on the fire and filled to the brim. Three pounds of black soap were then melted into the water. The hot suds were poured over the flannel, which was in a sort of casing made by taking our own door off the hinges and doing the same to a couple of neighbours' doors. Men took off their trousers and went into this casing to kick the flannel. Heavy work it was, too. The women often took their turn at it; the nice white clean skin you would have after a day scouring flannel.

It was a great day when you grew beyond your mother's scissors and the tailor made your suit. Man alive, you would be watching the road for him for a week, and the sight of him coming to your house was as good as a feed of boxty. The tailor brought his scissors, tape and needles, and we had the thread, lining and buttons and the cloth. He charged one and six for a man's coat and trousers, and from ninepence to a shilling for boys'. He sewed sitting up on the table. When any youngster came in from a neighbour's house, he wouldn't let anybody tell him whose child it was, only puzzle out the stock for himself.

PATRICK GALLEGHER
Paddy the Cope

THE HIRING FAIR

When I was ten years of age I was in the second book, but until I had passed into the third book I would not be looked upon as a scholar. But I could not wait. The year before had been a bad year in Scotland, and my father had not enough money home with him to pay the rent and the shop debts. It was the same with the neighbours. A crowd of us boys were got ready for the hiring fair at Strabane. Boys, oh, boys, but we were glad. The big people warned us we would not have such a rush in our feet when we had the thirty-seven miles' tramp to Ballybofey past us, but we only laughed at them.

I'll always mind the morning I first left home to go to the Lagan; that was what we called the countryside beyond the mountains where boys went on hire. I think I see my mother as she handed me my four shillings for the journey. She was crying. She kissed me again and again. I can't say whether I was crying or not, though it's likely I was, for to this day it's easy to make me cry. It was in Irish she spoke and this is the sense of what she said: "Paddy, son, here is four shillings. Two shillings will take you to the fair. If you hire, keep the other two shillings till you come home; if you don't hire, it will take you back to me. Wherever you go and wherever you be, say your prayers night and morning and say three Hail Marys to the Blessed Virgin that God will keep you from the temptations of the devil." Everywhere you looked some mother was saying something to her own boy or girl, and I think they were all crying too. But anyway we got started. We were all barefooted; we had our boots in our bundles. There was not much weight in our bundles. There was nothing in mine, only two shirts, some patches, thread, buttons and a couple of needles.

We made a lot of noise along the road but there was still plenty of walk in us when we had finished the thirty-seven miles to Ballybofey. We lodged in a sort of barn, twenty-six boys of us on shake-downs on the floor. The old-fashioned fellows who went over the roads before advised us to take off our shirts to save ourselves from vermin. In the hurry in the morning the shirts got mixed up, but the one I got was as good as the one I lost. We paid threepence each for our night's lodging. We ate what we had left over of our pieces and started for the station. The train fare for the rest of our journey was one and twopence, so I still had one two-shilling piece, a sixpence and a penny.

When we reached Strabane we all cuddled together, and were scared at first, but the big fellows told us to scatter out so as the farmers would see us. They made us walk up and down to see how we were set up and judge what mettle was in us. Anybody who looked tired or faulty in any way was passed over. The strong boys were picked up quickly, and I was getting scared I would be left. In the end two men came to me.

"Well," said one of them. "Wee fellow, what wages do you want for the six months?"

I said, "Three pounds ten."

He said, "Get out, you would be dear at your meat.

Walk up there to the market clock until I see what you are like."

I walked up, he followed me and made me walk back to where I started from. I heard him whispering to the other fellow, "He is wee, but the neck is ' good,'" and he then offered me two pounds ten.

The other man caught both our hands in his, hit our hands a slap, and said, "Bought and sold for three pounds."

We both agreed. My master took my bundle from me and told me to meet him there at that spot in an hour.

PATRICK GALLEGHER
Paddy the Cope

AFTER THE STORM

Next morning the tempest was still high, and venturing upon the strand, I there saw, as at Valentia, crowds of females busied; and speaking to one, she replied, "These stawrmy nights, ma'am, blow good luck to the poor; they wash up the say-weed, and that's why ye see so many now at work."

The company increased, till I counted more than sixty; and busy, merry work they made of it; running with heavy loads upon their heads, dripping with wet, exultingly throwing them down, and bounding away in glee. Truly, "A merry heart doeth good like a medicine," "And are you not cold?" "Oh no, ma'am, the salt say keeps us warm; the salt say, ma'am never let us take cold." "And how many days must you work in this way, before you get a supply?" "Aw, sometimes not fawrty, but scores of days." "And all you have for your labour is the potato?" "That's all, ma'am, that's all; and it's many of us that can't get the sup of milk with 'em, no, nor the salt; but we can't help it, we must be content with what the good God sends us."

She hitched her basket over her shoulder, and in company with one older than herself, skipped upon the sand made wet with rain, and turning suddenly about, gave me a pretty specimen of Kerry dancing, as practised by the peasantry. "The sand is too wet, ma'am, to dance right well on," and again shouldering her basket, with a "God speed ye on yer journey," leaped away.

I looked after them among the rocks, more with admiration for the moment than with pity; for what hearts, amid splendour and ease, lighter than these? And what heads and stomachs, faring sumptuously every day, freer from aches than theirs, with the potato and sup of milk? This woman, who danced before me, was more than fifty, and I do not believe that the daughter of Herodias herself was more graceful in her movements, more beautiful in complexion or symmetry, than was this dark-haired matron of the mountains of Kerry.

ASENATH NICHOLSON (*c.* 1840)
The Bible in Ireland

A DROVER

To Meath of the pastures,
From wet hills by the sea,
Through Leitrim and Longford
Go my cattle and me.

I hear in the darkness
Their slipping and breathing.
I name them the bye-ways
They're to pass without heeding.

Then the wet, winding roads,
Brown bogs with black water;
And my thoughts on white ships
And the King o' Spain's daughter.

O! farmer, strong farmer!
You can spend at the fair
But your face you must turn
To your crops and your care.

And soldiers—red soldiers!
You've seen many lands;
But you walk two by two.
And by captain's commands.

O! the smell of the beasts,
The wet wind in the morn;
And the proud and hard earth
Never broken for corn;

And the crowds at the fair,
The herds loosened and blind,
Loud words and dark faces,
And the wild blood behind.

(O! strong men with your best
I would strive breast to breast
I could quiet your herds
With my words, with my words.)

I will bring you, my kine,
Where there's grass to the knee;
But you'll think of scant croppings
Harsh with salt of the sea.

PADRAIC COLUM (b. 1881)

FOUR DUCKS ON A POND

Four ducks on a pond,
A grass-bank beyond,
A blue sky of spring,
White clouds on the wing;
What a little thing
To remember for years—
To remember with tears!

WILLIAM ALLINGHAM (1824-1889)

MERRY CHRISTMAS, 1778

Close to the kennel of his hounds my father had built a
small cottage, which was occupied solely by an old
huntsman, his older wife, and his nephew, a whipper-in.
The chase, and the bottle, and the piper were the enjoyments of winter, and nothing could recompense a
suspension of these enjoyments.

My elder brother justly apprehending that the frost
and snow of Christmas might probably prevent their
usual occupation of the chase, determined to provide
against any listlessness during the shut-up period by an
uninterrupted match of what was called "hard-going"
till the weather should break up.

A hogshead of superior claret was, therefore, sent to
the cottage of old Quin, the huntsman; and a fat cow,
killed and plundered of her skin, was hung up by the
heels. All the windows were closed to keep out the light.
One room, filled with straw and numerous blankets, was
destined for a bed-chamber in common, and another was
prepared as a kitchen for the use of the servants. Claret,

cold, mulled, or buttered, was to be the beverage for the whole company, and in addition to the cow above mentioned, chickens, bacon and bread were the only admitted viands. Wallace and Hosey, my father's and brother's pipers, and Boyle, a blind but a famous fiddler, were employed to enliven the banquet, which it was determined should continue till the cow became a skeleton, and the claret should be on its stoop.

My two elder brothers; two gentlemen of the name of Taylor, one of them afterwards a writer in India; a Mr. Barrington Lodge, a rough songster; Frank Skelton, a jester and a butt; Jemmy Moffat, the most knowing sportsman of the neighbourhood; and two other sporting gentlemen of the county, composed the permanent bacchanalians. A few visitors were occasionally admitted.

As for myself, I was too unseasoned to go through more than the first ordeal, which was on a frosty St. Stephen's Day, when the "hard-goers" partook of their opening banquet, and several neighbours were invited, to honour the commencement of what they called their "shut-up pilgrimage."

The old huntsman was the only male attendant, and his ancient spouse, once a kitchen-maid in the family, now somewhat resembling the amiable Leonarda in Gil Blas, was the cook, whilst the drudgery fell to the lot of the whipper-in. A long knife was prepared to cut collops from the cow; a large turf fire seemed to court the gridiron; the pot bubbled up as if proud of its contents, whilst plump white chickens floated in crowds upon the surface of the water; the simmering potatoes, just bursting their drab surtouts, exposed the delicate whiteness of their mealy bosoms; the claret was tapped, and the long earthen wide-mouthed pitchers stood gaping under the impatient cock, to receive their portions. The pipers plied their chants, the fiddler tuned his Cremona, and never did any feast commence with more auspicious appearances of hilarity and dissipation, appearances which were not doomed to be falsified.

I shall never forget the attraction this novelty had for my youthful mind. All thoughts but those of good cheer were for the time totally obliterated. A few curses were, it is true, requisite to spur on old Leonarda's skill, but at length the banquet entered: the luscious smoked bacon, bedded in its cabbage mattress, and partly obscured by its own savoury steam, might have tempted the most fastidious of epicures; whilst the round trussed chickens, ranked by the half dozen on hot pewter dishes, turned up their white plump merry-thoughts, exciting equally the eye and appetite; fat collops of the hanging cow, sliced indiscriminately from her tenderest points, grilled over the clear embers upon a shining gridiron, half-drowned in their own luscious juices, and garnished with little pyramids of congenial shallots, smoked at the bottom of the well-furnished board. A prologue of cherry-bounce (brandy) preceded the entertainment, which was enlivened by hob-nobs and joyous toasts.

Numerous toasts, in fact, as was customary in those days, intervened to prolong and give zest to the repast—every man shouted forth his fair favourite, or convivial pledge; and each voluntarily surrendered a portion of his own reason in bumpers to the beauty of his neighbour's toast. The pipers jerked from their bags appropriate planxties to every jolly sentiment; the jokers cracked the usual jests and ribaldry; one songster chanted the joys of wine and women; another gave, in full glee, the pleasures of the fox chase; the fiddler sawed his merriest jigs; the old huntsman sounded his horn, and thrusting his forefingers into his ear, to aid the quaver, gave the view halloa! of nearly ten minutes' duration, to which melody tally ho! was responded by every stentorian voice. A fox's brush stuck into a candlestick, in the centre of the tables, was worshipped as a divinity! Claret flowed, bumpers were multiplied, and chickens, in the garb of spicy spitchcocks, assumed the name of devils to whet the appetites which it was impossible to conquer!

My reason gradually began to lighten me of its burden, and in its last efforts kindly suggested the straw-chamber as my asylum. Two couple of favourite hounds had been introduced to share in the joyous pastime of their friends and master; and the deep bass of their throats, excited by the shrillness of the huntsman's tenor, harmonised by two rattling pipers, a jiggling fiddler, and twelve voices, in twelve different keys, all bellowing in one continuous unrelenting chime, was the last point of recognition which Bacchus permitted me to exercise, for my eyes began to perceive a much larger company than the room actually contained; the lights were more than doubled, without any virtual increase of their number, and even the chairs and tables commenced dancing a series of minuets before me. A faint tally ho! was attempted by my reluctant lips; but I believe the effort was unsuccessful, and I very soon lost, in the straw-room, all that brilliant consciousness of existence in the possession of which the morning had found me so happy.

Just as I was closing my eyes to a twelve hours' slumber, I distinguished the general roar of "stole away!" which rose almost up to the very roof of old Quin's cottage.

At noon, next day, a scene of a different nature was exhibited. I found, on waking, two associates by my side, in as perfect insensibility as that from which I had just aroused. Our piper seemed indubitably dead! but the fiddler, who had the privilege of age and blindness, had taken a hearty nap, and seemed as much alive as ever.

The room of banquet had been re-arranged by the old

woman; spitchcocked chickens, fried rashers, and broiled marrow-bones appeared struggling for precedence. The clean cloth looked itself fresh and exciting; jugs of mulled and buttered claret foamed hot upon the re-furnished table, and a better or heartier breakfast I never in my life enjoyed.

A few members of the jovial crew had remained all night at their posts, but, I suppose, alternately took some rest, as they seemed not at all affected by their repletion. Soap and hot water restored at once their spirits and their persons; and it was determined that the rooms should be ventilated and cleaned out for a cock-fight, to pass time till the approach of dinner.

In this battle-royal every man backed his own bird, twelve of which courageous animals were set down together to fight it out, the survivor to gain all. In point of principle, the battle of the Horatii and Curiatii was reacted, and in about an hour one cock crowed out his triumph over the mangled body of his last opponent, being himself, strange to say, but little wounded. The other eleven lay dead, and to the victor was unanimously voted a writ of ease, with sole monarchy over the hen-roost for the remainder of his days; and I remember him for many years the proud commandant of his poultry-yard and seraglio. Fresh visitors were intro-duced each successive day, and the seventh morning had arisen before the feast broke up. As that day advanced, the cow was proclaimed to have furnished her full quantum of good dishes; the claret was upon its stoop, and the last gallon, mulled with a pound of spices, was drunk in tumblers to the next merry meeting! All now retired to their natural rest, until the evening announced a different scene.

An early supper, to be partaken of by all the young folks of both sexes in the neighbourhood, was provided in the dwelling-house to terminate the festivities. A dance, as usual, wound up the entertainment, and what

was then termed a "raking pot of tea" put a finishing
stroke, in jollity and good humour, to such a revel
as I never saw before, and, I am sure, shall never see
again.

SIR JONAH BARRINGTON (1760-1834)
Personal Sketches

THE TRAGEDY OF SIR KIT

The bride might well be a great fortune—she was a
Jewish by all accounts, who are famous for their great
riches. I had never seen any of that tribe or nation
before, and could only gather that she spoke a strange
kind of English of her own, that she could not abide
pork or sausages, and went neither to church nor mass.
Mercy upon his honour's poor soul, thought I; what will
become of him and his, and all of us, with his heretic
blackamoor at the head of the Castle Rackrent estate? . . .
There were no balls, no dinners, no doings; the
country was all disappointed—Sir Kit's gentleman said
in a whisper to me, it was all my lady's own fault,
because she was so obstinate about the cross.
"What cross?" says I; "is it about her being a heretic?"
"Oh, no such matter," says he; "my master does not
mind her heresies, but her diamond cross—it's worth I
can't tell you how much, and she has thousands of
English pounds concealed in diamonds about her, which
she as good as promised to give up to my master before
he married; but now she won't part with any of them,
and she must take the consequences."
Her honeymoon, at least her Irish honeymoon, was
scarcely well over, when his honour one morning said
to me, "Thady, buy me a pig!" and then the sausages
were ordered, and here was the first open breaking-out
of my lady's troubles. My lady came down herself into
the kitchen to speak to the cook about the sausages, and

desired never to see them more at her table. Now my
master had ordered them, and my lady knew that. The
cook took my lady's part, because she never came down
into the kitchen and was young and innocent in housekeeping, which raised her pity; besides, said she, at her
own table, surely my lady should order and disorder
what she pleases. But the cook soon changed her note,
for my master made it a principle to have the sausages,
and swore at her for a Jew herself, till he drove her
fairly out of the kitchen; then, for fear of her place, and
because he threatened that my lady should give her no
discharge without the sausages, she gave up, and from
that day forward always sausages, or bacon, or pig-meat
in some shape or other, went up to table; upon which
my lady shut herself up in her own room, and my master
said she might stay there, with an oath; and to make
sure of her, he turned the key in the door, and kept it
ever after in his pocket. We none of us ever saw or heard
her speak for seven years after that: he carried her
dinner himself. Then his honour had a great deal of
company to dine with him, and balls in the house, and
was as gay and gallant, and as much himself as before
he was married; and at dinner he always drank my Lady
Rackrent's good health and so did the company, and he
sent out always a servant with his compliments to my
Lady Rackrent, and the company was drinking her
ladyship's health, and begged to know if there was
anything at table he might send her, and the man came
back, after the sham errand, with my Lady Rackrent's
compliments, and she was very much obliged to Sir Kit
—she did not wish for anything, but drank the company's
health.

The country, to be sure, talked and wondered at my
lady's being shut up, but nobody chose to interfere or
ask any impertinent questions, for they knew my master
was a man very apt to give a short answer himself, and
likely to call a man out for it afterwards; he was a famous

shot, had killed his man before he came of age, and nobody scarce dared look at him whilst at Bath. Sir Kit's character was so well known in the country that he lived in peace and quietness ever after, and was a great favourite with the ladies, especially when in process of time, in the fifth year of her confinement, my Lady Rackrent fell ill and took entirely to her bed, and he gave out that she was now skin and bone, and could not last through the winter. In this he had two physicians' opinions to back him (for now he called in two physicians for her), and tried all his arts to get the diamond cross from her on her death-bed, and to get her to make a will in his favour of her separate possessions, but there she was too tough for him. He used to swear at her behind her back after kneeling to her face, and call her in the presence of his gentleman his stiff-necked Israelite, though before he married her that same gentleman told me he used to call her (how he would bring it out, I don't know) "my pretty Jessica!" To be sure it must have been hard for her to guess what sort of a husband he reckoned to make her.

When she was lying, to all expectation, on her death-bed of a broken heart, I could not but pity her, though she was a Jewish, and considering it was no fault of hers to be taken with my master, so young as she was at the Bath, and so fine a gentleman as Sir Kit was when he courted her; and considering too, after all they had heard and seen of him as a husband, there were now no less than three ladies in our county talked of for his second wife, all at daggers drawn with each other, as his gentleman swore, at the balls, for Sir Kit for their partner—I could not but think them bewitched, but they all reasoned with themselves that Sir Kit would make a good husband to any Christian but a Jewish, I suppose, and especially as he was now a reformed rake; and it was not known how my lady's fortune was settled in her will, nor how the Castle Rackrent estate was all mortgaged, and bonds out against him, for he was never cured of his gaming tricks; but that was the only fault he had, God bless him!

My lady had a sort of fit, and it was given out that she was dead, by mistake; this brought things to a sad crisis for my poor master. One of the three ladies showed his letters to her brother, and claimed his promises, whilst another did the same. I don't mention names. Sir Kit, in his defence, said he would meet any man who dared to question his conduct; and as to the ladies, they must settle it amongst them who was to be his second, and his third, and his fourth, while his first was still alive, to his mortification and theirs. Upon this, as upon all former occasions, he had the voice of the country with him, on account of the great spirit and propriety he acted with. He met and shot the first lady's brother; the next day he called out the second, who had a wooden leg, and their place of meeting by appointment being in a new-ploughed field, the wooden-leg man stuck fast in it. Sir Kit, seeing his situation, with great candour fired his pistol over his head; upon which the seconds interposed, and convinced the parties there had been a slight misunderstanding between them; thereupon they shook hands cordially and went home to dinner together. This gentleman, to show the world how they stood together, and by the advice of the friends of both parties, to re-establish his sister's injured reputation, went out with Sir Kit as his second, and carried his message next day to the last of his adversaries.

I never saw him in such fine spirits as that day he went out—sure enough he was within an ace of getting quit handsomely of all his enemies; but unluckily, after hitting the tooth-pick out of his adversary's finger and thumb, he received a ball in a vital part, and was brought home, in little better than an hour after the affair, speechless on a hand-barrow to my lady. We got the key out of his pocket the first thing we did, and my son

Jason ran to unlock the barrack-room, where my lady had been shut up for seven years, to acquaint her with the fatal accident. The surprise bereaved her of her senses at first, nor would she believe but that we were putting some new trick upon her, to entrap her out of her jewels, till Jason bethought himself of taking her to the window, and showed her the man bringing Sir Kit up the avenue upon the hand-barrow, which had immediately the desired effect; for directly she burst into tears, and pulling her cross from her bosom, she kissed it with as great devotion as ever I witnessed, and lifting up her eyes to heaven uttered some ejaculation which none present heard; but I take the sense of it to be, she returned thanks for this unexpected interposition in her favour when she had least reason to expect it.

                              MARIA EDGEWORTH (1767-1849)
                                        Castle Rackrent

AT THE SHOW

The first competitor bucketed up to the starting-point, and at the same moment the discovery was made that there was no water in the water-jump, a space of perhaps a foot in depth by some five feet wide. Nothing but a thin paste of mud remained, the water having disappeared, unnoticed, during the hot hours of the morning.

Swift in expedient, the stewards supplied the deficiency with quicklime, which was scattered with a lavish hand in the fosse, and shone like snow through the barrier of furze bushes on the take-off side. If, as I suppose, the object was to delude the horses into the belief that it was a water-jump, it was a total failure; they immediately decided that it was a practical joke, dangerous, and in indifferent taste. If on the other side, a variety entertainment for the public was aimed at, nothing could have been more successful. Every known class of refusal was successfully exhibited. One horse endeavoured to climb the rails into the Grand Stand; another, having stopped dead at the critical point, swung round, and returned in consternation to the starting-point, with his rider hanging like a locket round his neck. Another, dowered with a sense of humour unusual among horses, stepped delicately over the furze-bushes, and, amidst rounds of applause, walked through the lime with a stoic calm. Yet another, a ponderous war-horse of seventeen hands, hung, trembling like an aspen on the brink, till a sympathiser, possibly his owner, sprang irrepressibly from his seat on the stand, climbed through the rails, and attacked him from behind with a large umbrella. It was during this three-cornered conflict that the green-eyed filly forced herself into the front rank of events. A chorus of "Hi! Hi! Hi!" fired at the rate of about fifty per second, volleyed in warning from the crowd round the starting-point, and a white-legged chestnut, with an unearthly white face and flying flounces of tawny mane and tail, came thundering down at the jump. Neither umbrella nor war-horse turned her by a hair's-breadth from her course, still less did her rider, a lean and long-legged country boy, whose single object was to keep on her back. Picking up her white stockings, she took off six feet from the jump, and whizzed like a driven grouse past the combatants and over the furze-bushes and the lime. Beneath her creamy fore-lock, I caught a glimpse of her amazing blue-green eyes.

She skimmed the hurdle, she flourished over the wall, flinging high her white heels with a twist that showed more consideration for their safety than that of her rider. She ramped over the big double bank, while the roars of approval swelled with each achievement, and she ended a faultless round by bolting into the heart of the crowd, which fled hilariously, and as hilariously, hived in round her again. . . .

Meanwhile, the war-horse, much embittered by the

umbrella, floundered through the lime, and, continuing his course, threw down the hurdle, made a breach in the wall that would, as my neighbour put it, give three hours' work to seven idlers, and came to a sudden conclusion in front of the bank, while his rider slowly turned a somersault that, by some process of evolution, placed him sitting on the fence, facing the large and gloomy countenance of his horse.

E. Œ. SOMERVILLE AND MARTIN ROSS
Experiences of an Irish R.M.

SPORT

"Sport is it? Divil so pleasant an afternoon ever you seen," replied Slipper. He leaned against a side table, and all the glasses on it jingled. "Does your honour know O'Driscoll?" he went on irrelevantly. "Sure you do. He was in your honour's stable. It's what we were all sayin'; it was a great pity your honour was not there, for the likin' you had to Driscoll."

"That's thrue," said a voice at the door.

"There wasn't one in the Barony but was gathered in it, through and fro," continued Slipper, with a quelling glance at the interrupter; "and there was tints for sellin' porther, and whisky as pliable as new milk, and boys goin' round the tints outside, feeling for heads with the big ends of their blackthorns, and all kinds of recreations, and the Sons of Liberty's piffler and dhrum band from Skebawn; though faith! there was more of thim runnin' to look at the races than what was playin' in it; not to mintion different occasions that the band-masther was atin' his lunch within in the whisky tint."

"But what about Driscoll?" said Flurry.

"Sure it's about him I'm tellin' ye," replied Slipper, with the practised orator's watchful eye on his growing audience. "'Twas within in the same whisky tint meself was, with the bandmasther and a few of the lads, an' we buyin' a ha'porth o' crackers, when I seen me brave Driscoll landin' into the tint, and a pair o' thim long boots on him; him that hadn't a shoe nor a stocking to his foot when your honour had him, picking grass out of the stones behind in your yard. 'Well,' said I to meself, 'We'll knock some spoort out of Driscoll.'

" ' Come here to me, acushla! ' says I to him; " I suppose it's some way wake in the legs y'are,' says I, ' an' the docthor put them on ye the way the people wouldn't thrample ye! '

" ' May the divil choke ye! ' says he, pleasant enough, but I knew by the blush he had he was vexed.

" ' Then I suppose 'tis a left-tenant colonel y'are,' says I; ' yer mother must be proud out o' ye,' says I, ' an' maybe ye'll lend her a loan o' thim waders when she's rinsin' yer bauneen in the river! ' says I.

" ' There'll be work out o' this! ' says he, lookin' at me both sour and bitther.

" ' Well, indeed, I was thinkin' you were blue moulded for want of a batin',' says I. He was for fightin' us then, but afther we had him pacificated, with about a quarther of a naggin o' sperrits, he told us he was goin' ridin' in a race.

" ' An' what'll ye ride? ' says I.

" ' Owld Bocock's mare,' says he.

" ' Knipes! ' says I, sayin' a great curse, ' is it that little stageen from the mountains; sure she's somethin' about the one age with meself,' says I. ' Many's the time Jamesy Geoghegan and meself used to be dhrivin' her to Macroom with pigs an' all soorts,' says I; ' an' is it leppin' stone walls ye want her to go now? '

" ' Faith, there's walls and every vari'ty of obstackle in it,' says he.

" ' It'll be the best o' your play, so,' says I, ' to leg it away home out o' this.'

" ' An' who'll ride her, so? ' says he.

"' Let the divil ride her,' says I."

Leigh Kelway, who had been leaning back seemingly half asleep, obeyed the hypnotism of Slipper's gaze, and opened his eyes.

"That was now all the conversation that passed between himself and meself," resumed Slipper, "and there was no great delay afther that till they said there was a race startin' and the dickens a one at all was goin' to ride only two, Driscoll, and one Clancy. With that then I seen Mr. Kinahane, the Petty Sessions clerk, goin' round clearin' the coorse, an' I gathered a few o' the neighbours, an' we walked the fields hither and over till we seen the most of th' obstackles.

"' Stand aisy now by the plantation,' says I; ' if they get to come as far as this, believe me ye'll see spoort,' says I, ' an' 'twill be a convanient spot to encourage the mare if she's anyway wake in herself,' says I, cuttin' somethin' about five foot of an ash sapling out o' the plantation.

"' That's yer sort!' says owld Bocock, that was thravellin' the racecoorse, peggin' a bit o' paper down with a thorn in front of every lep, the way Driscoll'd know the handiest place to face her at it.

"Well, I hadn't barely thrimmed the ash plant——"

"Have you any jam, Mary Kate?" interrupted Flurry, whose meal had been in no way interfered with by either the story or the highly-scented crowd who had come to listen to it.

"We have no jam, only thraycle, sir," replied the invisible Mary Kate.

"I hadn't the switch barely thrimmed," repeated Slipper firmly, "when I heard the people screechin', an' I see Driscoll an' Clancy comin' on, leppin' all before them an' owld Bocock's mare bellusin' an' powdherin' along, an' bedad! whatever obstackle wouldn't throw *her* down, faith, she'd throw *it* down, and there's the thraffic they had in it.

"'I declare to me sowl,' says I, 'if they continue on this way there's a great chance some one of thim'll win,' says I.

"'Ye lie!' says the bandmasther, bein' a thrifle fulsome after his luncheon.

"'I do not,' says I, 'in regard of seein' how soople them two boys is. Ye might observe,' says I, 'that if they have no convanient way to sit on the saddle, they'll ride the neck o' the horse till such time as they gets an an occasion to lave it,' says I.

"'Arrah, shut yer mouth!' says the bandmasther; 'they're puckin' out this way now, an' may the divil admire me!' says he, 'but Clancy has the other bet out, and the divil such leatherin' and beltin' of owld Bockock's mare ever you seen as what's in it!' says he.

"Well, when I seen them comin' to me, and Driscoll about the length of the plantation behind Clancy, I let a couple of bawls.

"'Skelp her, ye big brute!' says I. 'What good's in ye that ye aren't able to skelp her?'"

The yell and the histrionic flourish of his stick with which Slipper delivered this incident brought down the house. Leigh Kelway was sufficiently moved to ask me in an undertone if "skelp" was a local term.

"Well, Mr. Flurry, and gintlemen," recommenced Slipper, "I declare to ye when owld Bocock's mare heard thim roars she sthretched out her neck like a gandher, and when she passed me out she give a couple of grunts, and looked at me as ugly as a Christian.

"'Hah!' says I, givin' her a couple o' dhraws o' th' ash plant across the butt o' the tail, the way I wouldn't blind her; 'I'll make ye grunt!' says I, 'I'll nourish ye!'

"I knew she was very frightful of th' ash plant since the winter Tommeen Sullivan had her under a sidecar. But now, in place of havin' any obligations to me, ye'd be surprised if ye heard the blaspheemious expressions of that young boy that was ridin' her; and whether it was over-anxious he was, turnin' around the way I'd hear him cursin', or whether it was some slither or slide came to owld Bocock's mare, I dunno, but she was bet up agin the last obstackle but two, and before ye could say ' shnipes ' she was standin' on her two ears beyond in th' other field! I declare to ye, on the vartue of me oath, she stood that way till she reconnoithred what side would Driscoll fall, an' she turned about then and rolled on him as cosy as if he was meadow grass!"

Slipper stopped short: the people in the doorway groaned appreciatively; Mary Kate murmured "The Lord save us!"

"The blood was dhruv out through his nose and ears," continued Slipper, with a voice that indicated the cream of the narration, "and you'd hear his bones crackin' on the ground! You'd have pitied the poor boy."

"Good heavens!" said Leigh Kelway, sitting up very straight in his chair.

"Was he hurt, Slipper?" asked Flurry casually.

"Hurt, is it?" echoed Slipper in high scorn; "killed on the spot!" He paused to relish the effect of the *dénouement* on Leigh Kelway. "Oh, divil so pleasant an afthernoon ever you seen; and indeed, Mr. Flurry, it's what we were all sayin', it was a great pity your honour was not there for the likin' you had for Driscoll."

E. Œ. SOMERVILLE AND MARTIN ROSS
Experiences of an Irish R.M.

THE ROSCARBERRY FOXHOUNDS

"The defendant was referred to as if she kept a fashionable pack of hounds in elaborate kennels. The Roscarberry pack was certainly interesting by reason of its diversified character. Variety has a charm of its own.

What is unique is always attractive. The pack was composed of all sorts and conditions of hunting dogs— uniform neither in size nor pace nor breeding—and although it was styled ' The Roscarberry Foxhounds,' it could boast of only one pure-bred foxhound—*lucus a non lucendo*. The proclivities of the pack were as diversified as its composition; it pursued with equal ardour every description of quadruped, whatever the nature of the scent. I am not sure that the feathered tribe was alto- gether without some measure of attention. However, though the menage at Roscarberry was not quite up to Leicestershire standard, I feel quite certain that the heart of the young Master was, so far as related to physical courage, in the right place, and that he often afforded good sport, and that the followers of the pack had not infrequently, to use an expression amongst hunting men, ' a clinking run.' The mother's heart was proud, and the field was at once gratified and grateful. This was all very interesting and picturesque, but it did not at all involve that the mother held out her son as her general agent to buy horses."

Judgment by LORD O'BRIEN OF KILFENORA
Irish Law Reports 1907

THE MASTER OF HOUNDS

Black Daly was a man quite as dark as his soubriquet described him. He was tall, but very thin and bony, and seemed not to have an ounce of flesh about his face or body. He had large black whiskers,—coarse and jet black —which did not quite meet beneath his chin. And he wore no other beard, no tuft, no imperial, no mustachios; but when he was seen before shaving on a morning, he would seem to be black all over, and his hair was black, short and harsh; and though black, round about his ears it was beginning to be tinged with grey. He was now over fifty years of age; but the hair on his head was as thick as it had been when he first undertook the hounds. He had great dark eyes in his head, deep down, so that they seemed to glitter at you out of caverns. And above them were great, bushy eyebrows, every hair of which seemed to be black, harsh and hard. His nose was well-formed and prominent; but of cheeks he had apparently none. Between his whiskers and his nose, and the corners of his mouth, there was nothing but two hollow cavities. He was somewhat over six feet high, but from his extraordinary thinness gave the appearance of much greater height. His arms were long, and the waistcoat which he wore was always long; his breeches were very long, and his boots seemed the longest thing about him—unless his spurs seemed longer. He had no flesh about him, and it was boasted of him that, in spite of length, and in spite of his height, he could ride under twelve stone. Of himself, and of his doings, he never talked. They were secrets of his own, of which he might have to make money. And no one had a right to ask him questions. He did not conceive that it would be necessary for a gentleman to declare his weight unless he were about to ride a race. Now it was understood that for the last ten years Black Daly had ridden no races.

He was a man of whom it might be said that he never joked. Though his life was devoted in a peculiar manner to sport, and there may be thought to be something akin between the amusements and the lightness of life, it was all serious to him. Though he was bitter over it, or happy; triumphant, or occasionally in despair—as when the money was not forthcoming—he never laughed. It was all serious to him, and apparently sad, from the first note of a hound in the early covert, down to the tidings that a poor fox had been found poisoned near his earth. He had much to do to find sport for the country on such limited means, and he was always doing it.

He not only knew every hound in his pack, but he knew their ages, their sires, and their dams; and the sires and the dams of most of their sires and dams. He knew the constitution of each, and to what extent their noses were to be trusted. "It's a very heavy scent to-day," he would say, "because Gaylap carries it over the plow. It's only a catching scent because the drops don't hang on the bushes." His lore on all such matters was incredible, but he would never listen to any argument. A man had a right to his own opinion; but then the man that differed from him knew nothing. He gave out his little laws to favoured individuals; not by way of conversation, for which he cared nothing, but because it might be well that the favoured individual should know the truth on that occasion.

As a man to ride he was a complete master of his art. There was nothing which a horse could do with a man on his back, which Daly could not make him do; and when he had ridden a horse he would know exactly what was within his power. But there was no desire with him for the showing off of a horse. He often rode to sell a horse, but he never seemed to do so. He never rode at difficult places, unless driven to do so by the exigencies of the moment. He was always quiet in the field, unless when driven to express himself as to the faults of some young man. Then he could blaze forth in his anger with great power. He was constantly to be seen trotting along a road when hounds were running, because he had no desire to achieve for himself a character for hardriding. But he was always with his hounds when he was wanted, and it was boasted of him that he had ridden four days a week through the season on three horses, and had never lamed one of them. . . .

It is hardly necessary to say that Black Daly was an unmarried man. No one who knew him could conceive that he should have had a wife. His hounds were his children, and he could have taught no wife to assist him in looking after them with the constant attention and tender care which was given to them by Barney Smith, his huntsman. A wife, had she seen to the feeding of the numerous babies, would have given them too much to eat, and had she not undertaken this care, she would have been useless at Daly Bridge. . . .

But the personal appearance of Mr. Daly on hunting mornings, was not a matter of indifference. It was not that he wore beautiful pink tops, or came out guarded from the dust by little aprons, or had his cravat just out of the band-box or his scarlet coat always new, and in the latest fashion, nor had his hat just come from the shop in Piccadilly with the newest twist to its rim. But there was something manly, and even powerful about his whole apparel. He was always the same, so that by men even in his own county, he would hardly have been known in other garments. The strong broad-brimmed high hat with the cord passing down his back beneath his coat, that had known the weather of various winters; the dark-red coat with long swallow tails which had grown nearly black under many storms: the dark buff striped waistcoat with the stripe running downward, long, so as to come well down over his breeches; the breeches themselves, which were always of leather, but which had become nearly brown under the hands of Barney Smith or his wife, and the mahogany top-boots of which the tops seemed to be a foot in length, could none of them have been worn by any but Black Daly. His very spurs must have surely been made for him, they were in length and weight, and general strength of leather, so peculiarly his own. He was unlike other Masters of Hounds in this, that he never carried a horn, but he spoke to his hounds in a loud indistinct chirruping voice which all County Galway believed to be understood by every hound in the pack.

One other fact must be told respecting Mr. Daly. He

was a Protestant—as opposed to a Roman Catholic. No
one ever knew him to go to church, or speak a word in
reference to religion. He was equally civil or uncivil—
to priest or parson when priest or parson appeared in the
field. But on no account would he speak to either of
them if he could avoid it. But he had in his heart a
thorough conviction that all Roman Catholics ought to
be regarded as enemies by all Protestants, and that
the feeling was one entirely independent of faith and
prayer-books, or crosses and masses.   For him fox-
hunting—fox-hunting for others—was the work of his
life, and he did not care to meddle with what he did not
understand. But he was a Protestant, and Sir Nicholas
Bodkin was a Roman Catholic, and therefore an enemy
—as a dog may be supposed to declare himself a dog,
and a cat a cat, if called upon to explain the cause for
the old family quarrel.

ANTHONY TROLLOPE (1815-82)
The Land Leaguers

THE DESERTED VILLAGE

Sweet Auburn! loveliest village of the plain,
Where health and plenty cheered the labouring swain,
Where smiling spring its earliest visit paid,
And parting summer's lingering blooms delayed:
Dear lovely bowers of innocence and ease,
Seats of my youth, when every sport could please,
How often have I loitered o'er thy green,
Where humble happiness endeared each scene;
How often have I paused on every charm,
The sheltered cot, the cultivated farm,
The never-failing brook, the busy mill,
The decent church that topped the neighbouring hill,

The hawthorn bush, with seats beneath the shade,
For talking age and whispering lovers made!
How often have I blessed the coming day,
When toil remitting lent its turn to play,
And all the village train, from labour free,
Led up their sports beneath the spreading tree,
While many a pastime circled in the shade,
The young contending as the old surveyed,
And many a gambol frolicked o'er the ground,
And sleights of art and feats of strength went round,
And still as each repeated pleasure tired,
Succeeding sports the mirthful band inspired;
The dancing pair that simply sought renown,
By holding out, to tire each other down;
The swain mistrustless of his smutted face,
While secret laughter tittered round the place;
The bashful virgin's sidelong looks of love,
The matron's glance that would those looks reprove;
These were thy charms, sweet village! sports like these,
With sweet succession, taught even toil to please;
These round thy bowers their cheerful influence shed,
These were thy charms—But all these charms are fled.
   Sweet smiling village, loveliest of the lawn,
Thy sports are fled, and all thy charms withdrawn;
Amidst thy bowers the tyrant's hand is seen,
And desolation saddens all thy green:
One only master grasps the whole domain,
And half a tillage stints thy smiling plain.
No more thy glassy brook reflects the day,
But, choked with sedges, works its weedy way.
Along thy glades, a solitary guest,
The hollow-sounding bittern guards its nest;
Amidst thy desert walks the lapwing flies,
And tires their echoes with unvaried cries.
Sunk are thy bowers, in shapeless ruin all,
And the long grass o'ertops the mouldering wall,
And, trembling, shrinking from the spoiler's hand,

SCOTCH STREET, ARMAGH CITY
(Northern Ireland Tourist Board)

MARSH'S LIBRARY, DUBLIN
(Bord Fáilte)

DERRYCLARE LAKE, CONNEMARA, COUNTY GALWAY
(Bord Fáilte)

BEN BULBEN MOUNTAIN, COUNTY SLIGO
(Bord Fáilte)

Far, far away, thy children leave the land.
   Ill fares the land, to hastening ills a prey,
Where wealth accumulates, and men decay;
Princes and lords may flourish, or may fade;
A breath can make them, as a breath has made:
But a bold peasantry, their country's pride,
When once destroyed, can never be supplied.

OLIVER GOLDSMITH (1730-1774)
The Deserted Village

BUT A BOLD PEASANTRY . . .

It was not the famine killed them. God knows in that
     evil year
   He pressed us a little hard, but he spared our lives and
      joy.
Only the old and weak were taken. The rest stood clear,
   Quit of their debt to Death. God struck, but not to
      destroy . . .

It was a woman did it. Her father, the lawyer Blake,
   Purchased the land for a song—some say, or less, for
      a debt
Owed by the former lord, a broken spendthrift and rake—
   And left it hers when he died with all he could grip
      or get.

Timothy Blake was not loved. He had too much in his
      heart
   Of the law of tenures, for love. No word men spoke in
      his praise.
Yet, in his lawyer's way, and deeds and titles apart,
   All were allowed to live who paid their rent in his days.

6

Little Miss Blake was his daughter. A pink-faced school-
   girl she came
First from Dublin city to live in her father's house,
She and her dogs and horses, unconscious of shame or
   blame.
   Who would have guessed her cruel with manners meek
   as a mouse? . . .

She was fastidious too, with her English education,
   And pained at want and squalor, things hard she
   should understand.
The sight of poverty touched the sense of what was due
   to her station,
   And still in her earlier years she gave with an open
   hand.

The village was poor to look at, a row of houses, no
   more,
   With just four walls and the thatch in holes where the
   fowls passed through.
A shame to us all, she averred, and her, so near to her
   door.
   She sent us for slates to the quarry and bade us build
   them anew.

The chapel, too, was unsightly. A Protestant she, and
   yet
   Decency needs must be in a house of prayer, she said.
Perched on a rising ground in sight of her windows set,
   Its shapeless walls were her grief. She built it a new
   façade.

What was it changed her heart? God knows. I know
   not. Some say
   She set her fancy on one above her in rank and pride.

Young Lord Clair at the Castle had danced with her.
    Then one day
    Dancing and she were at odds. He had taken an English
      bride . . .

Rent—who speaks of the rent? We Irish, who till the
    soil,
    Are ever ready to pay the tribute your laws impose;
You, the conquering race, have portioned to each his toil,
    We, the conquered, bring the ransom due to our woes.

Here is no case of justice, of just debts made or unjust;
    Contracts 'twixt freemen are, not here, where but one
      is free.
No man argues of right, who pays the toll that he must;
    Life is dear to all, and rent is the leave to be.

No. None argued of rent. Each paid, or he could not
    pay,
    Much as the seasons willed, in fatness or hungry years.
Blake's old rental was high. She raised it, and none said
    nay;
    Then she raised it again, and made a claim for arrears.

Joyce was her agent now. The rules of Charity bind
    Somewhat my tongue in speech, for even truths wrongs
      endured;
All I will say is this, in Joyce you might see combined
    Three worst things, a lawyer, moneylender, and
      steward.

His was the triple method, to harass by legal plan,
    Ruin by note of hand, and serve with the Crown's
      decree;
One by one in his snare he trapped the poor to a man,
    Left them bare in the street, and turned in their doors
      the key . . .

Joyce was found on his doorstep, stone dead, one Sunday
    morning,
    Shot by an unknown hand, a charge of slugs in his
      chest.
The blow had fallen unheard, without either sign or
    warning,
    Save for the notice-to-quit found pinned to the dead
      man's breast.

The answer to Joyce's murder was swift. Two strokes of
    the pen,
    Set by Miss Blake's fair hand on parchment white as
      her face
Gave what remained of the parish, lands, tenements,
    chapel and mill,
    All to a Scotch stock farmer to hold on a single lease.

Here stands the story written. The parchment itself
    could show
    Hardly more of their death than this great desolate
      plain.
The poor potato trenches they dug, how greenly they
    grow,
    Grass, all grass for ever, the graves of our women and
      men!

WILFRID SCAWEN BLUNT (1840-1922)
The Canon of Aughrim

17TH CENTURY DUBLIN

We landed at a place called Ringsend about a mile from
Dublin. I was asked whether I would have a coach.
"Where are there any," said I, for I looked about me,
and could see nothing like a coach. The fellow looked

upon me to be a very ignorant person, because I understood not what he meant, and angrily spake thus: "By my gossip's hand, thou canst not see very much well, arre look here is one by thine own side." It was a great while before I could tell what language he spoke, he did so tone his words; neither could I understand him, till one standing by interpreted him. As for his Ringsend coach, as he called it, it was wheel-barrow fashion, only it had two wheels not much bigger than a large Cheshire cheese. The horse that drew this princely pygmy chariot, I at first mistook for an over-grown mastiff, but viewing him narrowly, found him the extract (by his shape) of a Scotch hobby. Well, up I mounted, but could not invent a name for the manner of my riding for I was neither coached nor carted, but I fancied myself (and that justly) as I was riding, to be some notorious malefactor drawn on a sledge to the place of execution, which afterwards experimentally I found Dublin to be. Many of its inhabitants call this city Divlin, quasi Divels Inn, and very properly it is by them so termed; for there is hardly a city in the world that entertains such variety of devil's imps as that doth. If any knavishly break, murder, rob, or are desirous of polygamy, they straightway repair thither, making that place, or the kingdom in general, their asylum, or sanctuary.

RICHARD HEAD (*c.* 1600)

DUBLIN STREET CRIES

And first perhaps there was never known a wiser institution than that of allowing certain persons of both sexes in large and populous cities to cry through the streets many necessaries of life; it would be endless to recount the conveniences which our city enjoys by this useful invention, and particularly strangers, forced hither by business, who reside here but a short time; for these having usually but little money, and being wholly ignorant of the town, might at an easy price purchase a tolerable dinner, if the several criers would pronounce the names of the goods they have to sell in any tolerable language. And therefore till our law-makers shall think it proper to interpose so far as to make these traders pronounce their words in such terms that a plain Christian hearer may comprehend what is cried, I would advise all newcomers to look out at their garret windows, and there see whether the thing that is cried be tripes or flummery, buttermilk or cowheels. For as things are now managed, how is it possible for an honest countryman, just arrived, to find out what is meant for instance by the following words, with which his ears are constantly stunned twice a day, " Mugs, jugs and porringers, up in the garret and down in the cellar." I say, how is it possible for any stranger to understand that this jargon is meant as an invitation to buy a farthing's worth of milk for his breakfast or supper, unless his curiosity draws him to the window, or till his landlady shall inform him? I produce this only as one instance, among a hundred much worse, I mean where the words make a sound wholly inarticulate, which give so much disturbance and so little informa-tion.

The affirmation solemnly made in the cry of herrings is directly against all truth and probability: "Herrings alive, alive here." The very proverb will convince us of this; for what is more frequent in ordinary speech than to say of some neighbour for whom the passing bell rings that he is "dead as a herring." And pray, how is it possible that a herring, which as philosophers observe cannot live longer than one minute, three seconds and a half out of water should bear a voyage in open boats from Howth to Dublin, be tossed into twenty hands and preserve its life in sieves for several hours? Nay, we have witnesses ready to produce that many thousands of these herrings, so impudently asserted to be alive, have been a day and a night upon dry land. But this is not the worst. What can we think of those impious wretches who dare in the face of the sun vouch the very same affirmative of their salmon and cry "Salmon, alive, alive"; whereas if you call the woman who cries it she is not ashamed to turn back her mantle and show you this individual salmon cut into a dozen pieces. I have given good advice to these infamous disgracers of their sex and calling without the least appearance of remorse, and fully against the conviction of their own consciences. I have mentioned this grievance to several of our parish ministers, but all in vain; so that it must continue till the Government shall think fit to interpose.

JONATHAN SWIFT (1667-1745)
An Examination of Certain Abuses

COCKLES AND MUSSELS

In Dublin's fair city,
Where the girls are so pretty,
 I first set my eyes on sweet Mollie Malone.
She wheeled her wheel-barrow
Through streets broad and narrow,
 Crying, "Cockles and mussels, alive, alive, oh!
   Alive, alive, oh!
   Alive, alive oh!"
 Crying, "Cockles and mussels, alive, alive, oh!"

She was a fishmonger,
But sure 'twas no wonder,

For so were her father and mother before.
And they both wheeled their barrow
Through streets broad and narrow,
    Crying, "Cockles and mussels, alive, alive, oh!
        Alive, alive, oh! etc.

She died of a fever,
And none could relieve her,
    And that was the end of sweet Mollie Malone.
But her ghost wheels her barrow
Through streets broad and narrow,
    Crying, "Cockles and mussels, alive, alive, oh!
        Alive, alive, oh! etc.

ANONYMOUS (19th cent.)

GOING TO THE DOGS

I remember one evening not so long ago noticing a man
I knew from the County Monaghan eating in a city
restaurant, accompanied by three other young men in
blue suits and salmon-coloured caps. When I asked
what had them in town, they said they were up with a
dog and a considerable sum of money in notes. I im-
plored them to tell me no more and in due course made
my way to Shelbourne Park. There I happened to meet
another man who had for many years impressed me by
the singular regularity with which he lost his money
on unsound betting transactions. In his earlier days,
he had devised a system entirely from his own head
which enabled him to lose his money many times more
quickly than was possible with the assistance of ordinary
bad luck. He was now content to lose heavily on single
bets instead of yielding to any catastrophic doubling-up
neurosis, but he assured me that things could not be

going worse with him. From his shabby and ill-nourished appearance, this seemed to be a fact. I gave him a quiet word of advice about the last race and then carefully lost him in the crowd.

The dog was unknown and the betting closed at sixes and sevens, which means that the price was very satisfactory, not disordered. The crowd thought that some other dog could not possibly be beaten and I watched the traps nervously as the hare came bobbing down the straight to the start. My own dog seemed to emerge miraculously through the grating of his trap before the others were released and to have shot round the first bend before there was any question of a race at all. When the others had gathered themselves into a pack and set off in pursuit, my own dog was almost in sight of home and he was probably well on his way back to Monaghan with the salmon-coloured caps before the other dogs were caught. Going out, my arm was taken by the shabby gambler. He thanked me with the simple words of a man who rarely finds it necessary to thank anybody. Then he drew my attention to the race itself. Never, he swore, had he seen anything so exciting, so heart-pounding, so full of the colour and fire of hard clean racing. What could be more cheering to the heart than to see six or seven lithe thoroughbreds streaking round a track with fair field and no favour, no hard feelings if your fancy loses provided the best dog wins? Was there anything in the world finer to watch than a race between those grand animals, hurtling onwards neck and neck to a fierce finish? To his dying day he would remember that great race.

I refrained from mentioning that there had been no race to speak of, knowing well what a good win can do to a man's head. I noticed that his face was beautiful, shining on me with the clear luminance of a better world. If he had died at that moment he would have gone straight to heaven. It goes to prove that how you leave Shelbourne Park is more important than how you enter it. If you leave it with the feel of strange greasy notes in your pocket, you will find it a wide clean fine place, magnificent well-appointed stands on each side and grass of an unusually green hue in the centre. Attendants in spotless white coats (which have been subjected to a patent antiseptic process) will be around you retrieving benign-faced hounds from an innocent after-race frolic. All around you handsome men and women will be walking with quiet dignity to their gleaming cars. They will be dressed in cool expensive linens and will carry in their faces the mark of clean living. A cool breeze will temper the genial evening.

But if you happen to depart leaving all your money in the bag of a bookmaker, you will be appalled at the dreariness of your surroundings. Thunderous clouds will be massed above the ramshackle stands, ready to vomit their contents on you when they get you away from cover. Loathsome dogs, their faces lined with vice, will leer at you in mockery. Your demoniacal fellow-degenerates, slinking out beside you, will look suspiciously like drug addicts. Every one of them will have lost his entire week's wages notwithstanding the fact that he has a wife and seven children to support, each of whom is suffering from an incurable disease. There will be a bad smell in evidence, probably from the bucket-strewn river. If you notice any odd patron walking out jauntily, it will be safe to infer on such an occasion that he has given himself the needle behind the grand-stand.

At Shelbourne Park and at every other park, there are two ways of it, and the pity is that you cannot be at the choice of them.

BRIAN O'NOLAN ("FLANN O'BRIEN") (b. 1912)
The Bell, Vol. I, No. 1

THE YELLOW BITTERN

The yellow bittern that never broke out
  In a drinking-bout, might as well have drunk;
His bones are thrown on a naked stone
  Where he lived alone like a hermit monk.
O yellow bittern! I pity your lot,
  Though they say that a sot like myself is curst—
I was sober a while, but I'll drink and be wise
  For fear I should die in the end of thirst.

It's not for the common birds that I'd mourn,
  The blackbird, the corncrake or the crane,
But for the bittern that's shy and apart
  And drinks in the marsh from the lone bog-drain.
Oh! if I had known you were near your death,
  While my breath held out I'd have run to you,
Till a splash from the Lake of the Son of the Bird
  Your soul would have stirred and waked anew.

My darling told me to drink no more
  Or my life would be o'er in a little short while;
But I told her 'tis drink gives me health and strength,
  And will lengthen my road by many a mile.
You see how the bird of the long smooth neck,
  Could get his death from the thirst at last-
Come, son of my soul, and drain your cup,
  You'll get no sup when your life is past.

In a wintering island by Constantine's halls,
  A bittern calls from a wineless place,
And tells me that hither he cannot come
  Till the summer is here and the sunny days.

When he crosses the stream there and wings o'er the sea,
  Then a fear comes to me he may fail in his flight—
Well, the milk and the ale are drunk every drop,
  And a dram won't stop our thirst this night.

CATHAL BUIDHE MACELGUN (c. 1750)
translated from the Irish by
THOMAS MacDONAGH (1878-1916)

AFTER HOURS

At ten o'clock on week nights, at half-nine on Saturday the tide ebbs suddenly, leaving the city high and dry. Unless you are staying at a hotel or visiting a theatre, you may not lawfully consume excisable liquors within the confines of the county borough. The city has entered that solemn hiatus, that almost sublime eclipse known as The Closed Hours. Here the law, as if with true Select Lounge mentality, discriminates sharply against the poor man at the pint counter by allowing those who can command transport and can embark upon a journey to drink elsewhere till morning. The theory is that all travellers still proceed by stage-coach and that those who travel outside become blue with cold after five miles and must be thawed out with hot rum at the first hostelry they encounter by night or day. In practice, people who are in the first twilight of inebriation are transported from the urban to the rural pub so swiftly by the internal combustion engine that they need not necessarily be aware that they have moved at all, still less comprehend that their legal personalities have undergone a mystical transfiguration. Whether this system is to be regarded as a scandal or a godsend depends largely on whether one owns a car. At present the city is ringed round with these "bona-fide" pubs, many of them well-run modern houses, and a considerable amount of the stock-in-trade is transferred to the stomachs of the customers at a time every night when the sensible and just are in their second sleeps ...

To go back to the city: it appears that the poor man does not always go straight home at ten o'clock. If his thirst is big enough and he knows the knocking-formula, he may possibly visit some house where the Demand Note of the Corporation has stampeded the owner into a bout of illicit after-hour trading. For trader and customer alike, such a life is one of excitement, tiptoe and hush. The boss's ear, refined to shades of perception far beyond the sensitiveness of any modern aircraft detector, can tell almost the inner thoughts of any police-man in the next street. At the first breath of danger all lights are suddenly doused and conversation toned down, as with a knob, to vanishing point. Drinkers reared in such schools will tell you that in inky blackness stout cannot be distinguished in taste from Bass and that no satisfaction whatever can be extracted from a cigarette unless the smoke is seen. Sometimes the police make a catch. Here is the sort of thing that is continually appearing in the papers:

Guard—said that accompanied by Guard—he visited the premises at 11.45 p.m. and noticed a light at the side door. When he knocked the light was extinguished, but he was not admitted for six minutes. When defendant opened eventually, he appeared to be in an excited con-dition and used bad language. There was nobody in the bar but there were two empty pint measures con-taining traces of fresh porter on the counter. He found a man crouching in a small press containing switches and a gas-meter. When he attempted to enter the yard to carry out a search, he was obstructed by the defendant, who used an improper expression. He arrested him, but owing to the illness of his wife, he was later released.

Defendant—Did you give me an unmerciful box in the mouth?

Witness—No.

Defendant—Did you say that you would put me and my gawm of a brother through the back wall with one good haymaker of a clout the next time I didn't open when you knocked?

Witness—No.

Justice—You look a fine block of a man yourself. How old are you?

Defendant—I'm as grey as a badger, but I'm not long past forty. (Laughter.)

Justice—Was the brother there at all?

Defendant—He was away in Kells, your worship, seeing about getting a girl for himself. (Laughter.)

Justice—Well, I think you could give a good account of yourself.

Witness—He was very obstreperous, your worship.

Witness, continuing, said that he found two men standing in the dark in an outhouse. They said they were there "for a joke." Witness also found an empty pint measure in an outdoor lavatory and two empty bottles of Cairnes.

Defendant said that two of the men were personal friends and were being treated. There was no question of taking money. He did not know who the man in the press was and did not recall having seen him before. He had given strict instructions to his assistant to allow nobody to remain on after hours. There was nobody in the press the previous day as the gas-man had called to inspect the meter. The two Guards had given him an unmerciful hammering in the hall. His wife was in ill-health, necessitating his doing without sleep for three weeks. A week previously he was compelled to send for the Guards to assist in clearing the house at ten o'clock. He was conducting the house to the best of his ability and was very strict about the hours.

Guard—said that the defendant was a decent hard-working type but was of an excitable nature. The house had a good record.

Remarking that the defendant seemed a decent sort and that the case was distinguished by the absence of perjury, the Justice said he would impose a fine of twenty shillings, the offence not to be endorsed. Were it not for extenuating circumstances he would have no hesitation in sending the defendant to Mountjoy for six months. He commended Guards for smart police work.

Not many publicans, however, will take the risk. If they were as careful of their souls as they are of their licences, heaven would be packed with those confidential and solicitous profit-takers and, to please them, it might be necessary to provide an inferior annex to paradise to house such porter-drinkers as would make the grade.

BRIAN O'NOLAN ("FLANN O'BRIEN")
The Bell, Vol. 1 No. 2

People Great and Small

A FAIR PEOPLE

The Irish are not in a conspiracy to cheat the world by
false representations of the merits of their countrymen.
No, sir; the Irish are a fair people—they never speak
well of one another.

SAMUEL JOHNSON (1709-84)
Boswell's Life of Johnson

THESE IRISH

No nation in Europe is less given to industry or is more
phlegmatic than this. They do not concern themselves
with ecclesiastical or political amelioration.

RINUCINNI (*c.* 1641)

THESE FRIENDLY IRISH

In a couple of hours' talk an Englishman will give you
his notions on trade, politics, the crops; the last run with
the hounds or the weather; it requires a long sitting,
and a bottle of wine at the least, to induce him to laugh
cordially or to speak unreservedly; and if you joke with
him before you know him, he will assuredly set you
down as a low impertinent fellow. In two hours, and
over a pipe, a German will be quite ready to let loose
the easy floodgates of his sentiment, and confide to you

many of the secrets of his soft heart. In two hours a Frenchman will say a hundred and twenty smart, witty, brilliant, false things, and will care for you as much then as he would if you saw him every day for twenty years, that is, not one single straw; and in two hours an Irishman will have allowed his jovial humour to unbutton, and gambolled and frolicked to his heart's content. Which of these, putting Monsieur out of the question, will stand by his friend with the most constancy, and maintain his steady wish to serve him? That is a question which the Englishman (and I think with a little of his ordinary cool assumption) is disposed to decide in his own favour; but it is clear that for a stranger the Irish ways are the pleasantest, for here he is at once made happy and at home.

WILLIAM MAKEPEACE THACKERAY (1811-63)
Irish Sketch Book

NICE BUT—

It was altogether a very jolly life that I led in Ireland. I was always moving about, and soon found myself to be in pecuniary circumstances which were opulent in comparison with those of my past life. The Irish people did not murder me, nor did they even break my head. I soon found them to be good-humoured, clever—the working classes much more intelligent than those of England—economical and hospitable. We hear much of their spendthrift nature; but extravagance is not the nature of an Irishman. He will count the shillings in a pound much more accurately than an Englishman and will with much more certainty get twelve pennyworth from each. But they are perverse, irrational, and but little bound by the love of truth.

ANTHONY TROLLOPE (1815-82)
Autobiography

DECENT PEOPLE

Laugh at me as you may, I cannot but think that there is, amongst the lower orders of Irish, a delicacy of feeling which is not generally to be met in the same rank in England; if it be not refinement, it very much resembles it, and produces the same effect upon the manners. There is a laughing, blushing modesty about the young women which is pleasing from its very artlessness, and which, in the upper ranks, affectation often seeks in vain to imitate. There is, too, a degree of decency, a personal reserve, which I have never met with in the English peasant. If they come to ask for medicine, their symptoms are detailed in a whisper, and are explained in terms as little offensive as possible. When they desire to buy one of the undergarments provided by the kindness of our English friends, it must not be examined in the presence of the other sex, or, if that cannot be avoided, they turn their back, taking care to hold the obnoxious article so as least to be observed.

ANONYMOUS
Letter, 1825

TEMPERAMENT

A gentleman in the County Cavan had complained most bitterly of the injury done to him by some arrangement of the post office. The nature of his grievance has no present significance; but it was so unendurable that he had written many letters, couched in the strongest language. He was most irate, and indulged in that scorn which is so easy to an angry mind.

The place was not in my district, but I was borrowed, being young and strong, that I might remove the edge of his personal wrath. It was mid-winter, and I drove up to his house, a squire's country seat, in the middle of a snow-storm, just as it was becoming dark. I was on an open jaunting-car, and was on my way from one little town to another, the cause of his complaint having reference to some mail conveyance between the two. I was certainly very cold, and very wet, and very uncomfortable, when I entered his house. I was admitted by a butler, but the gentleman himself hurried into the hall. I at once began to explain my business.

"God bless me!" he said, "you are wet through. John, get Mr. Trollope some brandy and water—very hot." I was beginning my story about the post again when he himself took off my great-coat, and suggested that I should go up to my bedroom before I troubled myself with business.

"Bedroom!" I exclaimed. Then he assured me that he would not turn a dog out on such a night as that, and into a bedroom I was shown, having first drunk the brandy and water standing at the drawing-room fire. When I came down I was introduced to his daughter, and the three of us sent into dinner. I shall never forget his righteous indignation when I again brought up the postal question on the departure of the young lady. Was I such a Goth as to contaminate wine with business? So I drank my wine, and then heard the young lady sing while her father slept in his arm-chair.

I spent a very pleasant evening, but my host was too sleepy to hear anything about the post office that night. It was absolutely necessary that I should go away the next morning after breakfast, and I explained that the matter must be discussed then. He shook his head and wrung his hands in unutterable disgust—almost in despair. "But what am I to say in my report?" I asked. "Anything you please," he said. "Don't spare me, if you want an excuse for yourself. Here I sit all the day, with nothing to do; and I like writing letters." I did report that Mr. —— was now quite satisfied with the postal arrangement of his district; and I felt a soft regret that I should have robbed my friend of his occupation. Perhaps he was able to take up the Poor Law Board, or to attack the Excise. At the post office nothing more was heard of him.

ANTHONY TROLLOPE (1815-82)
Autobiography

CAROLAN

Of all the bards this country ever produced, the last and the greatest was CAROLAN THE BLIND. He was at once a poet, a musician, a composer, and sung his own verses to his harp. The original natives never mention his name without rapture; both his poetry and the music they have by heart; and even some of the English themselves, who have been transplanted there, find his music extremely pleasing. A song beginning "O Rourke's noble fare will ne'er be forgot," transplanted by Dean Swift, is of his composition; which, though perhaps by this means the best known of his pieces, is yet by no means the most deserving. His songs, in general, may be compared to those of Pindar, as they have frequently the same flights of imagination, and are composed (I don't say written, for he could not write) merely to flatter some man of fortune upon some excellence of the same kind. In these one man is praised for the excellence of his stable (as in Pindar), another for his hospitality, and a third for the beauty of his wife and children, and a fourth for the antiquity of his family. Whenever any of the original natives of distinction were assembled at feasting or revelling, Carolan was generally there, where he was always ready with his harp to celebrate their praises. He seemed by nature formed for his profession; for as he was born blind, so also he was possessed of a most astonishing memory, and a facetious turn of thinking, which gave his entertainers infinite satisfaction. Being once at the house of an Irish nobleman, where there was a musician present who was eminent in the profession, Carolan immediately challenged him to a trial of skill. To carry the jest forward, his lordship persuaded the musician to accept the challenge, and he accordingly played over on his fiddle the fifth concerto of Vivaldi. Carolan, immediately taking his harp, played over the whole piece after him, without missing a note, though he had never heard it before; which produced some surprise: but their astonishment increased when he assured them he could make a concerto in the same taste himself, which he instantly composed, and that with such spirit and elegance that it may compare (for we have it still) with the finest compositions of Italy.

His death was not more remarkable than his life. Homer was never more fond of a glass than he; he would drink whole pints of usquebaugh, and, as he used to think, without any ill consequence. His intemperance, however, in this respect, at length brought on an incurable disorder; and when just at the point of death, he called for a cup of his beloved liquor. Those who were standing round him, surprised at the demand, endeavoured to persuade him to the contrary; but he persisted, and, when the bowl was brought him, attempted to drink, but could not; wherefore, giving away the bowl, he observed, with a smile, that it would be hard if two such friends as he and the cup should part at least without kissing, and then expired.

OLIVER GOLDSMITH (1730-74)
Prose Works

OLIVER GOLDSMITH

Who, of the millions whom he has amused, does not love him? To be the most beloved of English writers, what a title that is for a man! A wild youth, wayward but full of tenderness and affection, quits the country village where his boyhood has been passed in happy musing, in idle shelter, in fond longing to see the great world out of doors, and achieve name and fortune —and after years of dire struggle, and neglect, and poverty, his heart turning back fondly to his native place, as it had longed eagerly for change when sheltered there, he writes a book and a poem, full of the recollections and feelings of home—he paints the friends and scenes of his youth, and peoples Auburn and Wakefield with remembrances of Lissoy. Wander he must, but he carries away a home-relic with him, and dies with it on his breast. His nature is truant; in repose it longs for change: as on the journey it looks back for friends and quiet. He passes to-day in building an air-castle for to-morrow, or in writing yesterday's elegy; and he would fly away this hour, but that a cage of necessity keeps him. What is the charm of his verse, of his style and humour? His sweet regrets, his delicate compassion, his soft smile, his tremulous sympathy, the weakness which he owns? Your love for him is half pity. You come hot and tired from the day's battle, and this sweet minstrel sings to you. Who could harm the kind vagrant harper? Whom did he ever hurt? He carries no weapon—save the harp on which he plays to you; and with which he delights great and humble, young and old, the captains in the tents, or the soldiers round the fire, or the women and children in the villages, at whose porches he stops and sings his simple songs of love and beauty.

WILLIAM MAKEPEACE THACKERAY (1811-63)
English Humorists

SIR BOYLE ROCHE

I will now advert to Sir Boyle Roche, who certainly was, without exception, the most celebrated and entertaining anti-grammarian in the Irish Parliament. I knew him intimately. He was of a very respectable Irish family, and in point of appearance, a fine, bluff, soldier-like old gentleman. He had numerous good qualities; and, having been long in the army, his ideas were full of honour and etiquette—of discipline and bravery. He had a claim to the title of Fermoy, which, however, he never pursued; and was brother to the famous Tiger Roche, who fought some desperate duel abroad, and was near being hanged for it. Sir Boyle was perfectly well-bred in all his habits; had been appointed gentleman-usher at the Irish court, and executed the duties of that office to the day of his death, with the utmost satisfaction to himself, as well as to everyone in connection with him. He was married to the eldest daughter of Sir John Cave, Bart.; and his lady, who was a "bas bleu" prematurely injured Sir Boyle's capacity (it was said) by forcing him to read Gibbon's *Rise and Fall of the Roman Empire* whereat he was so cruelly puzzled without being in the least amused, that in his cups he often stigmatised the great historian as a low fellow, who ought to have been kicked out of company wherever he was, for turning people's thoughts away from their prayers and their politics to what the devil himself could make neither head nor tail of.

His perpetually bragging that Sir John Cave had given him his *eldest* daughter, afforded Curran an opportunity of replying, "Ay, Sir Boyle, and depend on it, if he had an *older* one still he would have given her to you." Sir Boyle thought it best to receive the repartee as a compliment, lest it should come to her ladyship's ears, who, for several years back, had prohibited Sir Boyle from all allusions to chronology.

The baronet had certainly one great advantage over all other bull and blunder makers: he seldom launched a blunder from which some fine aphorism or maxim might not be easily extracted. When a debate arose in the Irish House of Commons on the vote of a grant which was recommended by Sir John Parnell, Chancellor of the Exchequer, as one not likely to be felt burdensome for many years to come—it was observed in reply, that the House had no just right to load posterity with a weighty debt for what could in no degree operate to their advantage. Sir Boyle, eager to defend the measure of Government, immediately rose, and in a very few words, put forward the most unanswerable argument which human ingenuity could possibly devise. "What, Mr. Speaker!" said he, "and so we are to beggar ourselves for fear of vexing posterity! Now, I would ask the honourable gentleman, and *still more* honourable House, why we should put ourselves out of our way to do anything for *posterity*; for what has *posterity* done for *us*?"

Sir Boyle, hearing the roar of laughter, which of course followed this sensible blunder, but not being conscious that he had said anything out of the way, was rather puzzled, and conceived that the House had misunderstood him. He therefore begged leave to explain, as he apprehended that gentleman had entirely mistaken his words: he assured the House that "by *posterity*, he did not at all mean *our ancestors*, but those who were to come *immediately* after *them*." Upon hearing this *explanation*, it was impossible to do any serious business for half an hour.

Sir Boyle was induced by Government to fight as hard as possible for the Union; so he did, and I really believe fancied, by degrees, that he was right. On one occasion, a general titter arose at his florid picture of the happiness which must proceed from this event. "Gentlemen," said Sir Boyle, "may titther, and titther, and titther, and may think it a bad measure; but their heads at present are hot, and will remain so till they grow cool again; and so they can't decide right now; but when the *day of judgment* comes, *then* honourable gentlemen will be satisfied at this most excellent union. Sir, there is no Levitical degree between nations, and on this occasion I can see neither sin nor shame in *marrying our own sister*."

He was a determined enemy to the French Revolution, and seldom rose in the House for several years without volunteering some abuse of it. "Mr. Speaker," said he, in a mood of this kind, "if we once permitted the villainous French masons to meddle with the buttresses and walls of our ancient constitution, they would never stop, nor stay, sir, till they brought the foundation-stones tumbling down about the ears of the nation! There," continued Sir Boyle, placing his hand earnestly on his heart, his powdered head shaking in unison with his loyal zeal, while he described the probable consequences of an invasion of Ireland by the French republicans; "there, Mr. Speaker! if those Gallican villains should invade us, sir, 'tis on *that very table*, maybe, these honourable members might see their own destinies lying in heaps on top of one another! Here perhaps, sir, the murderous Marshal-law-men (Marseillais) would break in, cut us to mince-meat and throw our bleeding heads upon that table to stare us in the face!"

SIR JONAH BARRINGTON (1760-1834)
Personal Sketches

THE FORGETFUL POET

August 7th, 1843

Dear Moore,

The following articles have been found in your room and forwarded by the Great Western! A right-hand glove, an odd stocking, a sheet of music-paper, a missal, several letters, apparently from ladies, an Elegy on Phelim O'Neil. There is also a bottle of eau de Cologne. What a careless mortal you are!

God bless you.

SYDNEY SMITH
Letter to Thomas Moore

A LOYALIST

"You never saw more elegant lodgings than these, captain," said the master of the house, a tall, handsome and athletic man, who came up while our little family were seated at dinner late in the afternoon of the day of our arrival; "they beat anything in this town of Clonmel. I do not let them for the sake of interest, and to none but gentlemen in the army, in order that myself and my wife, who is from Londonderry, may have the advantage of pleasant company, a genteel company;

ay Protestant company, captain. It did my heart good when I saw your honour ride in at the head of all those fine fellows, real Protestants, I'll engage, not a Papist among them, they are too good-looking and honest-looking for that. So I no sooner saw your honour at the head of your army, with that handsome young gentleman holding by your stirrup, than I said to my wife, Mistress Hyne, who is from Londonderry, ' God bless me,' said I, ' what a truly Protestant countenance, what a noble bearing, and what a sweet young gentleman. By the silver hairs of his honour—and sure enough I never saw hairs more regally silver than those of your honour—by his honour's grey silver hairs, and by my own soul, which is not worthy to be mentioned in the same day with one of them—it would be no more than decent and civil to run out and welcome such a father and son coming in at the head of such Protestant military.' And then my wife, who is from Londonderry, Mistress Hyne, looking me in the face like a fairy as she is, ' You may say that,' says she. ' It would be but decent and civil, honey.' And your honour knows how I ran out of my own door and welcomed your honour riding in company with your son, who was walking; how I welcomed ye both at the head of your royal regiment, and how I shook your honour by the hand, saying I am glad to see your honour, and your honour's son, and your honour's royal military Protestant regiment. And now I have you in the house, and right proud I am to have ye one and all; one, two, three, four, true Protestants every one, no Papists here; and I have made bold to bring up a bottle of claret which is now waiting behind the door; and when your honour and your family have dined, I will make bold too to bring up Mistress Hyne, from Londonderry, to introduce to your honour's lady, and then we'll drink to the health of King George, God bless him; to the ' glorious and immortal '—to Boyne water—to your honour's speedy promotion to be Lord Lieutenant, and to the speedy downfall of the Pope and Saint Anthony of Padua."

GEORGE BORROW (1803-81)
Lavengro

A MAN OF THE WORLD

One man, however, who died not long ago, claimed to have reached one hundred and two with a show of likelihood; for several old people remember his first appearance in a certain district as a man of middle age, about the year of the Famine, in 1847 or 1848. This man could hardly be classed with ordinary tramps, for he was married several times in different parts of the world, and reared children of whom he seemed to have forgotten, in his old age, even the names and sex. In his early life he spent thirty years at sea, where he sailed with someone he spoke of afterwards as "Il mio capitane," visiting India and Japan, and gaining odd words and intonations that gave colour to his language. When he was too old to wander in the world, he learned all the paths of Wicklow, and till the end of his life he could go the thirty miles from Dublin to the Seven Churches without, as he said, "putting out his foot on a white road, or seeing any Christian but the hares and moon." When he was over ninety he married an old woman of eighty-five. Before many days, however, they quarrelled so fiercely that he beat her with his stick, and came out again on the roads. In a few hours he was arrested at her complaint, and sentenced to a month in Kilmainham. He cared nothing for the plank-bed and uncomfortable diet; but he always gathered himself together, and cursed with extraordinary rage, as he told how they had cut off the white hair which had grown down upon his shoulders. All his pride and his half-conscious feeling for the dignity of his age seemed to have set themselves on this long hair, which marked him out from the other people of his district; and I have often heard him saying to himself, as he sat beside me under a ditch: "What use is an old man without his hair? A man has only his bloom like the trees; and what use is an old man without his white hair?"

J. M. SYNGE (1871-1909)
In Wicklow and West Kerry

RICHARD ADAMS, LIMERICK COUNTY COURT JUDGE

He had most of the qualities that the position called for. He was born on the shores of Bantry Bay among the peasantry with whom he sympathised and whose ways he understood. He had periods of genius. Self-educated, he was widely and deeply read in all literature save law, and he knew enough law to assist his experience and common sense. Unfortunately, he had not always control of his tongue. He was incomparably witty without effort, but his wit resembled Dean Swift's, and outrageous and ludicrous phrases escaped his lips before they had entered his mind. His position on the Bench afforded him no self-restraint. His worst offences against propriety were perpetrated in court. His proceedings, if not always wise were never dull, and his actual decisions were thoroughly good, though delivered sometimes in terms that were not conventional.

"Some people," said he, "may think that my jurisdiction is limited to cases not exceeding £50. It is not. I can give a decree for fifty pounds, costs on the higher scale, enormous expenses, and a load of abuse from the dirtiest tongue in Christendom."

"It is time for Crown business," he would exclaim. "The crier will please search the public-houses and bring in the Magistrates."

At Rathkeale, two gentlemen were remarkably regular in their attendance as spectators during the sittings of the court. Both were mad, one amusingly so, the other dangerously, and they were inseparables, until one retired to an institution and the other committed murder. The proceedings at Rathkeale used to open with an application by the harmless lunatic for leave to wear his hat on the ground that he had no skull and therefore his brain uncovered by a hat was liable to catch cold. To save time, permission to this effect was added to the crier's proclamation of the opening of the court, which accordingly ran, "Hear ye all manner of persons that this court is now open and any desirous of transacting business herein come forward and you shall be heard and Mr. Jones may wear his hat, God save the King!"

Notwithstanding this, one morning, Mr. Jones advanced as of old to the foot of the table. "Yes, certainly," said Adams in anticipation. "You may wear your hat." "But your Honour——" "Wear it, I tell you, and for Heaven's sake, sit down." "But I can't, your Honour. That's what I want to tell you. I went home to tea last evening with my friend, Mr. Frost" (his fellow lunatic) "and he offered to show me a trick if I laid myself down on the billiard table, but he tied me with a rope, your Honour, and he beat me until he broke the cues, and I shall never sit down any more." "I wish he had killed you," said the Judge, "then you'd be dead, and he'd be hanged and I'd be rid of both of you."

Adams delighted in luring on a tipsy witness to creating an uproar of laughter and turning on the poor man a flood of righteous corrective. On one occasion, however, he was disarmed. A rural authority was sued for destroying a cow under the rabies order. If destroyed on suspicion, the cow should be paid for, but if prior to destruction, it had been proved rabid, no payment need be made. Legal proof of the existence of rabies had been held to require microscopic examination of the spinal cord, so defence appeared hopeless. These defendants, however, produced as a witness a local cow doctor who knew nothing of microscopics or spinal cords, though something perhaps about the taste of alcohol. "That cow had rabies," he swore, "by the infallible test." "What test did you apply?" "Bring a dog into the stall with the cow, and the cow sort of barks——that's the only infallible test." "Was that the only symptom you noticed in this case?" asked Adams. "N-no, in this case there was the sudden death of the cow." "Did she die suddenly?" "V-very suddenly." "Describe what happened." "I sh—ot her."

Jurors in the County of Limerick were the worst in Munster. At the end of the trial of a bad stabbing case, the usual verdict having been returned, Adams said to the accused, "Michael, I have now to discharge you. These twelve gentlemen on my left say that you are not guilty. Take a good look at them, Mike, so that you may know them again, for if you treat any one of them the way you treated the prosecutor in this case, you will not get one hour's imprisonment from me, even if you are convicted of it."

This jurist's definition of the limit of permissible perjury was as follows: "Look here, sir," he said to a litigant in the witness-box, "tell me no more unnecessary lies. Such lies as your attorney advised you are necessary for the presentation of your fraudulent case I will listen to though I shall decide against you whatever you swear, but if you tell me another unnecessary lie, I'll put you in the dock."

A. M. SULLIVAN (1871-1959)
Old Ireland

ADAMS AGAIN

It was perhaps that prisoner, or another in similar circumstances, that Adams dismissed with the words—"You have been acquitted by a Limerick jury, and you may now leave the dock without any other stain upon your character."

MAURICE HEALY (1859-1923)
The Old Munster Circuit

A PARSON

The Protestant clergyman at Headford, in whose parish Morony Castle was supposed to have been situated, was a thin, bigoted Protestant of that kind which used to be common in Ireland. Mr. Armstrong was a gentleman who held it to be an established fact that a Roman Catholic must necessarily go to the devil. In all the moralities he was perfect. He was a married man with a wife and six children, all of whom he brought up and educated on £250 a year. He never was in debt, he performed all his duties—such as they were—and passed his time in making rude and unavailing attempts to convert his poorer neighbours. There was a Union —or poor-house—in the neighbourhood, to which he would carry morsels of meat in his pocket on Friday, thinking that the poor wretches who had flown in the face of their priest by eating the unhallowed morsels, would then have made a first step towards Protestantism. He was charitable, with so little means for charity; he was very eager in his discourses, in the course of which he would preach to a dozen Protestants for three quarters of an hour, and would confine himself to one subject, the iniquities of the Roman Catholic religion. . . . He had attempted to argue with Father Brosnan, but had been like a babe in his hands. He ate and drank of the poorest, and clothed himself so as just to maintain his clerical aspect. All his aspirations were of such a nature as to entitle him to a crown of martyrdom. But they were certainly not of a nature to justify him in expecting any promotion on this earth.

ANTHONY TROLLOPE (1815-82)
The Land Leaguers

MISS MARTIN OF CONNEMARA

While Mrs. Martin was thus refreshing my spirits with anecdotes scandalous and humorous, her daughter Mary was either in her room or on a sofa opposite us with her legs on it and her head back, not hearing or heeding a word that was said, but wrapped in some philosophical abstraction of her own, which I should never have expected, had her mother not let me into her character. "My dear, you don't understand Mary. She is living in another world and has not the least knowledge or taste or care about this world as it goes. She does not hear one word we say, and the only thing that keeps her there is you as an authoress and celebrated person. She is exceptionally curious about celebrated people, and I know would delight in talking to you about books." In a dark closet in her own room it seems Miss Martin had books, though nought but a few religious books and an odd volume or two of the Edinburgh and Quarterly Review appeared in any other room in the house; Mary's apartment was on the other side of her mother's bedchamber. And: "Every morning," said Mrs. Martin, "she comes in to me while I am dressing

7

and pours out an inundation of learning of all sorts, fresh and fresh: all she has been reading for hours before I was up. She has read prodigiously, as you will find when you talk to her, or when she lets herself out to you. But she has no tact, no knowledge how to manage the quantity she has read and no taste for anything of humour or mere amusement. Now there may be too much of philosophy and science, you know, at least for me: very good all in its place and season, but there must be some relief. You feel that, I am sure, don't you?" And her way of saying this was so like Aunt Ruxton—and then her fear that she had prejudiced me against Mary, and her going back to apologise for her and explain that it wasn't pedantry, but mere simplicity.

I began to study Mary and found her really one of the most extraordinary persons I ever saw—in original talent not at all equal to her mother, I think, though nobody else in the house nor neighbourhood suspected it but myself. Her acquirements are indeed prodigious; she has more knowledge of books, both scientific and learned, than any female creature I ever saw or heard of at her age: heraldry, metaphysics, painting and painters' lives, and tactics. She had a course of tactics from a French officer, and of engineering from Mr. Nimmo. She understands Latin, Greek and Hebrew, and I don't know how many modern languages. I can answer for it that she speaks French perfectly, learned from the French officer who taught her fortification, M. du Bois, who was one of Bonaparte's legion of honour, and when the Emperor was ousted, fled from France and took refuge at Ballinahinch Castle, and earned his bread by teaching French. . . . She imbibed from him such an enthusiasm for Bonaparte, that she cannot bear a word said to his disparagement; and when Sir Culling sometimes offended in that way, Miss Martin's face and neck grew carnation colour, and

down to the tips of her fingers she blushed with
indignation. . . .

Mary has read all Sir Walter Scott's poetry and all of
Lord Byron's that is fit for a young lady to read; but
to give you an idea of the extreme care that her mother
has taken to preserve the purity of her mind, and to
show you her own perfect simplicity, I must tell you
that till Sir Culling alluded to them, she had not the
least suspicion that Byron was not a perfectly moral
man, and was quite taken in by his representations of
himself and his fine feelings in Childe Harold; you never
saw anything more breathless and amusing.   Her
memory for poetry and prose in all languages is, I
think really equal to the Admirable Crichton's.   When
any allusion was made to books, she could quote whole
passages from them, begin or end where you would,
and at dinner I have heard her going on in a low rumble
to herself with whole stanzas *à propos* to what had been
said, without any desire to attract attention, but only
for her own satisfaction.   In truth it could have been
for nobody else's, for among her other accomplishments
she had never learned to recite or read English tolerably,
but so fast and so oddly in such a Connemara accent and
words so fluid, running one into the other, that at first
I could not guess what language it was.   Not having
been ever in the least used to literary conversation or
sympathy in her literary pursuits, she does not know how
to manage, full of enthusiasm as she is and of her
herself.   She brings out whole bales whereas she should
produce only patterns—or draws for a thousand pounds
of sympathy at sight upon a bankrupt, and on the
strength of a commonplace simper, believes in the
profound intelligence of a pretended listener and real
sneerer.   She is, apparently, egotistic—she talks more of
herself than any well bred young lady or than anyone
taught by the least acquaintance with the world's cold-
ness and selfishness would venture to do; but though

she talks more of herself, I question whether she does
not think less, and more of others than many of the
accredited polite.

MARIA EDGEWORTH (1767-1849)
Tour in Connemara

MISS MAKEBELIEVE OF DUBLIN

Mary Makebelieve lived with her mother in a small
room at the very top of a big dingy house in a Dublin
back street. As long as she could remember she had
lived in that top back room. . . . There was but one
window in the room, and when she wished to look out
of it she had to push the window up, because the grime
of many years had so encrusted the glass that it was of
no more than the demi-semi-transparency of thin horn.
When she did look there was nothing to see but a bulky
array of chimney-pots crowning a next-door house, and
these continually hurled jays of soot against her window;
therefore, she did not care to look out often, for each
time she did so she was forced to wash herself, and as
water had to be carried from the very bottom of the
five-storey house up hundreds and hundreds of stairs to
her room, she disliked having to use too much water.

Her mother seldom washed at all. She held that wash-
ing was very unhealthy and took the natural gloss off
the face, and that, moreover, soap either tightened the
skin or made it wrinkle. Her own face was very tight
in some places and very loose in others, and Mary
Makebelieve often thought that the tight places were
spots which her mother used to wash when she was
young, and the loose parts were those which had never
been washed at all. She thought she would prefer to
be either loose all over her face or tight all over it, and,

therefore, when she washed she did it thoroughly, and when she abstained she allowed of no compromise. . . .

Every morning about six o'clock Mary Makebelieve left her bed and lit the fire. It was an ugly fire to light, because the chimney had never been swept, and there was no draught. Also they never had any sticks in the house, and scraps of paper twisted tightly into balls with the last night's cinders placed on them and a handful of small coals strewn on the top were used instead. Sometimes the fire blazed up quickly, and that made her happy, but at other times it went out three and four, and often half a dozen times; then the little bottle of paraffin oil had to be squandered—a few rags well steeped in the oil with a newspaper stretched over the grate seldom failed to coax enough fire to boil the saucepan of water; generally this method smoked the water, and then the tea tasted so horrid that one only drank it for the sake of economy.

Mrs. Makebelieve liked to lie in bed until the last possible moment. As there was no table in the room, Mary used to bring the two cups of tea, the tin of condensed milk, and the quarter of a loaf over to the bed, and there she and her mother took their breakfast.

From the time she opened her eyes in the morning her mother never ceased to talk. It was then she went over all the things that had happened on the previous day and enumerated the places she would have to go to on the present day, and the chances for and against the making of a little money. At this meal she used to arrange also to have the room re-papered and the chimney swept and the rat-holes stopped up—there were three of these, one was on the left-hand side of the fire grate, the other two were under the bed, and Mary Makebelieve had lain awake many a night listening to the gnawing of teeth on the skirting and the scamper of little feet here and there on the floor. Her mother further arranged to have a Turkey carpet placed on the floor, although she

admitted that oilcloth or linoleum was easier to clean,
but they were not so nice to the feet or the eye. Into
all these improvements her daughter entered with the
greatest delight. There was to be a red mahogany chest
of drawers against one wall and a rosewood piano
against the wall opposite. A fender of shining brass
with brazen furniture, a bright, copper kettle for boiling
water in, and an iron pot for cooking potatoes and
meat; there was to be a life-sized picture of Mary over
the mantelpiece and a picture of her mother near the
window in a golden frame, also a picture of a Newfound-
land dog lying in a barrel and a little wee terrier crawling
up to make friends with him, and a picture of a battle
between black people and soldiers.

Her mother knew it was time to get out of bed when
she heard a heavy step coming from the next room and
going downstairs. . . . When the door banged she
jumped up, dressed quickly, and flew from the room in
a panic of haste. Usually then, as there was nothing to
do, Mary went back to bed for another couple of hours.
After this she arose, made the bed and tidied the room,
and went out to walk in the streets, or to sit in the
St. Stephen's Green Park. . . . She loved to watch the
ducklings swimming after their mothers: they were
quite fearless, and would dash to the water's edge where
one was standing and pick up nothing with the greatest
eagerness and swallow it with delight. . . . Mary
Makebelieve thought it was very clever of the little
ducklings to be able to swim so well. She loved them,
and when nobody was looking she used to cluck at them
like their mother, but she did not often do this because
she did not know duck language really well, and feared
that her cluck might mean the wrong things, and that
she might be giving these innocents bad advice, and
telling them to do something contrary to what their
mother had just directed. . . .

After that, growing hungry, she would go home for

her lunch. She went home down Grafton Street and O'Connell Street. She always went along the right-hand side of the street going home, and looked in every shop window that she passed, and then, when she had eaten her lunch, she came out again and walked along the left-hand side of the road, looking at the shops on that side, and so she knew daily everything that was new in the city, and was able to tell her mother at night-time that the black dress with Spanish lace was taken out of Manning's window and a red gown with tucks at the shoulders and Irish lace at the wrists put in its place; or that the diamond ring in Johnson's marked One Hundred Pounds was gone from the case and that a slide of brooches of beaten silver and blue enamel was there instead.

In the night-time her mother and herself went round to each of the theatres in turn and watched the people going in and looked at the big posters. When they went home afterwards they had supper and used to try to make out the plots of the various plays from the pictures they had seen, so that generally they had lots to talk about before they went to bed. Mary Makebelieve used to talk most in the night-time, but her mother talked most in the morning.

JAMES STEPHENS (1881-1950)
The Charwoman's Daughter

A LANGUAGE ENTHUSIAST

A great old cock was O'Neill Russell, whom we never looked upon as an old man, despite his eighty years. How could we, since he was straight as a maypole, and went for walks of two-and-twenty miles among the Dublin mountains? He came back to me one day after one of these strolls, the news bubbling upon his lips that he had composed an entire scenario on the subject of an heroic adventure that had happened to an Irish king in the thirteenth century; but he would not stay to dinner, nor even to relate it; he was in too great a hurry to verify a fact in the National Library, to get his scenario down on paper. For one reason or another he never dined at my house, though he liked to come in after dinner for a talk on Saturday nights. It was no use offering him a cigar, he always begged to be allowed to smoke his pipe, and there being no spittoons in my dining-room the coal-scuttle was put by him. A great old cock, head up-reared, fine neck, grand shoulders, a stately piece of architecture, fine in detail as in general effect. A big nose divided the face, wandering grey eyes lit it. The large hands had worked for sixty years in America, in France, in the East. He had been all over the world, and had returned to Ireland with some seventy, eighty, perhaps a hundred pounds a year. He was gibed in songs, for he had gone away as a boy, speaking bad Irish, and come back after sixty years, speaking bad Irish still; so said the song's refrain, and a story followed at his heels that he had vilified a man for twenty years in the American newspapers, denouncing him as a renegade Irishman, because he had advocated a certain use of the genitive. A great old cock, as young as the youngest of the men that came to my house, were it not for a certain sadness—a very beautiful sadness, not for himself, but for his country. He had hoped all his life for Ireland's resurrection, but at the end of his life it seemed as distant as ever.

He haunted the Gaelic League offices, and the day he pushed the door open, entering the room with a great stride, I began to wonder who the intruder could be— this great tall man, dressed in a faded blue jacket and a pair of grey trousers and a calico shirt. The editor of the Claidheamh introduced us, and my heart went out to him at once, as every heart did, for he was the recognisable Irishman, the adventurer, the wild goose. And after that meeting we met frequently between five and six o'clock; the Gaelic League offices were then a pleasant resort; all kinds and conditions of men assembled there, and we discussed the Irish language sitting upon tables while smoking cigarettes. It appeared every week in the Claidheamh Soluis, and I liked to dictate a paragraph for somebody to turn into Irish before my eyes, and when the editor paused for an equivalent, every one ransacked his memory, but our dictionary was always O'Neill Russell—a rambling, incoherent, untrustworthy, old dictionary—but one that none of us would have willingly been without. It is pleasant to remember that he was in the offices of the League the day that I called to unfold my project for a little travelling company to the secretary and that he approved of it; but his conversation soon diverged from the matter in hand into an argument regarding the relative merits of Munster and Connaught Irish.

I'm afraid, he said, that you've come too late to revive the Irish language. There are only three men in Ireland who can write pure Irish. It's dialect, sir, they write.

GEORGE MOORE (1852-1933)
Hail and Farewell

A. E., YEATS, SYNGE AND MOORE

There were so many people whom she knew by sight; almost daily she saw these somewhere, and she often followed them for a short distance, with a feeling of friendship; for the loneliness of the long day often drew down upon her like a weight, so that even the distant companionship of these remembered faces that did not know her was comforting. She wished she could find out who some of them were.—There was a tall man with a sweeping brown beard, whose heavy overcoat looked as though it had been put on with a shovel; he wore spectacles, and his eyes were blue, and always seemed as if they were going to laugh; he, also, looked into the shops as he went along, and he seemed to know everybody. Every few paces people would halt and shake his hand, but these people never spoke because the big man with the brown beard would instantly burst into a fury of speech which had no intervals, and when there was no one with him at all he would talk to himself. On these occasions he did not see anyone, and people had to jump out of his way while he strode onwards swinging his big head from one side to the other, and with his eyes fixed on some place a great distance away. Once or twice, in passing, she heard him singing to himself the most lugubrious song in the world. There was another—a long, thin, black man— who looked young and was always smiling secretly to himself; his lips were never still for a moment, and, passing Mary Makebelieve a few times, she heard him buzzing like a great bee. He did not stop to shake hands with any one, and although many people saluted him he took no heed, but strode on smiling his secret smile and buzzing serenely. There was a third man whom she often noticed: his clothing seemed as if it had been put on him a long time ago and had never been taken off again. He had a long, pale face with a dark moustache drooping over a most beautiful mouth. His eyes were very big and lazy, and did not look quite human; they had a trick of looking sideways—a most intimate, personal look. Sometimes he saw nothing in the world but the pavement, and at other times he saw everything. He looked at Mary Makebelieve once, and she got a fright; she had a queer idea that she had known him well hundreds of years before and that he remembered her also. She was afraid of that man, but she liked him because he looked so gentle and so—there was something else he looked which as yet she could not put a name to, but which her ancestry remembered dimly. There was a short, fair, pale-faced man, who looked like the tiredest man in the world. He was often preoccupied, but not in the singular way the others were. He seemed to be always chewing the cud of remembrance, and looked at people as if they reminded him of other people who were dead a long time and whom he thought of but did not regret. He was a detached man even in a crowd and carried with him a cold atmosphere; even his smile was bleak and aloof. Mary Makebelieve noticed that many people nudged each other as he went by, and then they would turn and look after him and go away whispering.

JAMES STEPHENS (1881-1950)
The Charwoman's Daughter

YEATS

One could never claim to have known Yeats well. Unlike A. E., whose manner was benevolent, his attitude was haughty. A. E. muffled in his great tweed coat, peering pleasantly through a tangle of spectacles and beard, was always ready to talk with us, listen to our theories. Yeats, on the other hand, appeared to give only half his attention. In conversation, one got the impression that he looked through and beyond you towards another world.

Being at once a brilliant and rather mysterious person, apparently detached from the material things of life, he was the idol of most of the young people who filled the Dublin universities. His every move was followed closely during his visits from London, where he lived at the time. He was a striking figure, tall, commanding attention. He was dark complexioned, with a high forehead, jet-black hair, deep eyes. His full-lipped mouth gave him a rather sulky look at times. It is hardly accurate to say that he was wayward, but he was exceptionally strong-willed. During the years which followed, when he acquired the leadership of the Abbey, he carried it through some of its most critical years, fought all its battles, denounced its enemies and critics with a vigour almost terrifying in its finality. Those who moved on the outskirts of the theatrical movement used to say (not inaptly, really): "Yeats thrives in a row." I have frequently seen his whole being shaken by fits of the most uncontrollable rage.

Of course, being the foremost Irish writer of the time, surrounded by this aura of mystery, and already famous enough to be satirised by the wits in England, where many people admired him but few, surprisingly, understood him, he qualified as a sort of gibing-post in some circles in Dublin, and many humorous, but not altogether just, stories were told about him. It was understandable of course: he was on the one hand completely divorced from material considerations—an impression which his association with occult societies, and the strange unrealistic note which ran through some of his poetry helped to foster—on the other he was a fighter of the fiercest calibre who could descend completely from the plane which he usually occupied and crush all who opposed him by the sheer force of his personality. Later years were to show evidence of this trait—his attitude on the occasion of the first production of J. M. Synge's ill-fated *Playboy of the Western World* was one—but he had already proved himself a fighter during the furore in Dublin some years earlier over his *Countess Cathleen* when the audience rose in protest because his central character sold her soul to the devils. Yeats had completely surmounted all this opposition with an acid pen and a scathing word. Dublin, in fact, was still rather uncertain about him. He was a puzzle to some; he was admired and copied by others. Young literary-minded people looked at him with a sort of awe, were struck almost dumb when he spoke to them. If he saw the effect he was creating he seldom showed it. The witticisms which were woven around his actions, if he noticed them, he disregarded or glanced at with a sort of lofty detachment. Yeats was a *poseur* but he was never the insipid poet. He commanded the respect of men; the adoration of many women.

MAIRE NIC SHIUBHLAIGH and EDWARD KENNY
The Splendid Years

SYNGE

He was a gentle fellow, shy, with that deep sense of humour that is sometimes found in the quietest people. His bulky figure and heavy black moustache gave him a rather austere appearance—an impression quickly dispelled when he spoke. His voice was mellow, low; he seldom raised it. But for his quiet personality he might have passed unnoticed at any gathering. During rehearsals of his play, he would sit quietly in the background, endlessly rolling cigarettes. This was a typical gesture, born more of habit than of any desire for tobacco—he gave away more cigarettes than he smoked. At the first opportunity, he would lever his huge frame out of a chair and come up on to the stage, a half-rolled cigarette in each hand. Then he would look enquiringly round and thrust the little paper cylinders forward towards whoever was going to smoke them. In later years he became the terror of fire-conscious Abbey stage-managers. He used to sit timidly in the wings during plays, rolling cigarettes and handing them to the players as they made their exits.

MAIRE NIC SHIUBHLAIGH and EDWARD KENNY
The Splendid Years

GEORGE MOORE

I was Registrar of the Dublin National Gallery at one time. My man came in and said: "Mr. George Moore to see you, sir." "Ah," said I to myself, "the famous novelist that everybody talks about and nobody reads, and of whom I've never read a word either!" . . . "Show him in," said I.

In ten more seconds George Moore stepped into my lovely office. There were three or four pictures on each of my walls, and a beautiful fire in the grate. Moore looked very carefully at all my pictures before he looked at me, and said: "Ah, copies, I presume."

"I think not," I replied, "but you are more of an expert than I am." Moore sat down. "You are an expert *ex officio*," said he. "Oh no," I answered. "I am merely a very superior official: my director is Quattrocento and my Board is Byzantine. They are our experts."

An odd thing happens when two writers meet. Without a word being uttered on the subject, each knows in thirty seconds whether the other has ever read a line of his work or not. Neither of us had, and we were both instantly aware that life is not perfect, but, while I was full of patience and hope, Moore was scandalised.

Still, literature was his subject, and this was so in a deeper sense than in any other writer I have ever met. In the way of being dedicated to the craft of writing, Moore was that. He lived for the prose way of thinking —wine, women and murder—and I am sure that when he was asleep he dreamed that he was writing a bigger and better book than any he had yet managed to produce. He loved the art of prose; for poetry he had the traditional reverence that we all have; but I fancy that he had small liking for it. . . .

"What are you working at now, Stephens?" said Moore.

"This morning," I replied, "I translated *The County of Mayo*."

"That is my own county," said he, "and so I am interested. But, my dear Stephens, that poem has been translated so many times already, that you are wasting your, ah, talent, yes, perhaps talent, on a job that every literate person in Ireland has done before you."

"Why, Moore?" said I.

Here he broke in, "Don't you think, Stephens, that I have come to the years in which younger men should address me as Mr. Moore?"

"Certainly, Mr. Moore," said I—and he smiled a grave, fattish and reprobating smile at me.

"You were going to say," he prompted, turning on me his pale fattish face and his sloping, thinnish shoulders, and his air of listening to me almost as through a keyhole.

"Only, sir, that a translation is never completed until it has become a piece of original verse in the new tongue."

"That is an excellent and beautifully impossible definition," said Moore. "Perhaps," he went on, "you would like to say the verses to me. How many are there?" he added hastily.

"Only four," I answered, "and as it is about your own county, sir, you should be the first one to hear them."

"Thank you, Stephens," said he, unnecessarily, for I intended to say that poem to someone. So I said the little poem, and he praised it highly, mainly I think because I had called him ' sir.'

"I must leave you very soon," said he, "for I have a lunch engagement, but if you ever need literary advice,

I hope you will write to me. In fact, I beg that you will do so, for I have a proposition to make to you."

"I am in need of advice right now, Mr. Moore," said I, "and although some might think the matter not literary I consider that everything that has to do with a speech problem has to do with literature."

Moore agreed. "Psychological problems," said he, "are women and religion and English grammar. All other problems are literary. Tell me the matter that is confusing you, Stephens."

"Well, sir," said I, "I have been invited to the first formal dinner party of my life."

"Your first dinner party?" he queried.

"I have eaten," I explained, "with every kind of person and at every kind of table, but I have never dined with anybody."

"At a dinner," said he, "formal or informal, you just eat your dinner."

"Oh, no, Mr. Moore," said I, "the problem has nothing to do with mastication and is quite a troublesome one. I shall be sitting at a strange table and on my right hand there will be a lady whom I have never seen before and may never see again."

"Quite," said he.

"On my left hand," I continued, "there will be another lady whom I've never seen before. In the name of heaven, Mr. Moore, what shall I say to these ladies?"

"Why," said Moore thoughtfully, "this is a problem that never struck me before. It is a very real one," said he, sitting up at me and at it. "If you were an Englishman," he went on, "you could talk a little about the weather, vaguely, you know, a number of Dirty Days and How are You's, and then you could say a few well-chosen words about the soup, and the meat, and subsequently about the pudding—pudding, Stephens."

"Dammit," said I.

"An Irishman," Moore said, "can always find something to say about the cattle, and the crops, the manure and the ... No, no," he continued energetically, "no manure—ladies think it is very strange stuff: they prefer to talk about the theatres—actors, I mean,—and hats. I'll tell you, talk to the first woman about how pretty her dress is; say that you have never seen so lovely a dress in your life. Then turn to the other hussy, and say that she is the most beautiful person in the room. Admire her rings: don't ask her where she got them: never ask a woman where or how she got anything whatever; questions like that often lead to divorce proceedings. In short, Stephens, talk to them about themselves, and you are pretty safe."

He enlarged on this matter; "You may talk to them about their hair and their eyes and their noses, but," he interrupted hastily, "don't say anything whatever about their knees."

"I will not, Mr. Moore," said I fervently.

"In especial, Stephens, do not touch their knees under any circumstances."

"I will not, Mr. Moore."

"Restraint at a formal dinner party, Stephens, is absolutely necessary."

"I quite understand, sir."

"Moreover, Stephens, women are strangely gifted creatures in some respects, all women have a sense akin to absolute divination about their knees."

"Ah, sir?" I queried.

"When a woman's knee is touched, Stephens, however delicately, the lady knows infallibly whether the gentleman is really caressing her or whether he is only wiping his greasy fingers on her stocking. But formal dinner parties are disgusting entertainments anyhow. Goodbye, Stephens."

"Goodbye, Mr. Moore," said I fervently, "and thank you very much for your help. I shall never forget those ladies' knees."

Moore smiled at me happily, almost lovingly. "Write to me about this dinner party, Stephens."

"I shall certainly do so, Mr. Moore."

And that was our first meeting.

JAMES STEPHENS (1881-1950)
from a radio broadcast, 1949

GEORGE MOORE

Moore had inherited a large Mayo estate, and no Mayo country gentleman had ever dressed the part so well. He lacked manners, but had manner; he could enter a room so as to draw your attention without seeming to, his French, his knowledge of painting, suggested travel and leisure. Yet nature had denied to him the final touch; he had a coarse palate. Edward Martyn alone suspected it. When Moore abused the waiter or the cook, he had thought, "I know what he is hiding." In a London restaurant on a night when the soup was particularly good, just when Moore had the spoon at his lips, he said: "Do you mean to say you are going to drink that?" Moore tasted the soup, then called the waiter, and ran through the usual performance. Martyn did not undeceive him, content to chuckle in solitude. Moore had taken a house in Upper Ely Place; he spent a week at our principal hotel while his furniture was moving in: he denounced the food to the waiter, to the manager, went down to the kitchen and denounced it to the cook. "He has written to the proprietress," said the manager, "that the steak is like brown paper. How can you believe a word such a man would say, a steak cannot be like brown paper." He had his own bread sent in from the baker and said on the day he left: "How can these people endure it?" "Because," said the admiring headwaiter, "they are not comme il faut." A little later I stayed with him and wrote to Lady

Gregory: "He is boisterously enduring the sixth cook."
Then from Sligo a few days later: "Moore dismissed
the sixth cook the day I left—six in three weeks. One
brought in a policeman, Moore had made so much noise.
He dragged the policeman into the dining-room and
said: 'Is there a law in this country to compel me to
eat this abominable omelette?'"

Sometimes Moore, instead of asking us to accept for
true some monstrous invention, would press a spon-
taneous action into deliberate comedy; starting in bad
blood or blind passion, he would all in a moment see
himself as others saw him. When he arrived in Dublin,
all the doors in Upper Ely Place had been painted white
by an agreement between the landlord and the tenants.
Moore had his door painted green, and three Miss Beams
—no, I have not got the name quite right—who lived
next door protested to the landlord. Then began a
correspondence between Moore and the landlord wherein
Moore insisted on his position as an art critic, that
the whole decoration of his house required a green
door—I imagine that he had but wrapped the green
flag around him—then the indignant young women
bought a copy of *Esther Waters*, tore it up, put the
fragments into a large envelope, wrote thereon: "Too
filthy to keep in the house," dropped it into his letter-box.
I was staying with Moore, I let myself in with a latch-
key some night after twelve, and found a note on the
hall table asking me to put the door on the chain. As
I was undressing, I heard Moore trying to get in; when
I had opened the door and pointed to the note he said:
"Oh, I forgot. Every night I go out at eleven, at twelve,
at one, and rattle my stick on the railing to make the
Miss Beams' dogs bark." Then I saw in the newspapers
that the Miss Beams had hired organ-grinders to play
under Moore's window when he was writing, that he
had prosecuted the organ-grinders. Moore had a large
garden on the other side of the street, a blackbird sang

there; he received his friends upon Saturday evening and made a moving speech upon the bird. "I enjoy its song. If I were the bad man people say I am, could I enjoy its song?" He wrote every morning at an open window on the ground floor, and one morning saw the Miss Beams' cat cross the street, and thought, "That cat will get my bird." He went out and filled his pocket with stones, and whenever he saw the cat, threw a stone. Somebody, perhaps the typist, must have laughed, for the rest of the tale fills me with doubt. I was passing through Dublin just on my way to Coole; he came to my hotel. "I remembered how early that cat got up. I thought it might get the blackbird if I was not there to protect it, so I set a trap. The Miss Beams wrote to the Society for the Prevention of Cruelty to Animals, and I am carrying on a correspondence with its secretary, cat versus bird." (Perhaps after all, the archives of the Society do contain that correspondence. The tale is not yet incredible.) I passed through Dublin again, perhaps on my way back. Moore came to see me in seeming great depression. "Remember that trap?" "Yes." "Remember that bird?" "Yes." "I have caught the bird."

W. B. YEATS (1865-1939)
Dramatis Personae

THE GREAT LADY AND THE GREAT MAN

I

Casey told me he is a labourer, and, as we talked of masons, said he had "carried the hod." He said, "I was among books as a child, but I was sixteen before I learned to read or write. My father loved books, he had a big library. I remember the look of the books high up on shelves."

I asked why his father had not taught him and he said, "He died when I was three years old through those same books. There was a little ladder in the room to get to the shelves, and one day when he was standing on it, it broke and he fell and was killed."

I said, "I often go up the ladder in our library at home," and he begged me to be careful.

He is learning what he can about art, has bought books on Whistler and Raphael, and takes *The Studio*. All this was as we watched the crowd.

I forget how I came to mention the Bible, and he asked "Do you like it?" I said, "Yes. I read it constantly, even for the beauty of the language." He said he admires that beauty, he was brought up as a Protestant but has lost belief in religious forms. Then, in talking of our war here, we came to Plato's *Republic*, his dream city, whether on earth or in heaven not far away from the city of God. And then we went into the play. He says he sent us a play four years ago, *The Frost in the Flower*, and it was returned, but marked, "not far from being a good play." He has sent others, and says how grateful he was to me because when we had to refuse the Labour one, *The Crimson In the Tri-colour*, I had said, "I believe there is something in you and your strong point is characterisation." And I had wanted to pull that play together and put it on to give him experience, but Yeats was down on it. Perrin says he offered him a pass sometimes when he happened to come in, but he refused and said, "No one ought to come into the Abbey Theatre without paying for it." He said, "All the thought in Ireland for years past has come through the Abbey. You have no idea what an education it has been to the country." That, and the fine audience on this our last week, put me in great spirits.

LADY GREGORY (1852-1932)
The Journals

2

There she was waiting for him—a trim, stout, sturdy figure, standing upright and still on the platform, ready to guide him safely down to Gort, grimly patient in the midst of the talkative, quickly-moving crowd. A strange, lone figure she looked in a third-class carriage, stuck tight in a mass of peasants and small farmers, and they with baskets on their laps, or live fowls clutched in their hands; while one woman, young and lively, had a big goose, its legs and wings tied with cord, at her feet, so that it could only gabble, mixing its comic cries with the eager, animated chatter of the crowd.

—Der, said Lady Gregory, suddenly pointing out of a window, der's Craughwell where the police were always half-afraid to stir eating, drinking, and sleeping behind iron doors, thick walls, and steel-shuttered windows. We'll pass Ardrahan later on, remembering what Davis sang,

> And fleet as deer, deh Normans ran
> Tro Curlew's Pass and Ardrahan.

—An' will again, please God, murmured a quiet voice from a corner.

She has a bit of lisp, thought Sean, and I only after noticing it now. Look at her there, with all her elegance, well at ease among the chattering crowd of common people; so why shouldn't I be steady in my mind at coming to a Big House, among rare silver and the best of china, sleeping in a bounteous bed, and handling divers tools at food never seen before. And he took heart, and felt strong, looking at the calm, handsome, old face, smiling at the chatter of the people and the frightened cackling of the fowl.

SEAN O'CASEY (1880-1964)
Inishfallen, Fare Thee Well

3

March 8, 1924. In the evening to the Abbey with
W. B. Yeats, *Juno and the Paycock* (*Sean O' Casey's*)—a long
queue at the door, the theatre crowded, many turned
away, so it will be run on next week. A wonderful and
terrible play of futility, of irony, humour, tragedy.
When I went round to the Green-room I saw Casey and
had a little talk with him. He was very happy.

I asked him to come to tea the next day, the matinee,
as I had brought up a barmbrack for the players,
but he said, "No. I can't come. I'll be at work
till the afternoon and I'm working with cement, and
that takes such a long time to get off."

"But after that?"

"Then I have to cook my dinner. I have but one room
and I cook for myself since my mother died."

He is, of course, happy at the great success of his play,
and I said, "You must feel now that we were right in
not putting on that first one you sent in—*The Crimson
and the Tri-colour*. I was inclined to put it on because
some of it was so good and I thought you might learn
by seeing it on the stage, though some was very poor,
but Mr. Yeats was firm."

He said, "You were right not to put it on. I can't read
it myself now. But I will tell you that it was a bitter
disappointment for I had not only thought at the time
it was the best thing I had written, but I thought that
no one in the world had ever written anything so fine."

Then he said, "You had it typed for me, and I don't
know how you could have read it as I sent it in with the
bad writing and the poor paper. But at that time it
was hard for me to afford even the paper it was written
on."

And he said, "I owe a great deal to you and Mr. Yeats
and Mr. Robinson, but to you above all. You gave me
encouragement. And it was you who said to me upstairs

in the office—I could show you the very spot where you stood—' Mr. Casey, your gift is characterisation.' And so I threw over my theories and worked at characters and this is the result."

LADY GREGORY (1852-1932)
The Journals

4

But Lady Gregory wasn't afraid of the child's cry or the creak of the lumbering cart; and she stayed to speak warm words to the ploughman splashing the wintry mould. She trotted fearlessly beside all these things, sad or merry; listened to their tales, sang songs with them when they were merry; and mourned with them when a silver cord was sundered or a golden bowl was broken. The taste of rare wine mingled with that of home-made bread on the tip of her tongue; her finely-shod feet felt the true warmth of the turf fire, and beside its glow she often emptied the sorrows of her own heart into the sorrows of others. Out of her plush and plum, she came to serve the people, body and mind, with whatever faculties God had given her.

SEAN O'CASEY (1880-1964)
Inishfallen, Fare Thee Well

THE STORYTELLER

The Tailor, when I knew him first, was over eighty, a crippled little Kerryman with soft, round, rosy cheeks exactly like a baby's and two brilliant, mischieveous baby eyes. His eyes were the first thing that attracted you. He had no teeth, and he spoke very fast from far back in his throat, and talk and laughter mixed and bubbled like water and wind in a pipe. Most fine days he sat on the road outside his house, maybe minding the cow, but never doing anything much else in the nature of work; the most approachable man in the world, for he had no slyness and distrusted no human being, wherever he might come from. If a Chinese had happened to pass the way, the Tailor would have saluted him politely and asked him how the divil things were by them in China, and, if the man was an intelligent, conversible sort of man who could pass a shrewd comment or crack a joke, the Tailor would have brought him home to Anstey, his wife, and accepted him as a friend along with Kirsten, the Danish girl, Ripley, the American, Seumas, the sculptor, and the English colonel—his "scholars," as he called them.

Not only did he not distrust people, but, what is much rarer in Ireland, country or town, he did not distrust ideas or conventions. I could not say if this was charity, natural good breeding or simple intellectual independence, but, if someone had dropped in in an autogiro and offered the Tailor a lift, the old man would have gone without giving it a thought, in spite of the shrieks and curses of Anstey. "Take the world easy and the world will take you easy," the Tailor told her, but he never managed to get her to appreciate it, because she was a woman of the ancient world, and love and hatred stuck like hooks in her heart.

There are only two dialects of Irish, plain Irish and toothless Irish, and, lacking a proper acquaintance with the latter, I think I missed the cream of the old man's talk, though his English was very colourful and characteristic. But I noticed how almost every phrase he spoke was rounded off by an apt allusion. When Anstey hurried, the Tailor, enthroned on his butter-box by the fire, reproved her and instantly followed up with the story of the Gárlach Coileánach's mother. "A year is past since my mother was lost; she'd be round the lake since then." Or when someone spoke of a girl having a baby he came back with: "She's having last year's laugh's cry." In Irish, poems, rhymes and proverbs tumbled from him literally in hundreds.

He had all the traditional stuff—the pisherogues about the fairies and the pookas, and the witch-doctors born on Good Friday and christened on Easter Sunday, whose power was entirely in their thumbs. . . . He was excellent on the history of the parish, on the old days and the faction fights between Cork and Kerrymen which took place in these mountains. . . .

But the Tailor was at his best as a yarn-spinner, and I never heard a better. Unlike the usual traditional story-tellers, whose stories have been transmitted to them from previous generations and whose own creative powers seem to be non-existent, the Tailor could take a simple little incident of life in the valley, embroider it here and there with a traditional touch, and it became a masterpiece. So, for instance, with the story of the inquest in Mr. Cross's book on him, and with the story of his friend Jerry Coakley, "The Captain." The Captain had a cat called Moonlighter, who, according to the Tailor, was so bleddy human that he always joined in the Captain's favourite patriotic song, "We'll plant a tree in Ould Ireland." One night the Captain, who slept stark naked, found himself with a terrible toothache. In anguish he left his little hut and ran down the road towards the river, followed by Moonlighter. He buried his face in the icy water till the shock killed the toothache, and then, seeing that it was a fine moonlight night, he thought he might as well put in a little poaching. He caught a salmon and tossed it on the bank, but Moonlighter dug his teeth in the salmon, who gave a mighty leap which carried himself and Moonlighter back into the river, where the Captain had the divil's own job to rescue the cat.

The pleasantest Christmas of my life was spent in the inn in Gougane Barra, though most of the day I was with the Tailor and Anstey. . . . Their cottage was nearly full after supper, a row of old men sitting on the settle with their hats down over their eyes and their sticks between their knees, while the Tailor sat by the fire in front of them on his butter-box. I brought the whisky and the Tailor supplied the beer. I have never seen the Tailor in better form. He knew I wanted the words and music of a beautiful song which had never been recorded, and he had brought down the only old man in the locality who knew it. The talk began with stories of ghosts and pookas, and then the Tailor sang his favourite song, a version of the Somerset song, "The Herring." . . .

Then it was the turn of the other old man, and he hummed and hawed about it.

"'Tis a bit barbarous."

"Even so, even so," said the Tailor, who had his own way with censorships, "'twasn't you made or composed it."

When the evening was fair and the sunlight was yellow—

"That's a powerful line," interjected the singer after the Gaelic words *buidheachtan na gréine*. "There's a cart-load of meaning in that line."

> When the evening was fair and the sunlight was yellow
> I halted beholding a maiden bright,
> Coming to me by the edge of the mountain;
> Her cheeks had a berry-bright, rosy light;
> The honey-gold hair down her shoulders was twining,
> Swinging and billowing, surging and shining,
> Sweeping the grass as she passed by me smiling,
> Driving her geese at the fall of night.

The tune was exquisite and there was nothing in the song you could call barbarous except the young woman's warmly expressed objection to sleeping alone instead of having a companion to "drive the geese" with her. But with the whisky it loosened the tongues of the old men, and they quoted with gusto the supposed dying words of Owen Roe O'Sullivan and told scandalous stories about the neighbours, and then the Tailor sang his party piece about the blacksmith! . . .

Late that night as we stumbled out along the little causeway from the cabin to the road one of the old men slapped me vigorously on the shoulder and roared: "Well, thanks be to the Almighty God, Frinshias, we had wan grand dirty night." I admit that at the time I was a little surprised, but, remembering it afterwards, I felt that to thank God for a good uproariously bawdy party was the very hallmark of a deeply religious mind. I don't know, but I commend the idea to moralists.

FRANK O'CONNOR (1903-1966)
Leinster, Munster and Connacht

A TELEPHONE OPERATOR

COUNTY CORK

Even to get a call through on the telephone may entail a conversation. "Hold on a while now and I'll see if I can get him for you. I have an idea he was away shooting for the week-end, but I'll see if I can get him. Isn't it a grand day? Yerra, 'tis like summer. Another fortnight now and we'll be into spring. Tell me, who am I speaking to? Oh, to be sure, I know you well. I saw you the other night. 'Who's that?' said I to Paddy Riordan. You remember Paddy, he lived at the cross below you. 'Sure, that's Bob Gibbings,' says he, 'the fellow is writing a book about Cork.' Hold on a while, I think you're through. Ah, you're not. I'm Mick Ahern that lived at Curraheen. You wouldn't remember me, but—hold on a while—'tis wonderful weather. Did you see any widgeon when you were down at Imokilly? They tell me the place is full of

them. Oh, indeed, yes, I saw you getting on to the bus.
'Tis a grand spot down there. Hold on a while, you're
through. Good-bye now and good luck, you're through."

ROBERT GIBBINGS (1889-1958)
Lovely is the Lee

EPITAPHS

1

Here lies the body
Of Jonathan Swift,
Dean of this Cathedral,
Where savage indignation
Can lacerate his heart no more.
Go, traveller,
And imitate, if you can,
His gallant fight for human liberty.

JONATHAN SWIFT (1667-1745)

2

George Moore
Born Moore Hall 1852 Died 1933 London
  He forsook his family and friends
    for his art
but because he was faithful to his art
  his family and friends
  reclaimed his ashes for Ireland
    Vale

W. B. YEATS
Dramatis Personæ

3

Cast a cold eye
On life, on death
Horseman, pass by.

W. B. YEATS (1865-1939)
Under Ben Bulben

Humour, Romance and Sentiment

RIGHTEOUS ANGER

Stephens was modest enough to ascribe the original poem to David O'Bruadair. It is, perhaps, sufficient to say that in the original the two final lines are separated!

The lanky hank of a she in the inn over there
Nearly killed me for asking the loan of a glass of beer:
May the devil grip the whey-faced slut by the hair,
And beat bad manners out of her skin for a year.

That parboiled imp, with the hardest jaw you will see
On virtue's path, and a voice that would rasp the dead,
Came roaring and raging the minute she looked at me,
And threw me out of the house on the back of my head!

If I asked her master he'd give me a cask a day;
But she, with the beer at hand, not a gill would arrange!
May she marry a ghost and bear him a kitten, and may
The High King of Glory permit her to get the mange.

JAMES STEPHENS (1881–1950)
Collected Poems

THE BREWER'S MAN

Have I a wife? Bedam I have!
  But we was badly mated.
I hit her a great clout one night
  And now we're separated.

222

And mornin's going to me work
I meets her on the quay:
"Good mornin' to you, ma'am!" says I,
"To hell with ye!" says she.

L. A. G. STRONG (1896-1958)
Dublin Days

SMART BOY

One day, in my first job, a lady fell in love with me. It was quite unreasonable, of course, for I wasn't wonderful: I was small and thin, and I weighed much the same as a largish duck-egg. I didn't fall in love with her, or anything like that. I got under the table, and stayed there until she had to go wherever she had to go to.

I had seen an advertisement—"Smart boy wanted," it said. My legs were the smartest things about me, so I went there on the run. I got the job.

At that time there was nothing on God's earth that I could do, except run. I had no brains, and I had no memory. When I was told to do anything I got into such an enthusiasm about it that I couldn't remember anything else about it. I just ran as hard as I could, and then I ran back, proud and panting. And when they asked me for the whatever-it-was that I had run for, I started, right on the instant, and ran some more.

The place I was working at was, amongst other things, a theatrical agency. I used to be sitting in a corner of the office floor, waiting to be told to run somewhere and back. A lady would come in—a music-hall lady that is—and, in about five minutes, howls of joy would start coming from the inner office. Then, peacefully enough, the lady and my two bosses would come out, and the lady always said, "Splits! I can do splits like no one." And one of my bosses would say, "I'm keeping your

splits in mind." And the other would add, gallantly,—
"No one who ever saw your splits could ever forget
'em."

One of my bosses was thin, and the other one was fat.
My fat boss was composed entirely of stomachs. He
had three baby-stomachs under his chin: then he had
three more descending in even larger engloblings nearly
to the ground: but, just before reaching the ground,
the final stomach bifurcated into a pair of boots. He
was very light on these and could bounce about in the
neatest way.

He was the fattest thing I had ever seen, except a
rhinoceros that I had met in the Zoo the Sunday before
I got the job. That rhino was *very* fat, and it had a smell
like twenty-five pigs. I was standing outside its palisade,
wondering what it could possibly feel like to be a rhinoceros, when two larger boys passed by. Suddenly they
caught hold of me, and pushed me through the bars of
the palisade. I was very skinny, and in about two
seconds I was right inside, and the rhinoceros was
looking at me.

It was very fat, but it wasn't fat like stomachs, it
was fat like barrels of cement and when it moved it
creaked a lot, like a woman I used to know who creaked
like an old bedstead. The rhinoceros swaggled over to
me with a bunch of cabbage sticking out of its mouth.
It wasn't angry or anything like that, it just wanted to
see who I was. Rhinos are blindish: they mainly see by
smelling, and they smell in snorts. This one started at
my left shoe, and snorted right up that side of me to
my ear. He smelt that very carefully: then he switched
over to my right ear, and snorted right down that side
of me to my right shoe: then he fell in love with my
shoes and began to lick them. I, naturally, wriggled my
feet at that, and the big chap was so astonished that he
did the strangest step-dance backwards to his pile of
cabbages, and began to eat them.

COBH, COUNTY CORK
(Bord Fáilte)

CAHIR CASTLE, COUNTY TIPPERARY
(Bord Fáilte)

DERRY CITY
(Northern Ireland Tourist Board)

INCH STRAND, COUNTY KERRY
(Bord Fáilte)

I squeezed myself out of his cage and walked away. In a couple of minutes I saw the two boys. They were very frightened, and they asked me what I had done to the rhinoceros. I answered, a bit grandly, perhaps, that I had seized it in both hands, ripped it limb from limb and tossed its carcase to the crows. But when they began shouting to people that I had just murdered a rhinoceros I took to my heels, for I didn't want to be arrested and hanged for a murder that I hadn't committed.

Still, a man can't be as fat as a rhinoceros, but my boss was as fat as a man can be. One day a great lady of the halls came in, and was received on the knee. She was very great. Her name was Maudie Darling or thereabouts. My bosses called her nothing but "Darling" and she called them the same. When the time came for her to arrive the whole building got palpitations of the heart. After waiting a while my thin boss got angry, and said—"Who does the woman think she is? If she isn't here in two twos I'll go down to the entry, and when she does come I'll boot her out." The fat boss said—"She's only two hours late, she'll be here before the week's out."

Within a few minutes there came great clamours from the courtyard. Patriotic cheers, such as Parnell himself never got, were thundering. My bosses ran instantly to the inner office. Then the door opened, and the lady appeared.

She was very wide, and deep, and magnificent. She was dressed in camels and zebras and goats: she had two peacocks in her hat and a rabbit muff in her hand, and she strode among these with prancings.

But when she got right into the room and saw herself being looked at by three men and a boy she became adorably shy: one could see that she had never been looked at before.

"Oh," said she, with a smile that made three and a

8

half hearts beat like one, "O," said she, very modestly, "is Mr. Which-of-'em-is-it really in? Please tell him that Little Miss-Me would be so glad to see and to be——"

Then the inner door opened, and the large lady was surrounded by my fat boss and my thin boss. She crooned to them—"Oh, you dear boys, you'll never know how much I've thought of you and longed to see you."

That remark left me stupefied. The first day I got to the office I heard that it was the fat boss's birthday, and that he was thirty years of age: and the thin boss didn't look a day younger than the fat one. How the lady could mistake these old men for boys seemed to me the strangest fact that had ever come my way. My own bet was that they'd both die of old age in about a month.

After a while they all came out again. The lady was helpless with laughter: she had to be supported by my two bosses. "O," she cried, "you boys will kill me." And the bosses laughed and laughed, and the fat one said—"Darling, you're a riot."

And then . . . she saw me! I saw her seeing me the very way I had seen the rhinoceros seeing me: I wondered for an instant would she smell me down one leg and up the other. She swept my two bosses right away from her, and she became a kind of queen, very glorious to behold: but sad, startled. She stretched a long, slow arm out and out and out and then she unfolded a long, slow finger, and pointed it at me—"Who is THAT?" she whispered in a strange whisper that could be heard two miles off.

My fat boss was an awful liar—"The cat brought that in," said he.

But the thin boss rebuked him; "No," he said, "it was not the cat. Let me introduce you; darling, this is James. James, this is the darling of the gods."

"And of the pit," said she, sternly.

She looked at me again. Then she sank to her knees and spread out both arms to me——

"Come to my Boozalum, angel," said she in a tender kind of way.

I knew what she meant, and I knew that she didn't know how to pronounce that word. I took a rapid glance at the area indicated. The lady had a boozalum you could graze a cow on. I didn't wait one second, but slid, in one swift, silent slide, under the table. Then she came forward and said a whole lot of poems to me under the table, imploring me, among a lot of odd things, to "come forth and gild the morning with my eyes," but at last she was reduced to whistling at me with two fingers in her mouth, the way you whistle for a cab.

I learned after she had gone that most of the things she said to me were written by a poet fellow named Spokeshave. They were very complimentary, but I couldn't love a woman who mistook my old bosses for boys, and had a boozalum that it would take an Arab chieftain a week to trot across on a camel.

The thin boss pulled me from under the table by my leg, and said that my way was the proper way to treat a rip, but my fat boss said, very gravely, "James, when a lady invites a gentleman to her boozalum a real gentleman hops there as pronto as possible, and I'll have none but real gentlemen in this office."

"Tell me," he went on, "what made that wad of Turkish Delight fall in love with you?"

"She didn't love me at all, sir," I answered.

"No?" he enquired.

"She was making fun of me," I explained.

"There's something in that," said he seriously, and went back to his office.

JAMES STEPHENS (1881-1950)
Irish Writing

THE NIGHT BEFORE LARRY WAS STRETCHED

The night before Larry was stretched,
  The boys they all paid him a visit;
A bait in their sacks, too, they fetched;
  They sweated their duds till they riz it:
For Larry was ever the lad,
  When a boy was condemned to the squeezer,
Would fence all the duds that he had
  To help a poor friend to a sneezer,
    And warm his gob 'fore he died.

The boys they came crowding in fast,
  They drew all their stools round about him,
Six glims round his trap-case were placed,
  He couldn't be well waked without them.
When one of them asked could he die
  Without having truly repented,
Says Larry "That's all in my eye;
  And first by the clergy invented,
    To get a fat bit for themselves."

"I'm sorry, dear Larry," says I,
  "To see you in this situation;
And blister my limbs if I lie,
  I'd as lieve it had been my own station,"
"Ochone! it's all over," says he,
  "For the neck-cloth I'll be forced to put on,
And by this time tomorrow you'll see
  Your poor Larry as dead as a mutton,"
    Because why, his courage was good.

"And I'll be cut up like a pie,
   And my nob from my body be parted."
"You're in the wrong box, then" says I,
   "For blast me if they're so hard-hearted;
A chalk on the back of your neck
   Is all that Jack Ketch dares to give you;
Then mind not such trifles a feck
    For why should the likes of them grieve you?
     And now, boys, come tip us the deck."

The cards being called for, they played,
   Till Larry found one of them cheated;
A dart at his napper he made
   (The boy being easily heated);
"Oh, by the hokey, you thief,
   I'll scuttle your nob with my daddle [1]!
You cheat me because I'm in grief,
   But soon I'll demolish your noddle,
    And leave you your claret to drink."

Then the clergy came in with his book,
   He spoke him so smooth and so civil;
Larry tipped him a Kilmainham look,
   And pitched his big wig to the devil;
Then sighing, he threw back his head,
   To get a sweet drop of the bottle,
And pitiful sighing, he said:
   "Oh, the hemp will be soon round my throttle,
    And choke my poor windpipe to death."

"Though sure it's the best way to die,
   Oh, the devil a better aliving!
For sure when the gallows is high
   Your journey is shorter to Heaven:
But what harasses Larry the most,
   And makes his poor soul melancholy,

            [1] daddle=fist.

Is to think on the time when his ghost
    Will come in a sheet to sweet Molly—
      Oh, sure, it will kill her alive!"

So moving these last words he spoke,
    We all vented our tears in a shower;
For my part, I thought my heart broke
    To see him cut down like a flower.
On his travels we watched him next day,
    Oh, the throttler, I thought I could kill him!
But Larry not one word did say,
    Nor changed till he came to King William—
      Then, musha, his colour grew white.

When he came to the nubbing-cheat,[1]
    He was tucked up so neat and so pretty,
The rumbler jogged off from his feet,
    And he died with his face to the city;
He kicked too, but that was all pride,
    And soon you might see 'twas all over;
Soon after the noose was untied,
    And at darkee we waked him in clover,
      And sent him to take a ground sweat.

ANONYMOUS (19th cent.)

[1] nubbing-cheat=gallows.

THE OLD ORANGE FLUTE

In the County Tyrone, in the town of Dungannon,
Where many a ruction myself had a han' in,
Bob Williamson lived, a weaver by trade
And all of us thought him a stout Orange blade.
On the Twelfth of July as around it would come,
Bob played on the flute to the sound of the drum.
You may talk of your harp, your piano or lute
But there's nothing compared with the ould Orange
    flute.

But Bob the deceiver he took us all in,
For he married a Papish called Brigid McGinn,
Turned Papish himself, and forsook the old cause
That gave us our freedom, religion, and laws.
Now the boys of the place made some comment upon it,
And Bob had to fly to the Province of Connacht.
He fled with his wife and his fixings to boot,
And along with the latter his old Orange flute.

At the chapel on Sundays, to atone for past deeds,
He said Paters and Aves and counted his beads,
Till after some time, at the priest's own desire,
He went with his old flute to play in the choir.
He went with his old flute to play for the Mass,
And the instrument shivered, and sighed: "Oh, alas!"
And blow as he would, though it made a great
        noise,
The flute would play only "The Protestant Boys."

Bob jumped, and he started, and got in a flutter,
And threw his old flute in the blest Holy Water;
He thought that this charm would bring some other
        sound
When he blew it again, it played "Croppies lie down";
And for all he could whistle, and finger, and blow,
To play Papish music he found it no go;
"Kick the Pope," "The Boyne Water," it freely would
        sound,
But one Papish squeak in it couldn't be found.

At a council of priests that was held the next day,
They decided to banish the old flute away
For they couldn't knock heresy out of its head
And they bought Bob a new one to play in its stead.
So the old flute was doomed and its fate was pathetic,
'Twas fastened and burned at the stake as heretic,

While the flames roared around it they heard a strange
    noise—
'Twas the old flute still whistling "The Protestant Boys."
ANONYMOUS (19th cent.)

EATING ENGLISH HALFPENCE

Before I conclude, I must beg leave in all humility to
tell Mr. Wood that he is guilty of great indiscretion by
causing so honourable a name as that of Mr. Walpole to
be mentioned so often, and in such a manner upon this
occasion: a short paper printed at Bristol and reprinted
here reports Mr. Wood to say that he wonders at the
impudence and insolence of the Irish in refusing his
coin, and what he will do when Mr. Walpole comes to
town. Where, by the way, he is mistaken, for it is the
true English people of Ireland who refuse it, although
we take it for granted that the Irish will do so too
whenever they are asked. He orders it to be printed in
another paper that Mr. Walpole will cram this brass
down our throats: sometimes it is given out that we
must either take these half-pence or eat our brogues,
and in another news letter but of yesterday, we read
that the same great man hath sworn to make us swallow
his coin in fire-balls. . . .

As for the threat of making us eat our brogues, we
need not be in pain; for if his coin should pass, that
unpolite covering for the feet would no longer be a
national reproach; because then we should have neither
shoe nor brogue left in the kingdom. But here the
falsehood of Mr. Wood is fairly detected; for I am
confident Mr. Walpole never heard of a brogue in his
whole life.

As to swallowing these half-pence in fire-balls, it is a
story equally improbable. For to execute this operation

the whole stock of Mr. Wood's coin and metal must be melted down and moulded into hollow balls with wild-fire, no bigger than a reasonable throat can be able to swallow. Now the metal he hath prepared and already coined will amount to at least fifty millions of half-pence to be swallowed by a million and a half of people; so that allowing two half-pence to each ball, there will be about seventeen balls of wild-fire apiece to be swal-lowed by every person in this kingdom, and to admin-ister this dose there cannot be conveniently fewer than fifty thousand operators, allowing one operator to every thirty, which, considering the squeamishness of some stomachs and the peevishness of young children, is but reasonable. Now, under correction of better judgments, I think the trouble and charge of such an experiment would exceed the profit, and therefore I take this report to be spurious, or at least only a new scheme of Mr. Wood himself, which to make it pass the better in Ireland he would father upon a Minister of State.

JONATHAN SWIFT (1667-1745)
The Drapier's Fourth Letter

THE TAILOR ON CULTURE

"Writing a book? Yerra, manalive, I've thought of many more things than that, but somehow I have not had the time. . . . Did you ever see a book called *The Book of Knowledge*? It was that which partly turned me away from the idee. It was Cork Echo who first saw the advertisement, and it was he who told the others and persuaded them all to put their money together and buy it. I was against the business from the begin-ning, for I did not see how there could be anything printed in a book that could ever be of any use to any man. The only knowledge that is of any use or any value to a man is that which he learns himself by living.

"But the rest of them were soon clean mad for it. They thought that if only they had it they could sit on their backsides for the rest of their lives, and the world would come to them, and they would be the whole push. Yerra, they thought that they would be better than anything that was ever in a circus.

"Well, I joined in to make the money up, and Cork Echo wrote to the address in London where they had the book and told them to send it along, and he sent them earnest money, and told them that he would send the rest when we had the book got.

"After a week or two they wrote to him and told him that the book was waiting for him at Macroom station and he must come in for it with a horse and cart, and that there were five pounds to pay, and that he would not get the book until he paid the money.

"There was a big fair in Macroom a couple of days later, and happen Cork Echo himself was going in with a couple of fat pigs, so he said that he would have a look at the book as well, and see was it worth the money.

"He went along to the station, and right enough there was a case for him, a bloody great case. He knew the man of the station, a decent man he was too. He had a near relation to him by marriage. He told him his business, and the man agreed that you did not want to be spending all that money without seeing what you were getting, so they opened the case and there were dozens of books inside.

"The first one was all about Architecture and Archæology. They put that one back. That was no damned use at all. The second one was about 'Bogwrappy' and Botany, and they pitched that to hell. So they opened three or four, but they both said you would need a dictionary to read the titles let alone what was inside them. Cork Echo said that the only use he could see for them was to build a fence to a field, and he already had enough stones in his fields to fence all the fields in Ireland.

"The man of the station thought that it would be a great waste of money to spend five pounds on a lot of books with queer titles like that, and maybe some of them were the works of the devil, and you couldn't tell what might happen if you read them. You might be changed into a goat, whereas you did know where you were if you spent the money on porter.

"So they nailed the case up again and sent it back to London, but the people in London wrote several letters wanting to be paid for it. But we devised a plan and wrote back to them that, if they really knew so much as to be able to write a book called the book of knowledge, they ought to have known that we were not going to buy it, and not to be wasting any more time writing."

ERIC CROSS
The Tailor And Ansty

THE TAILOR AND CHRONOLOGY

"I tell you, those were the airy times and those were the airy people. But all that happened a long time ago. It could be thirty years ago the next holy day in August——"

"Thirty years ago!" spat Ansty, who had sat through the story without a sound. "Thirty years ago! Is it taking leave of your senses that you are with your—thirty years ago?"

The Tailor is a little startled by the unexpected interruption, but after a moment he recovers his balance and continues, "—thirty years ago on the next holy day in August."

"I tell you it is not!" interrupted Ansty again.

"Thon amon dieul!" answered the Tailor, with rising anger. "As sure as there is a tail on a cat it was thirty years ago."

"It's clean mad you are with your thirty years ago."

There was a silent pause while the Tailor reflected. Then he started in again, like a leading counsel laying a complicated trap.

"Wasn't it thirty years ago that Jack the Ram was married?"

"Am Bostha! if it was, what has that to do with it at all?"

"Wasn't that the year that I sold the black heifer calf in Bantry fair? Wasn't that the year that Timmy Johnny went to America? Wasn't that the year—?"

"Listen to him, will you, with his ' wasn't that the year.' You'd think it was saying his beads he was."

The Tailor returned to the defence with a new tack. "How old is Denny Mary Jamesy? Wasn't he thirty-one years last Christmas, and wasn't his father married to the Loughra woman the year before at the same time as the ' Redbreast '? ... Well, so!"

"Leave me alone with him! Didn't the Loughra woman marry the Yank? Wasn't she a first cousin to Mary John the Pub? And she only had the two girls, and one of them went away to America, and the other married Jim—Jimmy Faddy."

"She was not, I tell you. There was no relation at all unless it was on her mother's side, for her mother was a Kerry woman from near to Morley's Bridge, and there may have been a relationship far out, but no more. Her father was a Leary of Carrigdubh. Didn't I know him as well as I know you? Wasn't it many the piece of a night that we spent together card-playing? Wasn't his sister married over in America to Paddy Pat Buie, and haven't I a relation myself to him, for the Pat Buies were near related to my brother's wife's people. Thon amon dieul, woman! Talk sense."

"Talk sense! Listen to who's telling me to ' talk sense.' I tell you, you're half cracked!"

"Have it so. There is no one thinks themselves so sound in the head as the mad people."

While the Tailor carelessly enjoys his moment of victory, Ansty puzzles and returns to the attack.

"Didn't the ' Redbreast' marry the daughter of Long John? And hasn't Johnny Mary Jamesy been the age of the pension since last October and—."

"Hould your whist, woman. I tell you you haven't a bit of the head. You do get up too early in the morning, worrying about the cow. I am sorry for you."

"Sorry me eye! I tell you it was so."

There is a pause. The Tailor becomes aware of his audience again, and takes up the lost thread.

"—that happened about nineteen hundred and ten!"

He has won the last round.

"Nineteen hundred and ten!" echoes Ansty without comprehension. "Glory be! Nineteen hundred and ten! Fancy that!"

ERIC CROSS
The Tailor And Ansty

MR. LIGHTFOOT IN THE GREEN ISLE

It *is* a long way to Tipperary, and I suppose it *was* the song that sent me there. Wondrous, is it not, the insignificant motives that inspire some complicated efforts?

"Let you be giving me a penny, sir," said the old woman to me. I had but just started upon that sunny journey, and she hailed me.

"Let you be giving me a penny, sir." I gave it.

"May the Great God take ye to heaven, sir," said she,

and then I wished I'd given her a shilling, for, thought I, if I get to heaven for a penny, the Lord Himself might forgive me a great deal for the odd elevenpence.

And indeed, then I am specially blessed, for as the old woman goes wending away I stand looking back at her, and there by the highway I see a little group of farm buildings and trees just sitting across the top of a low bank, so very green, soft as silk it was, with no blemish upon it. Across that green some white ducks go a-travelling; the wind blows their voices to me. There is, too, a line of poplar springs, very slender and fan-like, their stems no bigger than altar candles, and they sigh like women in their grieving.

I got out a post card, one of those rarely tinted and admirably chased with a golden edge which I carry for the purpose, and, licking my pencil stub like a green-grocer's boy, I made a poem, one of those things with no rhyme in it, and with rhythms like a mangled cork-screw, with some lines as short as a full stop, and some unending ones on which you peg out very sweet notions as indiscriminately as a washerwoman hangs out her underwear, and then magnify with an exclamation mark.

"Go on, now," said I to myself then, and go on I did, like a sheep. It is not uncommon to feel yourself convincingly bullied by yourself into doing the thing you would not want to do. I'd love to be standing in that place, with a coin of gold in my hand, this very minute, until I'd become a pillar of salt with looking at it, but I went on until I came to the borheen.

Now, a borheen is a lean lane, full of deceitful notions, with hedges as high as a workhouse wall and brambles like the midriff of a great fish. Within the borheen the travelling stranger is beset as completely as the slice of meat in a sandwich, no more view of the surrounding world, no more will of his direction. Does a serpent twist? Then a borheen is a serpent bereft of its reason.

What is the longest thing in the world? A borheen, for it's longer than a sad Sunday. In ten miles or in twenty miles you may happen upon a cabin. You approach it, you drop a glance over the half-door, and you perceive an old, old woman sitting on some steps leading to a loft. There may be a pig sitting before her, apparently worshipping her, and there will certainly be hens, very furtive hens, and a cauldron. The old woman regards you with apprehension, with awe. You ask to be directed and she tells you to go on and inquire at the next house. You indulge this vain pursuit for as long as your sanity survives, or until you meet a pig coming towards you. There will be no more than just room for him to pass you, and so you will stand like one Christian meeting another, or like any man with a gush of charity in his breast. But this pig will fear you, he will turn tail, and behold you have a pig upon your hands, for, wherever you go now, you have upon you the appearance of driving that poor pig before you. You will endeavour to conciliate him, or persuade him of your passionate friendship, but there is no mortal man can appease a pig and it not wanting. He will behave like a Kaffir, and finally you will dislike him—and tell him so.

"A great nuisance was that pig to me," I said when I regained freedom upon the high road once more, "and a great pity that I only bought a pennyworth of blessing of that good old woman. I'll go no more into those borheens, so go upon your journey now." And I was just going when I heard the stir of a vast noise behind me. A great grey ass was standing in the road and braying as if he were the king of all asses, as indeed he was, for, look you, along the road a car came flying with military persons in it. The horn went Honk! Honk! but the ass went He! Haw! and lay down in the road before them, lashing his heels as if he'd tear the skin off the sky, and screaming triumphantly as the car came to a stop upon his very neck.

"Get out of it, or we'll break your heart," yelled the soldiers, and the car pumped noises at him like a big gun, but the ass trailed his carcass in the road with no fear at all, until someone leaped out of the car, kicked him where there was no dignity, and then pushed him into the borheen, where, I thought, if he meets that little pig of mine, it will not be Greek meeting Greek, for it's just Ajax to a sunflower that he will destroy my little pig and devour him. "But go on now," said I to myself, and I walked on into Tip, where I got some interesting food—but it was queer feeding. Better a fly in the ointment, believe me, than one in the blancmange. You will always have a cosy for the teapot in Ireland, and a slop basin, but there will be something odd and incinerated about the teapot; there will always be insects in the milk, cracks in the cup, and things in the sugar basin besides sugar!

"Waiter," I said, "this tea is very weak!"

"Is it, begod, sir, then I'll just put another half-pound in it," and, taking from his waistcoat pocket a thimbleful of tea wrapped in a screw of paper, that had once contained tobacco, he emptied it into my teapot, saying soothingly, "It 'ull be all right now."

In the evening I went into a bar. She had eyes as soft as darkness and a voice like a singing swallow. "A drop!" I cried to her, for she was reading on a book and did not heed me. When she had given me the whisky, she resumed her book.

"May I be stricken to my doom this minute," said I, quite to myself, "if it is not poetry and new poetry that girl is reading." At that a handsome young man came in and stood before her.

"Good evening, Mary."

"What is it you're wanting, Peter?"

"Stout," said he; "and what is it you're reading, Mary?"

"Poetry," said she; "listen to this, Peter," and she

read out, in the soft voice that was like the singing of swallows, some verses. Mary went on reading the poems, and there was no laughter upon the handsome young man; we were both filled with delight.

Pleasant thoughts I had that night as I pulled the quilt up to my neck, for pleasant it is to sleep in a country where the very donkeys are valiant, and even the barmaids woo you to the muses.

A. E. COPPARD (1878-1957)
Fishmonger's Fiddle

JEALOUSY

Love like heat and cold
Pierces and passes soon;
Jealousy pierces too
But sticks in the marrowbone.

ANONYMOUS (16th cent.)
translated from the Irish by
FRANK O'CONNOR

A LEARNED MISTRESS

Tell him the thing is a lie!
  I love him as much as my life.
He needn't be jealous of me:
  I love him, and loathe his wife.

If he kill me through jealousy now
  His wife will perish of spite;
He'll die of grief for his wife—
  That's three of us dead in a night.

All blessings from heaven to earth
　　On the head of the woman I hate!
And the man I love as my life,
　　Sudden death be his fate!

　　　　　　　ANONYMOUS (16th cent.)
　　　　　　　translated from the Irish by
　　　　　　　FRANK O'CONNOR

TO TOMAUS COSTELLO AT
THE WARS

Here's pretty conduct, Hugh O'Rourke!
　　Great son of Brian, blossoming bough!
Noblest son of noble kin!
　　What do you say of Costello now?

If you are still the man I loved
　　Hurry and aid me while you can.
Do you not see him at my side,
　　A walking ghost? What ails you, man?

Brian's son, goal of my song!
　　If any thought of losing me
Grieve you, strong pillar of my love,
　　Beseech this man to let me be.

Yet there's such darkness in his ways,
　　Though he a thousand oaths repeat,
You must not on your life believe
　　But he will try to have me yet.

And if the river of my shame
　　He ford but once, that frontier crossed,
You will not rule the land again:
　　Beyond my will my heart is lost.

Fearsome the forms he courts me in;
  Myriad and strange the arts he plies;
Desire, enchantment of the sight
  Never dons twice the same disguise.

Sometimes I turn, and there he stands,
  An unfledged stripling, bashful-eyed,
And swift as ever hawk can swoop
  The heart he snatches from my side.

Or as if I were a whore he comes,
  A young blood curious of my fame,
With sensual magic and dark rhymes,
  To woo and mock me in my shame.

Far to the Ulster wars he flies;
  Some town he sacks—I am the town;
With some light love he charms the night—
  Beguiling her, he brings me down.

Sometimes he comes into my room,
  So much like you in voice and shape,
I am in his arms before I know
  Who holds me—how can I escape?

But when he comes in his own form,
  With his own voice, I stand transfixed;
My love deserts its wonted place,
  My sense no longer holds it fixed.

Dearest, unless you pity me,
  And keep my wavering fancy set,
And drive that phantom from my side,
  I swear that he will have me yet.

I cannot tear myself in two,
  My love, your love within my mind
Pants like a bird within its cage—
  My lover, must you be unkind?

If 'tis not wasted time to plead,
  Sweet son of Shuretan, let me be!
The women of the world are yours;
  I am my husband's; let me be.

O sun-mist of the summer's day,
  You will find I am no easy game,
No graceless, love-sick, moony girl,
  I am not dazzled by a name.

What of the things the neighbours say!
  I am no harlot as you think:
I was a girl when first I loved;
  I have not strayed; you must not wink.

The enchantment of desire is vain;
  I see through every mask you don.
You rascal, pity my good name!
  You thief of laughter, get you gone!

You bandit of the heart, away!
  I shall not give your lust release.
Smother the frontier posts in flame,
  But let my foolish heart in peace.

Bright blossom of the scented wood,
  Yellow Shuretan's hope and pride,
For love, for money, or for rank,
  I cannot leave my husband's side.

And since I never can be yours,
  Take up your father's trade anew,
And magnify the northern blood—
  The light of poetry are you—

The stirring of the coals of love,
  The voice with which old griefs are healed,
The mast of the rolling sail of war—
  I may be yours; I shall not yield.

And yet, and yet, when all is said,
  All my scolding seems untrue;
My mind to each rebuke replies
  If love I must, I must love you.

And now God bless you, and good-bye,
  The time has come for you to go;
For all the grief of parting, I
  Could never grieve my husband so.

Silence, my darling! This is he!
  Go now, although my heart should crack!
Be silent! Quick! (God help me now!)
  My love!—O God, do not look back!

ANONYMOUS (c. 1680)
translated from the Irish by
FRANK O'CONNOR

THE SWIMMER

"Do not come out," said Ailill, "till you bring me a branch of the rowan there on the river-bank. I love its berries."

(Fraech) went off and broke off a branch of the tree

and brought it with him on his back through the water.

What Findabair used to say afterwards was that whatever beautiful thing she saw she thought Fraech more beautiful, seeing him across the dark pool, his body brilliantly white and his hair most beautiful, his face shapely and his eye grey; a tender lad without fault or stain, his face narrow below and broad above, strong-limbed and immaculate, and the branch with the red berries between the throat and the bright face. What Findabair used to say was that nothing else was half or a third as beautiful.

ANONYMOUS (8th cent.)
translated from the Irish by
FRANK O'CONNOR

INTO EXILE

What better fortune can we find
Than with the girl that pleased our mind
To leave our home and friends behind,
And sail on the first favouring wind?

ANONYMOUS (10th cent.?)
translated from the Irish by
FRANK O'CONNOR

THE HEART'S A WONDER

PEGEEN [*radiantly, wiping his face with her shawl*]: Well, you're the lad, and you'll have great times from this out when you could win that wealth of prizes, and you sweating in the heat of noon!

CHRISTY [*looking at her with delight*]: I'll have great times if I win the crowning prize I'm seeking now,

and that's your promise that you'll wed me in a fortnight, when our banns is called.

PEGEEN [*backing away from him*]: You've right daring
to go ask me that, when all knows you'll be starting
to some girl in your own townland, when your
father's rotten in four months, or five.

CHRISTY [*indignanty*]: Starting from you, is it? [*He
follows her*] I will not, then, and when the airs is
warming, in four months or five, it's then yourself
and me should be pacing Neifin in the dews of night,
the times sweet smells do be rising, and you'd see a
little, shiny new moon, maybe, sinking on the hills.

PEGEEN [*looking at him playfully*]: And it's that kind of
a poacher's love you'd make, Christy Mahon, on the
sides of Neifin, when the night is down?

CHRISTY: It's little you'll think if my love's a poacher's,
or an earl's itself, when you'll feel my two hands
stretched around you, and I squeezing kisses on your
puckered lips, till I'd feel a kind of pity for the Lord
God is all ages sitting lonesome in His golden chair.

PEGEEN: That'd be right fun, Christy Mahon, and any
girl would walk her heart out before she'd meet a
young man was your like for eloquence, or talk at all.

CHRISTY [*encouraged*]: Let you wait, to hear me talking,
till we're astray in Erris, when Good Friday's by,
drinking a sup from a well, and making mighty
kisses with our wetted mouths, or gaming in a gap of
sunshine, with yourself stretched back unto your
necklace, in the flowers of the earth.

PEGEEN [*in a low voice, moved by his tone*]: I'd be nice so,
is it?

CHRISTY [*with rapture*]: If the mitred bishops seen you
that time, they'd be the like of the holy prophets, I'm
thinking, do be straining the bars of Paradise to lay
eyes on the Lady Helen of Troy, and she abroad,
pacing back and forward, with a nosegay in her
golden shawl.

PEGEEN [*with real tenderness*]: And what is it I have, Christy Mahon, to make me fitting entertainment for the like of you, that has such poet's talking, and such bravery of heart.

CHRISTY [*in a low voice*]: Isn't there the light of seven heavens in your heart alone, the way you'll be an angel's lamp to me from this out, and I abroad in the darkness, spearing salmons in the Owen or the Carrowmore?

PEGEEN: If I was your wife I'd be along with you those nights, Christy Mahon, the way you'd see I was a great hand at coaxing bailiffs, or coining funny nicknames for the stars of the night.

CHRISTY: You, is it? Taking your death in the hailstones, or in the fogs of dawn.

PEGEEN: Yourself and me would shelter easy in a narrow bush; [*with a qualm of dread*] but we're only talking, maybe, for this would be a poor thatched place to hold a fine lad is the like of you.

CHRISTY [*putting his arm around her*]: If I wasn't a good Christian, it's on my naked knees I'd be saying my prayers and paters to every jackstraw you have roofing your head, and every stony pebble is paving the laneway to your door.

PEGEEN [*radiantly*]: If that's the truth I'll be burning candles from this out to the miracles of God that have brought you from the south to-day, and I with my gowns bought ready, the way that I can wed you, and not wait at all.

CHRISTY: It's miracles, and that's the truth. Me there toiling a long while, and walking a long while, not knowing at all I was drawing all times nearer to this holy day.

PEGEEN: And myself, a girl, was tempted often to go sailing the seas till I'd marry a Jew-man, with ten kegs of gold, and I not knowing at all there was the like of you drawing nearer, like the stars of God.

CHRISTY: And to think I'm long years hearing women talking that talk, to all bloody fools, and this the first time I've heard the like of your voice talking sweetly for my own delight.

PEGEEN: And to think it's me is talking sweetly, Christy Mahon, and I the fright of seven townlands for my biting tongue. Well, the heart's a wonder; and, I'm thinking, there won't be our like in Mayo, for gallant lovers, from this hour to-day.

J. M. SYNGE (1871-1909)
The Playboy of the Western World

LEGAL AID

I have never forgotten a trial in Cork, probably in March 1905, when a little barefoot post-boy was charged with having got a girl of less than statutory age into trouble. Such cases were rare in Ireland; this one was indeed a case of true love gone too impetuously forward. I cannot remember whether there was an actual trial or whether the accused pleaded guilty; but I do know that Stephen Ronan, the Crown Prosecutor, thought it necessary to read a number of letters which the lover had written to his lady; and one phrase burned itself into my brain, and survives to this day, although the rest which I have forgotten were all in tune with it. Barefooted, with no education beyond what a National School could give, this bucolic Petrarch addressed to his Laura the following lovely words:

"Far away from where I am now there is a little gap in the hills, and beyond it the sea; and 'tis there I do be looking the whole day long, for it's the nearest thing to yourself that I can see."

I watched the Judge; there was a tear trickling down his nose. "Mr. Ronan," he said, "these young people seem to be very fond of one another. Why couldn't they get married?"

Stephen Ronan sniggered; there was not much romance in his nature, and he had a trick of speech which made every sentence seem to begin with a sneering smile. "Heh!" he said. "Marriage is easy enough where there is money to provide for it, heh!" "I don't suppose it would cost a lot," said Billy. "Heh! More than these young people could afford!" cried Ronan. "Will the Post Office take him back if I bind him over?" asked the Judge. There proved to be little difficulty about that. "Come up here, my girl," said Billy kindly. The little girl, heavy with child, came into the witness-box. "Do you love the boy?" "I do, me Lord." "Will you marry him?" "I will if he'll ax me, me Lord." "Now, prisoner, do you hear that? Will you marry her?" "There's nothing I'm more wishful for, me Lord." "There, now; that's all settled; are the girl's people there?" A little procession went into the Judge's room, where the bride was promptly endowed out of his own pocket; and I hope they all lived happily ever afterwards.

MAURICE HEALY (1859-1923)
The Old Munster Circuit

THE END OF DEIRDRE

There was great contention as to who would invite Fergus to the most ale-feats, on Conchobar's advice because the Sons of Uisliu said that they would not eat in Ireland unless they first ate with Conchobar. But Fergus' son, Fiacha, went with the Sons of Uisliu while Fergus and Dubthach remained behind, and these went on till they reached the green at Emain. It was at this time that Eogan son of Durthacht, King of Farney, went to make peace with Conchobar because they had been enemies for a long time. Conchobar gave him the task of killing the Sons of Uisliu while his own soldiers stood round Conchobar so that these could not reach him.

The Sons of Uisliu were standing in the middle of the green and the women sitting on the walls of Emain. Eogan made for them with his troops over the green. Fergus' son went and stood side by side with Noisi. Eogan greeted them with a heavy thrust of a big spear through Noisi that burst through his back. Then Fergus' son threw himself on Noisi with his two arms round him so that Noisi was below and he above, and Noisi was killed through the body of Fergus' son. Then everyone was killed over the green so that no man escaped from it except on the spear's point or the sword's thrust; and Deirdre was brought over to Conchobar and placed beside him with her hands tied behind her back.

She was a year with Conchobar as his mistress and she never smiled, and never took enough food or sleep, nor raised her head from her knee.

"What do you most hate of all you see?" asked Conchobar.

"You indeed," she said, "and Eogan Durthacht's son."

"Then you shall spend a year as Eogan's mistress," said Conchobar.

Then Conchobar handed her over to Eogan. Next day they went to the fair of Emain. She was standing behind Eogan in the chariot. She had sworn that never would she see two of her bedmates on earth at the one time.

"Aha, Deirdre," said Conchobar, "between me and Eogan your look is that of a sheep between two rams."

There was a great boulder facing them. She dashed her head off the boulder and made bits of it, and died.

That is the Exile of the Sons of Uisliu and the Exile of Fergus and the Death of the Sons of Uisliu and of Deirdriu.

ANONYMOUS (9th cent.)
translated from the Irish by
FRANK O'CONNOR

GRIEF

"Let it be, Loingseachan," said Suibhne, "since it was ordained for us, but have you news of my own country for me?"

"I have," said Loingseachan. "Your father is dead."

"That is a great grief to me," said Suibhne.

"Your mother has died too," said the servant.

"Now men may cease to pity me," said Suibhne.

"Your brother is dead," said Loingseachan.

"My heart is pierced by the news," said Suibhne.

"Your daughter is dead," said Loingseachan.

"A heart's needle is an only daughter," said Suibhne.

"The little son who used to call you 'Daddy' is dead," said Loingseachan.

"You have said it," said Suibhne. "There is the grip that brings the man to ground."

ANONYMOUS (12th cent.)
translated from the Irish by
FRANK O'CONNOR

TRAGEDY AND TRIUMPH

MARY CAHEL: There is lasting kindness in Heaven when no kindness is found upon earth. There will surely be mercy found for him, and not the hard judgment of men! But my boy that was best in the world, that never rose a hair of my head, to have died with his name under blemish, and left a great shame on his child! Better for him have killed the whole world than to give any witness at all! Have you no word to say, Mary Cushin? Am I left here to keen him alone?

MARY CUSHIN [*who has sunk on to the step before the door, rocking herself and keening*]: Oh, Denis, my heart is broken you to have died with the hard word upon you! My grief you to be alone now that spent so many nights in company!

What way will I be going back through Gort and through Kilbecanty? The people will not be coming out keening you, they will say no prayer for the rest of your soul!

What way will I be the Sunday and I going up the hill to the Mass? Every woman with her own comrade, and Mary Cushin to be walking her lone!

What way will I be the Monday and the neighbours turning their heads from the house? The turf Denis cut lying on the bog, and no well-wisher to bring it to the hearth!

What way will I be in the night time, and none but the dog calling after you? Two women to be mixing a cake, and not a man in the house to break it!

What way will I sow the field, and no man to drive the furrow? The sheaf to be scattered before spring-time that was brought together at the harvest!

I would not begrudge you, Denis, and you leaving praises after you. The neighbours keening along with me would be better to me than an estate.

But my grief your name to be blackened in the time of the blackening of the rushes! Your name never to rise up again in the growing time of the year! [*She ceases keening and turns towards the old woman*] But tell me, Mary, do you think would they give us the body

of Denis? I would lay him out with myself only;
I would hire some man to dig the grave.

The GATEKEEPER *opens the gate and hands out
some clothes.*

GATEKEEPER: There now is all he brought in with him;
the flannels and the shirt and the shoes. It is little
they are worth altogether; those mountainy boys do
be poor.

MARY CUSHIN: They had a right to give him time to
ready himself the day they brought him to the magistrates. He to be wearing his Sunday coat, they would
see he was a decent boy. Tell me where they will
bury him, the way I can follow after him through
the streets? There is no other one to show respect
to him but Mary Cahel, his mother, and myself.

GATEKEEPER: That is not to be done. He is buried
since yesterday in the field that is belonging to the
gaol.

MARY CUSHIN: It is a great hardship that to have been
done, and not one of his own there to follow after
him at all.

GATEKEEPER: Those that break the law must be made
an example of. Why would they be laid out like a well
behaved man? A long rope and a short burying, that
is the order for a man that is hanged.

MARY CUSHIN: A man that was hanged! O Denis, was it
they that made an end of you and not the great God
at all? His curse and my own curse upon them that
did not let you die on the pillow! The curse of God
be fulfilled that was on them before they were born!
My curse upon them that brought harm on you, and
on Terry Fury that fired the shot!

MARY CAHEL [*standing up*]: And the other boys, did they
hang them along with him, Terry Fury and Pat
Ruane that were brought from Daire-caol?

GATEKEEPER: They did not, but set them free twelve

hours ago. It is likely you may have passed them in the night time.

MARY CUSHIN: Set free is it, and Denis made an end of? What justice is there in the world at all?

GATEKEEPER: He was taken near the house. They knew his footmark. There was no witness given against the rest worth while.

MARY CAHEL: Then the sergeant was lying and the people were lying when they said Denis Cahel had informed in the gaol?

GATEKEEPER: I have no time to be stopping here talking. The judge got no evidence and the law set them free.

He goes in and shuts gate after him.

MARY CAHEL [*holding out her hands*]: Are there any people in the streets at all till I call on them to come hither? Did they ever hear in Galway such a thing to be done, a man to die for his neighbour?

Tell it out in the streets for the people to hear, Denis Cahel from Slieve Echtge is dead. It was Denis Cahel from Daire-caol that died in the place of his neighbour!

It is he was young and comely and strong, the best reaper and the best hurler. It was not a little thing for him to die, and he protecting his neighbour!

Gather up, Mary Cushin, the clothes for your child; they'll be wanted by this one and that one. The boys crossing the sea in the springtime will be craving a thread for a memory.

One word to the judge and Denis was free, they offered him all sorts of riches. They brought him drink in the gaol, and gold, to swear away the life of his neighbour!

Pat Ruane was no good friend to him at all, but a foolish, wild companion; it was Terry Fury knocked a gap in the wall and sent in the calves to our meadow.

Denis would not speak, he shut his mouth, he would

never be an informer. It is no lie he would have said at all giving witness against Terry Fury.

I will go through Gort and Kilbecanty and Druimdarod and Daroda; I will call to the people and the singers at the fairs to make a great praise for Denis!

The child he left in the house that is shook, it is great will be his boast in his father! All Ireland will have a welcome before him, and all the people in Boston.

I to stoop on a stick through half a hundred years, I will never be tired with praising! Come hither, Mary Cushin, till we'll shout it through the roads, Denis Cahel died for his neighbour!

LADY GREGORY (1852-1932)
The Gaol Gate

Customs and Beliefs

IRISH COURTSHIP—I

Once when Naoisi was outside alone Deirdre slipped out to him as if she were going past him and he did not recognise her.

"That's a nice heifer that's going by me," he said.

"Heifers ought to be big," she said, "wherever there are no bulls."

"You have the bull of the province," he said, meaning the King of Ulster.

"I'd choose between you," she said, "and take a little young bull like you."

"No," he said. "Not after Cathbad's prophecy!"

"Are you saying that because you don't want me?"

"I am surely," said he.

She made a rush at him and grabbed his two ears.

"Then two ears of shame and mockery on you," she said, "unless you take me with you."

"Go on, woman!" he said.

"You'll have it," she said.

ANONYMOUS (9th cent.)
translated from the Irish by
FRANK O'CONNOR

IRISH COURTSHIP—II

My dear Mrs. Williams,

This is to certify that you are my best and dearest love, the regenerator of my heart, the holiest joy of my soul, my treasure, my salvation, my rest, my reward, my darling youngest child, my secret glimpse of heaven, my angel of the Annunciation, not yet herself awake, but rousing me from a long sleep with the beat of her unconscious wings, and shining upon me with her beautiful eyes that are still blind.

Also to observe incidentally that Wednesday is the nearest evening that shows blank in my diary.

Yours truly

Joseph Mazzini Walker

BERNARD SHAW (1856-1950)
Letters To Florence Farr

IRISH COURTSHIP—III

Fountain Court,
The Temple.
(December 1895)

My Dear S. S. D. D. has the magical armageddon begun at last? I notice that the *Freeman's Journal*, the only Irish paper I have seen has an article from its London correspondent announcing inevitable war and backing it up with excellent argument from the character of Cleveland. The war would fulfil the prophets and especially a prophetic vision I had long ago with the Mathers', and so far be for the glory of God but what a dusk of the nations it would be? for surely it would drag in half the world. What have your divinations said or have they said anything? When will you be in town next? Could you come and see me on Monday and have tea and perhaps divine for armageddon?

Yours ever

W. B. Yeats

Letters to Florence Farr

COUNTRY MARRIAGE

Country marriage in Ireland follows an ancient and widespread pattern. It is called "match-making" and it is the sort of *mariage de convenance* involving parental negotiations and a dowry which is nearly universal in Europe. In Ireland its importance is such as to make it the crucial point of rural social organization.

To describe the match one has to sink one's teeth into the countryman's way of life. For the match is made up of many things. It unites transfer of economic control and advance to adult status. It is the only respectable method of marriage and the usual method of inheritance in the Irish countryside. It is embedded in the Gaelic tongue, in joke and story, and in folklore.

A match usually begins when a farmer casts round for a suitable wife for one of his sons. The son to be married is to inherit the farm. The farmer has full power to choose among his sons. A hundred years ago, before famine, clearances and land reform, all the sons and daughters could hope to be provided for on the land. Such a situation is still an ideal, but little more. One cannot subdivide one's holding any longer, and new farms are hard to get. Today the farmer looks forward, ordinarily, to "settling" only one son "on the land."

"When a young man is on the lookout for a young lady," a farmer of Inagh in mid-Clare told me, "it is put through his friends for to get a suitable woman for him for his wife. It all goes by friendship and friends and meeting at public-houses." I think we can remember from the last lecture what he means. Getting married is no carefree, personal matter; one's whole kindred help, even to suggesting candidates.

"The young man," the farmer goes on, "sends a

' speaker ' to the young lady and the speaker will sound
a note to know what fortune she has, will she suit, and
will she marry this Shrove? She and her friends will
inquire what kind of a man he is, is he nice and steady.
And if he suits, they tell the speaker to go ahead and
' draw it down.' So then he goes back to the young
man's house and arranges for them to meet in such
a place, on such a night and we will see about it." With
this, the first step in the delicate negotiations is safely
passed.

The Inagh farmer goes on: "The speaker goes with
the young man and his father that night, and they meet
the father of the girl and his friends or maybe his son
and son-in-law. The first drink is called by the young
man; the second by the young lady's father.

"The young lady's father asks the speaker what fortune
do he want. He asks him the place of how many cows,
sheep, and horses is it? He asks what makings of a
garden are in it; is there plenty of water or spring
wells? Is it far in from the road, or on it? What
kind of house is in it, slate or thatch? Are the cabins
good, are they slate or thatch? If it is too far in from
the road, he won't take it. Backward places don't grow
big fortunes. And he asks, too, is it near a chapel and
the school, or near town?"

The Inagh countryman could pause here; he had
summarized a very long and important negotiation.

"Well," he went on, getting to the heart of the matter,
"if it is a nice place, near the road, and the place of eight
cows, they are sure to ask £350 fortune. Then the
young lady's father offers £250. Then maybe the boy's
father throws off £50. If the young lady's father still
has £250 on it, the speaker divides the £50 between them.
So now it's £275. Then the young man says he is not
willing to marry without £300—but if she's a nice girl
and a good housekeeper, he'll think of it. So, there's
another drink by the young man, and then another by

the young lady's father, and so on with every second drink till they're near drunk. The speaker gets plenty and has a good day."

The farmer paused here again; for the match is developing marvellously. "All this is one day's work," he continued. "After this, they appoint a place for the young people to see one another and be introduced. The young lady takes along her friends, maybe another girl, and her brother and her father and mother. The young man takes along his friends and the speaker.

"If they suit one another, then they will appoint a day to come and see the land. If they don't, no one will reflect on anybody, but they will say he or she doesn't suit. They do not say plainly what is wrong.

"The day before the girl's people come to see the land, geese are killed, the house is whitewashed, whiskey and porter bought. The cows get a feed early so as to look good; and maybe they get an extra cow in, if they want one." He said this last slyly, for to pretend to own more stock than one really has, is an unfair trick in the bargaining.

"Then next day comes the walking of the land. The young man stays outside in the street, but he sends his best friend in to show the girl's father round, but sure the friend won't show him the bad points.

"If the girl's father likes the land he returns, and there will be eating and drinking until night comes on them. Then they go to an attorney next day and get the writings between the two parties and get the father of the boy to sign over the land." With the writings, the match is made, and the wedding can go forward.

CONRAD ARENSBERG
The Irish Countryman

INNOCENT AMUSEMENT

1783

A Mr. Frank Skelton, one of the half-mounted gentlemen described in the early part of this work—a boisterous, joking, fat, young fellow—was prevailed on, much against his grain, to challenge the exciseman of the town for running the butt-end of a horsewhip down his throat the night before, while he lay drunk and sleeping with his mouth open. The exciseman insisted that snoring at a dinner-table was a personal offence to every gentleman in company, and would therefore make no apology.

Frank, though he had been very nearly choked, was very reluctant to fight; he said "he was sure to die if he did, as the exciseman could snuff a candle with his pistol-ball; and as he himself was as big as a hundred dozen of candles, what chance could he have?" We told him jocosely to give the exciseman no time to take aim at him, by which means he might, perhaps, hit his adversary first, and thus survive the contest. He seemed somewhat encouraged and consoled by the hint, and most strictly did he adhere to it.

Hundreds of the town's people went to see the fight on the green of Maryborough. The ground was regularly measured; and the friends of each party pitched a ragged tent on the green, where whiskey and salt beef were consumed in abundance. Skelton having taken his ground, and at the same time two heavy drams from a bottle his foster-brother had brought, appeared quite stout till he saw the balls entering the mouths of the exciseman's pistols, which shone as bright as silver, and were nearly as long as fusils. This vision made a palpable alteration in Skelton's sentiments: he changed colour, and looked about him as if he wanted some assistance. However, their seconds, who were of the same rank and description, handed to each party his case of pistols, and half-bellowed to them—"Blaze away, boys!"

Skelton now recollected his instructions, and *lost no time:* he cocked *both* his pistols at once; and as the exciseman was deliberately and most scientifically coming to his "dead level," as he called it, Skelton let fly.

"Holloa!" said the exciseman, dropping his level, "I'm battered, by Jasus!"

"The devil's cure to you!" said Skelton, instantly firing his second pistol.

One of the exciseman's legs then gave way, and down he came on his knee, exclaiming "Holloa! holloa! you blood-thirsty villain! do you want to take my life?"

"Why, to be sure I do!" said Skelton. "Ha! ha! have I *stiffened* you, my lad?" Wisely judging, however, that if he stayed till the exciseman recovered his legs, he might have a couple of shots to stand, he wheeled about, took to his heels, and got away as fast as possible. The crowd shouted; but Skelton, like a hare when started, ran the faster for the shouting.

Jemmy Moffit, his own second, followed, overtook, tripped up his heels, and cursing him for a disgraceful rascal, asked "why he ran away from the exciseman?"

"Ough, thunther!" said Skelton, with his chastest brogue, "how many holes did the villain want drilled in to his carcass? Would you have me stop to make a *riddle* of him, Jemmy?"

The second insisted that Skelton should return to the field, to be shot at. He resisted, affirming that he had done *all* that *honour* required. . . .

However, he was dragged up to the ground by his second, after agreeing to fight again, if he had another pistol given him. But, luckily for Frank, the last bullet had stuck so fast between the bones of the exciseman's leg that he could not stand. The friends of the latter then proposed to strap him to a tree, that he might be able to shoot Skelton; but this being positively objected to by Frank, the exciseman was carried home: his first wound was on the side of his thigh, and the second in his right leg; but neither proved at all dangerous.

SIR JONAH BARRINGTON (1760-1834)
Personal Sketches

A LANDLORD'S AMUSEMENT

A landlord in Ireland can scarcely invent an order which a servant, labourer or cottar dares to refuse to execute. Nothing satisfies him but an unlimited submission. Disrespect, or anything tending towards sauciness, he may punish with his cane or his horsewhip with the most perfect security; a poor man would have his bones broke if he offered to lift his hands in his own defence. Knocking-down is spoken of in the country in a manner that makes an Englishman stare. Landlords of consequence have assured me that many of their cottars would think themselves honoured by having their wives and daughters sent for to the bed of their master; a mark of slavery that proves the oppression under which such people must live. . . .

It must strike the most careless traveller to see whole strings of carts whipped into a ditch by a gentleman's footman to make way for his carriage; if they are over-turned or broken in pieces, no matter, it is taken in patience; were they to complain they would perhaps be horsewhipped. The execution of the laws lies very much in the hands of justices of the peace, many of whom are drawn from the most illiberal class in the kingdom. If a poor man lodges a complaint against a gentleman or any animal that chooses to call itself a gentleman, and the justice issues out a summons for his appearance, it is a fixed affront, and he will infallibly be called out. Where manners are in conspiracy against law, to whom are the oppressed people to have recourse?

ARTHUR YOUNG (1741-1820)
Tour in Ireland

AN IRISH ELECTION

18TH CENTURY

Every way it turned out fortunate for Sir Condy, for before the money was all gone there came a general election, and he being so well beloved in the country, and one of the oldest families, no one had a better right to stand candidate for the vacancy; and he was called upon by all his friends, and the whole county, I may say, to declare himself against the old member, who had little thought of a contest. My master did not relish the thoughts of a troublesome canvass and all the ill-will he might bring upon himself by disturbing the peace of the county, besides the expense, which was no trifle; but all his friends called upon one another to subscribe, and they formed themselves into a committee, and wrote all his circular-letters for him, and engaged all his agents, and did all the business unknown to him; and he was well pleased that it should be so at last, and my lady herself was very sanguine about the election; and there was open house kept night and day at Castle Rackrent, and I thought I never saw my lady look so well in her life as she did at that time. There were grand dinners, and all the gentlemen drinking success to Sir

Condy till they were carried off; and then dances and balls, and the ladies all finishing with a raking pot of tea in the morning. Indeed, it was well the company made it their choice to sit up all nights, for there were not half beds enough for the sights of people that were in it, though there were shake-downs in the drawing-room always made up before sunrise for those that liked it.

For my part, when I saw the doings that were going on, and the loads of claret that went down the throats of them that had no right to be asking for it, and the sights of meat that went up to the table and never came down, besides what was carried off to one or t'other below stair, I couldn't but pity my poor master, who was to pay for it all; but I said nothing, for fear of gaining myself ill-will. The day of election will come some time or other, says I to myself, and all will be over, and so it did, and a glorious day it was as any I ever had the happiness to see.

"Huzza! Huzza! Sir Condy Rackrent forever!" was the first thing I hears in the morning, and the same and nothing else all day, and not a soul sober only just when polling, enough to give their votes as became 'em, and to stand the browbeating of the lawyers, who came tight enough upon us; and many of our freeholders were knocked off, having never a freehold that they could safely swear to, and Sir Condy was not willing to have any man perjure himself for his sake, as was done on the other side. God knows; but no matter for that. Some of our friends were dumbfounded by the lawyers asking them: "Had they ever been upon the ground where their freeholds lay?" Now, Sir Condy, being tender of the consciences of them that had not even been on the ground, and so could not swear to a freehold when cross-examined by them lawyers, sent out for a couple of cleavefuls of the sods of his farm of Gultee-shinnagh; and as soon as the sods came into town, he set each man upon his sod, and so then, ever after, you know, they could fairly swear they had been upon the ground. We gained the day by this piece of honesty. I thought I should have died in the streets for joy when I seed my poor master chaired, and he bareheaded, and it raining as hard as it could pour; but all the crowds following him up and down, and he bowing and shaking hands with the whole town. . . .

After the election was quite and clean over, there comes shoals of people from all parts, claiming to have obliged my master with their votes, and putting him in mind of promises which he could never remember himself to have made: one was to have a freehold for each of his four sons; another was to have a renewal of a lease; another an abatement; one came to be paid ten guineas for a pair of silver buckles sold my master on the hustings, which turned out to be no better than copper gilt; another had a long bill for oats, the half of which never went into the granary to my certain knowledge, and the other half was not fit for the cattle to touch; but the bargain was made the week before the election, and the coach and saddle-horses were got into order for the day, besides a vote fairly got by them oats; so no more reasoning on that head. But then there was no end to them that were telling Sir Condy he had engaged to make their sons excisemen, or high constables, or the like; and as for them that had bills to give in for liquor, and beds, and straw, and ribands, and horses, and post-chaises for the gentlemen free-holders that came from all parts and other counties to vote for my master, and were not, to be sure, to be at any charges, there was no standing against all these; and worse than all, the gentlemen of my master's committee, who managed all for him, and talked how they'd bring him in without costing him a penny, and sub-scribed by hundreds very genteely, forgot to pay their subscriptions and had laid out in agents' and lawyers' fees and secret-service money to the Lord knows how much; and my master could never ask any of them for their subscription you are sensible, nor for the price of a fine horse he had sold one of them; so it all was left at his door.

He could never, God bless him again! I say, bring himself to ask a gentleman for money, despising such sort of conversation himself; but others, who were not gentlemen born, behaved very uncivil in pressing him at this very time, and all he could do to content 'em all was to take himself out of the way as fast as possible to Dublin, where my lady had taken a house fitting for him as a member of Parliament, to attend his duty in there all the winter. I was very lonely when the whole family was gone, and all the things they had ordered to go, and forgot, sent after them by the car. There was then a great silence in Castle Rackrent, and I went moping from room to room, hearing the doors clap for want of right locks, and the wind through the broken windows, that the glazier never would come to mend, and the rain coming through the roof and best ceilings all over the house for want of the slater, whose bill was not paid, besides our having no slates or shingles for that part of the old building which was shingled and burnt when the chimney took fire, and had been open to the weather ever since.

I took myself to the servants' hall in the evening to smoke my pipe as usual, but missed the bit of talk we used to have there sadly, and ever after was content to stay in the kitchen and boil my little potatoes and put up my bed there, and every post-day I looked in the newspaper, but no news of my master in the House; he never spoke good or bad, but, as the butler wrote down word to my son Jason, was very ill-used by the Government about a place that was promised him and never given, after his supporting them against his conscience very honourably, and being greatly abused for it, which hurt him greatly, he having the name of a great patriot in the country before.

MARIA EDGEWORTH (1767-1849)
Castle Rackrent

CARLYLE OBSERVES THE SAVAGES

I — CATHOLIC

Hooded monks, actually in brown, coarse woollen sacks, that reach to the knee, with funnel-shaped hood that can be thrown back; Irish physiognomy in a new guise! Labourers working in the field at hay, etc; *country* people they, I observe, *presided* over by a monk. Entrance; squalid hordes of beggars sit waiting. Irish *accent* from beneath the hood, as a "brother" admits us; learning the lordship's *quality*, he hastens off for "the prior," a tallish, lean, not very prepossessing Irishman of forty, who conducts us thenceforth. Banished from Mount Meilleraye in France, about 1830, for quasi-political reasons, the first of these Irishmen arrive penniless at Cork; know not what to do; a Protestant Sir Something gives them "waste land," wild, craggy moor on this upland of the Knockmeildowns; charitable Catholics intervene, with other help; they struggle, prosper, and are now as we see. Good bit of ground *cleared*, drained, and productive; more in clear progress thereto; big, simple square of buildings, etc. (*chapel* very grand, done by monks all the decorations), dormitory very large, wholly wooden and clean; bake-house, poor library, nasty *tubs* of cold stirabout (coarsest I ever saw) for beggars; silence; each monk, when bidden do anything, does it, folds hands over breast, and disappears with a *large* smile and a low bow; curious enough to look upon, indeed! Garden rather weedy, a few monks poking about in it; work rather make-believe, I feared; offices in the rear; extensive peat-stack, mill; *body* of hay-makers, one or two young monks actually *making* hay. Rise at 2 a.m. to their devotions; have really to go through a great deal of drill-exercise through the day, independently of work. One poor fellow in the library has been dabbling a bit in the elements of geometry—elemental, yet ingenious. "The other night lead spout has been torn off from our cowhouse there; new thing, theft from *us*." Excellent brown bread, milk and butter, is offered for viaticum; Lord Stuart, I see, smuggles some gift of money; and with blessings we are rolled away again. The new "Monastery" must have accumulated several thousand pounds of *property* in these seventeen or more or fewer years, in spite of its continual charities to beggars; but this itself, I take it, must be very much the result of public *charity* (Catholic Ireland much approving of them): and I confess the whole business had, lurking under it for me, at this year of grace, a certain *dramatic* character, as if they were "doing it." Inevitable at this year of grace, I fear! Hard work I didn't see monks doing: except it were one young fellow who was actually forking hay; food, glory, dim notion of getting to heaven, too, I suppose these are motive enough for a man of average Irish insight? The saddest fact I heard about these poor monks was that the prior had discovered some of them surveying the Youghal-and-Cappoquin steamer, watching its arrival, from their high moor, as the event of their day; and had reprovingly taken away their telescope; ah me!

THOMAS CARLYLE (1795-1881)
Reminiscences of My Irish Journey

2 — PROTESTANT

Church service; clean congregation of forty; red-haired young Irish parson, who is very evidently "performing" the service. Decency everywhere; poor little decent church with the tombs round it, and a tree or two shading it (on the top of a high rough green bank with a brook at the bottom): service here, according to the natural English method, "decently performed." I felt how decent English Protestants, or the sons of such, might with zealous affection like to assemble here once a week, and remind themselves of English purities and decencies and Gospel ordinances, in the midst of a black howling Babel of superstitious savagery—like Hebrews sitting by the streams of Babel: but I feel more clearly than ever how *impossible* it was that an extraneous son of Adam, first seized by the terrible conviction that he had a soul to be saved or damned, that he must rede the riddle of this universe or go to perdition everlasting, could for a moment think of taking this respectable "performance" as the solution of the mystery for him! Oh, heaven! never in this world! Weep ye by the stream of Babel, decent clean English-Irish; weep, for there is cause, till you can do something *better* than weep; but expect no Babylonian or any other mortal to concern himself with that affair of yours!

THOMAS CARLYLE (1795-1881)
Reminiscences of My Irish Journey

THE ART OF PERJURY

The Cork Assizes once contributed a leading case to the
law relating to the sale of goods: Wallis v. Russell. It
was tried before Pether O'Brien, who greatly enjoyed
himself. Mrs. Wallis had brought her action against
Messieurs Russell, who were well-known merchants in
Cork, in respect of a crab which had been purchased for
her supper, and which made her seriously ill. In those
days such actions were not common; but Mrs. Wallis
happened to be the mother of one of the most original
and courageous solicitors in Cork, who at a later date
distinguished himself by having his office premises
and their garden, situated in the main street of the town
of Midleton, declared to be a holding that was partly
agricultural or pastoral, and thus entitled to the benefits
of the Irish Land Acts. To a mind of such daring an
action about a diseased crab would be a trifle. And so
the case was launched. There was no doubt about
Mrs. Wallis's illness, or about its cause. The whole
point was, whether the salesman had warranted the
crab to be fit for human consumption. There is a section
of the Sale of Goods Act which deals with the matter;
and a young lady went into the box to describe her
purchase of the crab.

"I am a companion to Mrs. Wallis," she said. "I went
out to buy her some little tasty thing that she might
fancy for her tea; and I suddenly thought of a crab.
I knew that Russell's had cooked crabs; so I went in
there, and asked the shopman for a nice cooked crab,
telling him that I wanted it for Mrs Wallis's supper,
so as to make known to him the purpose for which it
was to be used." Pether pricked up his ears. "You said
that?" he asked. "Yes, my Lord." "In thothe very

wordth?" "Yes, my Lord." Pether reflected a moment. "Remarkable the thtrideth education ith taking," he commented. "Go on." The young lady took up her tale. "Well, then, when I had told him that, he looked at the crabs, and he selected one and gave it to me. So I, relying on his skill and judgment, took it——" "Thtop, thtop!" cried Pether. "You uthed thothe wordth also?" "Yes, my Lord." "Where were you educated?" "At the Ursuline Convent, Blackrock, my Lord." "And thinth when have the Urthuline Thithers included Thection Fourteen of the Thale of Goodth Act in their curriculum?" "I don't know, my Lord; I did not get beyond domestic economy." "Ah-h! That'th where it ith; they teach you to buy food?" "Yes, my Lord." "And they tell you, 'Never buy anything without telling the shopman what it ith for, tho that you can thay you have relied on his thkill and judgment'?" "Yes, my Lord." "What admirable nunth!" said Pether. "Go on!" But his sarcasm went for naught; the young lady's story was implicitly accepted by the jury; and Mrs. Wallis received such comfort as the law could afford her, and set a headline for the example of other persons unfortunate enough to poison themselves with unfit food.

MAURICE HEALY (1859-1923)
The Old Munster Circuit

THE PERJURER PURGED

There was a third Clareman whom I must mention; for he was one of the "characters" of the Circuit. Michael MacNamara, known far and wide as "Counsellor Mack," was an original. He was not alone a barrister; he was also a mapper; he was parish matchmaker to the parish of Kilshanny; but it is believed that his principal source of income was his skill at the game of "Forty-Five." He was also the Court interpreter in Irish. He professed to be a great etymologist; he wrote several learned pamphlets to prove that the Irish and Maori languages were inter-related (and who am I to suggest that he was wrong?); and when George V came to the throne, the Counsellor published a Coronation Ode, which began:

> Britannia's fame enlarges;
> Yes, Heaven gives and charges
> The mightiest of the Georges
>   To bless and guard her throne;

and it continued for several pages to the same effect. His Majesty was graciously pleased to accept a copy of the work, which was the next best thing to appointing the Counsellor Poet Laureate; and he would hardly have been worse than Alfred Austin.

On one occasion when the Counsellor was engaged for a plaintiff in the County Court, he had a great dread that the defendant would swear himself out of the debt by barefaced perjury. The fact that he was counsel in the case does not appear to have prevented him from acting as interpreter; and when the defendant came to take the oath, the Counsellor addressed him in Irish: "Listen carefully now to the terms of the oath, and repeat after me—'If I do not tell the truth in this case—'"

"'If I do not tell the truth in this case—'"

"May a murrain seize my cattle—"

"What's that, Counsellor? Sure that's not the oath?"

"Go on and repeat your oath: 'May a murrain seize my cattle—'"

"Oh! Glory be to God! 'May a murrain seize my cattle—'"

"May all my sheep be cliffted—" (i.e. fall over the cliff.)

"Yerra, Counsellor, what oath is that you're trying to get me to take? Sure, I never heard an oath like that before!"

"Go on, sir; don't argue with me; repeat your oath: ' May all my sheep be cliffted—'"

"Oh! God help us all! ' May all my sheep—' yerra, Counsellor, are you sure that's in the oath?"

"Go on, sir!"

"Oh! God! ' May all my sheep be cliffted! '"

"May my children get the falling sickness—"

"Arrah, Counsellor, tell his Honour that I admit the debt, and I only want a little time to pay!"

Some months after this I met Counsellor Mack in the King's Inns Library, and, having heard this story, and believing it to be an invention, proceeded to repeat it in his presence before an audience. To my surprise, the Counsellor not merely admitted its truth, but took great pride in it. "Wasn't I right?" he asked. "What is an oath? Isn't it a calling on God to punish you if you don't say what is true? And what was I doing but bringing home to him the perils he was running?"

MAURICE HEALY (1859-1923)
The Old Munster Circuit

STYLE

Or take this epitaph of an Irish Celt, Angus the Culdee, whose Felire, or festology, I have already mentioned—a festology in which, at the end of the eighth or beginning of the ninth century, he collected from "the countless hosts of the illuminated books of Erin" (to use his own words) the festivals of the Irish saints, his poem having a stanza for every day in the year. The epitaph on Angus, who died at Cluain Eidhnech, (Clonenagh) in Queen's County, runs thus:—

> Angus in the assembly of Heaven,
> Here are his tomb and his bed;
> It is from hence he went to death,
> In the Friday, to holy Heaven.
>
> It was in Cluain Eidhnech he was rear'd;
> In Cluain Eidhnech he was buried;
> In Cluain Eidhnech, of many crosses,
> He first read his psalms.

This is by no eminent hand; and yet a Greek epitaph could not show a finer perception of what constitutes propriety and felicity of style in compositions of this nature.

MATTHEW ARNOLD (1822-88)
The Study of Celtic Literature

SCHOLARS

> Scholars, regrettably, must yell
> In torment on the hob of hell
> While louts that never learned their letters
> Are perched in Heaven among their betters.

ANONYMOUS (9th cent.)
translated from the Irish by
FRANK O'CONNOR

THE STUDENT

The student's life is pleasant,
  And pleasant is his labour;
Search all Ireland over,
  You'll find no better neighbour.

Nor lords nor petty princes
  Dispute the student's pleasure;
Nor chapter stints his purse
  Nor stewardship his leisure.

None orders early rising,
  Calf-rearing nor cow-tending,
Nor nights of toilsome vigil;
  His time is his for spending.

He takes a hand at draughts,
  Or plucks a harp-string bravely,
And fills his nights with courting
  Some golden-haired light lady.

And when springtime is come
  The ploughshaft's there to follow—
A fistful of goosequills
  And a straight, deep furrow!

ANONYMOUS (16th cent.)
translated from the Irish by
FRANK O'CONNOR

CROW STREET THEATRE

From my youth I was attached to theatrical representations, and have still a clear recollection of many of the eminent performers of my early days. My grandmother, with whom I resided for many years, had silver tickets of admission to Crow Street theatre, whither I was very frequently sent.

The playhouse in Dublin were then lighted with tallow candles, stuck into tin circles hanging from the middle of the stage, which were every now and then snuffed by some performer; and two soldiers, with fixed bayonets, always stood like statues on each side of the stage, close to the boxes, to keep the audience in order. The galleries were very noisy and very *droll*. The ladies and gentlemen in the boxes always went dressed out nearly as for court; the strictest etiquette and decorum were preserved in that circle; while the pit, as being full of critics and wise men, was particularly respected, except when the young gentlemen of the university occasionally forced themselves in, to revenge some insult, real or imagined, to a member of their body; on which occasions, all the ladies, well-dressed men, and peaceable people generally, decamped forthwith, and the young gentlemen as generally proceeded to beat or turn out the rest of the audience, and to break everything that came within their reach. . . .

I remember . . . seeing old Mr. Sheridan perform the part of *Cato* at one of the Dublin theatres; I do not recollect which: but I well recollect his dress, which consisted of bright armour under a fine laced scarlet cloak, and surmounted by a huge, white, bushy, well-powdered wig (like Dr. Johnson's) over which was stuck his helmet. I wondered much how he could kill himself without stripping off the armour before he performed that operation! I also recollect him particularly (even as before my eyes now) playing *Alexander the Great*, and throwing the javelin at Clytus, whom happening to miss, he hit the cupbearer, then played by one of the hack performers, a Mr. Jemmy Fotterel. Jemmy very naturally supposed that he was hit *designedly*, and that it was some *new light* of the great Mr. Sheridan to slay the cupbearer in preference to his friend *Clytus* (which certainly would have been a less unjustifiable man-slaughter), and that therefore he ought to tumble down and make a painful end according to dramatic custom time immemorial. Immediately, therefore, on being struck, he reeled, staggered, and fell very naturally, considering it was his *first death*; but being determined on this unexpected opportunity to make an impression upon the audience, when he found himself stretched out on the boards at full length, he began to roll about, kick, and flap the stage with his hands most immoder-ately; falling next into strong convulsions, exhibiting every symptom of exquisite torture, and at length expiring with a groan so loud and so long that it paralyzed even the people in the galleries, while the ladies believed that he was really killed, and cried aloud. . . .

The actresses of both tragedy and genteel comedy formerly wore large hoops, and whenever they made a speech walked across the stage and changed sides with the performer who was to speak next, thus veering back-ward and forward, like a shuttlecock, during the entire performance. . . .

At one time, when the audience of Smock alley were beginning to flag, Old Sparkes told Ryder, if he would bring out the afterpiece of "The Padlock," and permit him to manage it, he would insure him a succession of good nights. Ryder gave him his way, and the bills announced a first appearance in the part of Leonora:

the *debutante* was reported to be a Spanish lady. The public curiosity was excited, and youth, beauty, and tremulous modesty, were all anticipated; the house overflowed; impatience was unbounded; the play ended in confusion, and the overture of "The Padlock" was received with rapture. Leonora at length appeared; the clapping was like thunder, to give courage to the *debutante*, who had a handsome face, and was very beautifully dressed as a Spanish donna, which it was supposed she really was. Her gigantic size, it is true, rather astonished the audience. However, they willingly took for granted that the Spaniards were an immense people, and it was observed that England must have had a great escape of the Spanish Armada, if the men were proportionably gigantic to the ladies. Her voice too was rather of the hoarsest, but that was accounted for by the sudden change of climate: at last, Leonora began her song of "Sweet Robin"—

> "Say, little foolish, fluttering thing,
>   Whither, ah whither, would you wing?"

and at the same moment Leonora's mask falling off, Old Sparkes stood confessed, with an immense gander which he brought from under his cloak, and which he had trained to stand on his hand and screech to his voice, and in chorus with himself. The whim took; the roar of laughter was quite inconceivable; he had also got Mungo played by a *real* black; and the whole was so extravagantly ludicrous, and so entirely to the taste of the Irish galleries at that time, that his "Sweet Robin" was encored, and the frequent repetition of the piece replenished poor Ryder's treasury for the residue of the season.

SIR JONAH BARRINGTON (1760-1834)
Personal Sketches

FIRST NIGHT AT THE ABBEY

The theatre opened for the first time on a Tuesday, December 27th, 1904. It is easy to describe. . . . As was only to be expected on such an occasion, we had a full house. It was the most fashionable theatrical event of the year. Distinguished-looking visitors kept drifting into the tiny vestibule, scrutinising the fittings and discussing the history of the society, standing in a little knots on the stairs. Yeats was impressive in evening dress, and kept coming behind the scenes every few minutes to see how things were getting along.

Back-stage, Willie Fay, dressed for his part in one of the new plays, a wild wig slipping sideways over his elfin face, swung unexpectedly from a batten high in the flys, arranging the lighting. Beneath him passed an endless procession of figures carrying ladders, tools, canvas screens, draperies. Idlers at the back of the drawn hessian curtain eyed the swelling audience; a muffled mumble of voices rose from the auditorium.

Standing as far out of the way as possible, those of us who were unoccupied, ate a scrap meal of bread and cocoa. It was all we had had to eat for hours. Every member of the society had been in the theatre since early afternoon.

In between bites we watched the auditorium through a crack in the curtain. The pit and gallery were full. The stalls were slower in filling, but the crowd was increasing all the time. A number of people sitting in front seemed oblivious of the pre-curtain chatter as they listened to the violin music of Arthur Darley, our one musician.

Darley was a great addition to the little company. A violinist of note, he was a well-known collector of

traditional Irish airs. Yeats had taken him along to
play between the acts when we were in the Molesworth
Hall. He used to stand in the corner of the stage, just
outside the curtain, fondling his violin self-consciously
and playing plaintive little pieces much appreciated by
audiences. Few reviews would have been complete
without mention of him. It turned out later that he
had known Synge in Paris before the writer came to us.
Both had played in the same orchestra.

The sound of a familiar voice drew our attention back-
stage again. In a dark corner, sitting on an upturned
property-basket, sat Synge himself, rolling the inevitable cigarette.

"God bless you," he said. "I hope you're as happy
as I am. I am so honoured that my little play should
be chosen for the first week."

In the Shadow of the Glen was billed for the second
night.

For our opening, we played a triple bill: Yeats' new
one-act *On Baile's Strand*; a revival of *Kathleen Ni
Houlihan*; and gave the first production of *Spreading the
News*, Lady Gregory's clever little cameo of an Irish
fair-day incident. During the following week, Synge's
play was shuffled with Lady Gregory's in support of
On Baile's Strand.

Many considered that Yeats' new play was his best.
In it, as one writer put it, he emerged from the shadows
with less of the mystic and more of the human element
in the composition than in some of his earlier verse
plays. The piece, a dramatic setting of the legend
telling of the slaying of his own son by the unwitting
Cuchullain, belonged to an older order of drama than
some of his other lyrical works. With the introduction
of Barach, the fool, Yeats approached the Shakesperian
model, but never sacrificed his own originality of
treatment, wrote the reviewers.

Fay adopted simplicity and the artistic blending of

colour as his keynote in the staging. Great emphasis was laid on lighting. Amber-coloured hangings draped the interior of a great hall. A huge door, closed, showed intricate Celtic interlacings on panel and lintel. When it was opened, a glimpse was revealed of a luminous blue sky over a bay. Two plain thrones stood in the centre; brilliant hand-painted medallions on the walls completed the fittings. A golden arc played across the front, helped the colourful costumes of kings, councillors and the resplendent Cuchullain of Frank Fay to blend into a pale background . . .

The evening progressed. In the auditorium, the audience, filling every seat, lining the walls of the balcony and pit, watched eagerly, a sea of faces stirring with enthusiasm. The subtle humour of Lady Gregory's new play, the first of her famous "Cloon" comedies, captured the heart of all. The overbearing "Removable Magistrate" and his dull-witted policeman, Jo Muldoon, seeking out the perpetrator of a crime that was never committed; the melancholy Bartley Fallon, hand-cuffed to the infuriated Jack Smith, whom he is supposed to have killed; his mournful fear that if they are put together in a cell, "murder will be done that time surely"—a perfect piece of dignified comedy by Willie Fay.

And then the scene had changed. The curtain had risen on the new Yeats play. I was standing in the wings, a forgotten prompt script in my hand. Willie Fay, the comedian, the business-like stage-manager of a few moments before was no more. He was transformed into a tiny ragged sprite, cringing before the glittering king of his brother. The other figures paled into the background. Frank Fay spoke, fondling his lines, and they flowed out across the footlights, hovering a moment over the hushed auditorium, his little figure gaining power through the beauty of his words; first as the proud king, hero of a thousand battles, then as the horrified, grief-stricken father, verging on madness, his anguish intensified by the quiet irony of the fool. That moment—a brief one in a memorable evening— will remain long in my memory. The Fays had never acted so well together.

That evening ended too soon. Silently we gathered on the darkened stage, the muffled roar of the applause coming through the fallen curtain. Yeats passed through the green-room door, crossed the set, then stepped in front of the audience. Faintly his words came back:

"We shall take as our mottoes those words written over the three gates of the City of Love of Edmund Spenser—over the first gate was ' Be bold! '; over the second, ' Be bold, be bold! And evermore be bold! '; and over the third, ' Yet be not too bold ' . . ."

More applause. The tiny building vibrating with the echoes. Then quiet, and the murmur of voices as the audience began to file out.

Back-stage, I remember, Frank Fay spoke first. He said: "This is only the beginning. . . ."

MAIRE NIC SHIUBHLAIGH and EDWARD KENNY
The Splendid Years

THE AMERICAN WAKE

At last everything was ready. Mrs. Feeney had exhausted all excuses for moving about, engaged on trivial tasks. She had to go into the big bedroom where Mary was putting on her new hat. The mother sat on a chair by the window, her face contorting on account of the flood of tears she was keeping back. Michael moved about the room uneasily, his two hands knotting a big red handkerchief behind his back. Mary twisted about in front of the mirror that hung over the black wooden mantelpiece. She was spending a long time with the hat. It was the first one she had ever worn, but it fitted her beautifully, and it was in excellent taste. It was given to her by the school-mistress, who was very fond of her, and she herself had taken it in a little. She had an instinct for beauty in dress and deportment.

But the mother, looking at how well her daughter wore the cheap navy blue costume and the white frilled blouse, and the little round black hat with a fat, fluffy, glossy curl covering each ear, and the black silk stockings with blue clocks in them, and the little black shoes that had laces of three colours in them, got suddenly enraged with . . . She didn't know with what she got enraged. But for the moment she hated her daughter's beauty, and she remembered all the anguish of giving birth to her and nursing her and toiling for her, for no other purpose than to lose her now and let her go away, maybe to be ravished wantonly because of her beauty and her love of gaiety. A cloud of mad jealousy and hatred against this impersonal beauty that she saw in her daughter almost suffocated the mother, and she stretched out her hands in front of her unconsciously and then just as suddenly her anger vanished like a puff of smoke, and she burst into wild tears, wailing: "My children, oh, my children, far over the sea you will be carried from me, your mother." And she began to rock herself and she threw her apron over her head.

Immediately the cabin was full of the sound of bitter wailing. A dismal cry rose from the women gathered in the kitchen. "Far over the sea they will be carried," began woman after woman, and they all rocked themselves and hid their heads in their aprons. Michael's mongrel dog began to howl on the hearth. Little Thomas sat down on the hearth beside the dog and, putting his arms around him, he began to cry, although he didn't know exactly why he was crying, but he felt

melancholy on account of the dog howling and so
many people being about.

In the bedroom the son and daughter, on their knees,
clung to their mother, who held their heads between
her hands and rained kisses on both heads ravenously.
After the first wave of tears she had stopped weeping.
The tears still ran down her cheeks, but her eyes gleamed
and they were dry. There was a fierce look in them as
she searched all over the heads of her two children
with them, with her brows contracted, searching with
a fierce terror-stricken expression, as if by the intensity
of her stare she hoped to keep a living photograph of
them before her mind. With her quivering lips she
made a queer sound like "im-m-m-m" and she kept
kissing. Her right hand clutched at Mary's left shoulder
and with her left she fondled the back of Michael's neck.
The two children were sobbing freely. They must have
stayed that way a quarter of an hour.

Then the father came into the room, dressed in his
best clothes. He wore a new frieze waistcoat, with a
grey and black front and a white back. He held his soft
black felt hat in one hand and in the other hand he
had a bottle of holy water. He coughed and said in a
weak gentle voice that was strange to him, as he touched
his son: "Come now, it is time."

Mary and Michael got to their feet. The father
sprinkled them with holy water and they crossed themselves. Then, without looking at their mother, who
lay in the chair with her hands clasped on her lap,
looking at the ground in a silent tearless stupor, they
left the room. Each hurriedly kissed little Thomas,
who was not going to Kilmurrage, and then, hand in
hand, they left the house. As Michael was going out
the door he picked a piece of loose whitewash from
the wall and put it in his pocket. The people filed
out after them, down the yard and on to the road, like
a funeral procession. The mother was left in the

house with little Thomas and two old peasant women from the village. Nobody spoke in the cabin for a long time.

LIAM O'FLAHERTY (*b.* 1897)
Going Into Exile

ARAN FUNERAL

The young man has been buried, and his funeral was one of the strangest scenes I have met with. People could be seen going down to his house from early in the day, yet when I went there with the old man about the middle of the afternoon, the coffin was still lying in front of the door, with the men and women of the family standing round beating it, and keening over it, in a great crowd of people. A little later every one knelt down and a last prayer was said. Then the cousins of the dead man got ready two oars and some pieces of rope—the men of his own family seemed too broken with grief to know what they were doing—the coffin was tied up, and the procession began. The old woman walked close behind the coffin, and I happened to take a place just after them, among the first of the men. The rough lane to the graveyard slopes away towards the east, and the crowd of women going down before me in their red dresses, cloaked with red petticoats, with the waist-band that is held round the head just seen from behind, had a strange effect, to which the white coffin and the unity of colour gave a nearly cloistral quietness.

This time the graveyard was filled with withered grass and bracken instead of the early ferns that were to be seen everywhere at the other funeral I have spoken of, and the grief of the people was of a different kind, as they had come to bury a young man who had died in his first manhood, instead of an old woman of eighty. For this reason the keen lost a part of its formal nature, and was recited as the expression of intense personal grief by the young men and women of the man's own family.

When the coffin had been laid down, near the grave that was to be opened, two long switches were cut out from the brambles among the rocks, and the length and breadth of the coffin were marked on them. Then the men began their work, clearing off stones and thin layers of earth, and breaking up an old coffin that was in the place into which the new one had to be lowered. When a number of blackened boards and pieces of bone had been thrown up with the clay, a skull was lifted out, and placed upon a gravestone. Immediately the old woman, the mother of the dead man, took it up in her hands, and carried it away by herself. Then she sat down and put it in her lap—it was the skull of her own mother— and began keening and shrieking over it with the wildest lamentation.

As the pile of mouldering clay got higher beside the grave a heavy smell began to rise from it, and the men hurried with their work, measuring the hole repeatedly with the two rods of bramble. When it was nearly deep enough the old woman got up and came back to the coffin, and began to beat on it, holding the skull in her left hand. This last moment of grief was the most terrible of all. The young women were nearly lying among the stones, worn out with their passion of grief, yet raising themselves every few moments to beat with magnificent gestures on the boards of the coffin. The young men were worn out also, and their voices cracked continually in the wail of the keen.

When everything was ready the sheet was unpinned from the coffin, and it was lowered into its place. Then an old man took a wooden vessel with holy water in it, and a wisp of bracken, and the people crowded round

POWERSCOURT HOUSE GARDENS, ENNISKERRY, COUNTY WICKLOW
(Bord Fáilte)

ROCK OF CASHEL, COUNTY TIPPERARY
(Bord Fáilte)

THE SKELLIGS, COUNTY KERRY
(Bord Fáilte)

NESS COUNTRY PARK, COUNTY DERRY
(Northern Ireland Tourist Board)

him while he splashed the water over them. They seemed eager to get as much of it as possible, more than one old woman crying out with a humorous voice—

> "*Tabhair dham braon eile, a Mhourteen.*"
> ("Give me another drop, Martin.")

When the grave was half filled in, I wandered round towards the north watching two seals that were chasing each other near the surf. I reached the Sandy Head as the light began to fail, and found some of the men I knew best fishing there with a sort of dragnet. It is a tedious process, and I sat for a long time on the sand watching the net being put out, and then drawn in again by eight men working together with a slow rhythmical movement.

As they talked to me and gave me a little poteen and a little bread when they thought I was hungry, I could not help feeling that I was talking with men who were under a judgment of death. I knew that every one of them would be drowned in the sea in a few years and battered naked on the rocks, or would die in his own cottage and be buried with another fearful scene in the graveyard I had come from.

J. M. SYNGE (1871-1909)
The Aran Islands

DUBLIN FUNERAL—I

The fact is, I am not always fortunate enough to arrive at these specially solemn concerts in the frame of mind proper to the occasion. The funeral march in the Eroica symphony, for instance, is extremely impressive to a man susceptible to the funereal emotions. Unluckily, my early training in this respect was not what it should have been. To begin with, I was born with an unreasonably large stock of relations, who have increased and multiplied ever since. My aunts and uncles were legion, and my cousins as the sands of the sea without number. Consequently, even a low death-rate meant, in the course of mere natural decay, a tolerably steady supply of funerals for a by no means affectionate but exceedingly clannish family to go to. Add to this that the town we lived in, being divided in religious opinion, buried its dead in two great ceme-teries, each of which was held by the opposite faction to be the ante-chamber of perdition, and by its own patrons to be the gate of paradise. These two cemeteries lay a mile or two outside the town; and this circum-stance, insignificant as it appears, had a marked effect on the funerals, because a considerable portion of the journey to the tomb, especially when the deceased had lived in the suburbs, was made along country roads. Now the sorest bereavement does not cause men to forget wholly that time is money. Hence, though we used to proceed slowly and sadly enough through the streets or terraces at the early stages of our progress, when we got into the open a change came over the spirit in which the coachmen drove. Encouraging words were addressed to the horses; whips were flicked; a jerk all along the line warned us to slip our arms through the broad elbow-straps of the mourning-coaches, which were balanced on longitudinal poles by enormous and totally inelastic springs; and then the funeral began in earnest. Many a clinking run have I had through that bit of country at the heels of some deceased uncle who had himself many a time enjoyed the same sport. But in the immediate neighbourhood of the cemetery the houses recommenced; and at that point our grief returned upon us with overwhelming force: we were able barely to crawl along to the great iron gates where a demonical black pony was waiting with a sort of primitive gun-carriage and a pall to convey our burden up the avenue to the mortuary chapel, looking as if he might be expected at every step to snort fire, spread a pair of gigantic bat's wings, and vanish, coffin and all, in thunder and brimstone. Such were the scenes which have disqualified me for life from feeling the march in the Eroica symphony as others do. It is that fatal episode where the oboe carries the march into the major key and the whole composition brightens and steps out, so to speak, that ruins me. The moment it begins, I instinctively look beside me for an elbow-strap; and the voices of the orchestra are lost in those of three men, all holding on tight as we jolt and swing madly to and fro, the youngest, a cousin, telling me a romantic tale of an encounter with the Lord Lieutenant's beautiful consort in the hunting-field (an entirely imaginary incident); the eldest, an uncle, giving my father an interminable account of an old verge watch which cost five shillings and kept perfect time for forty years subsequently; and my father speculating as to how far the deceased was cut short by his wife's temper, how far by alcohol, and how far by what might be called natural causes. When the sudden and somewhat unprepared relapse of the movement into the minor key takes place, then I imagine that we have come to the houses again. Finally I wake up completely, and realize that for the last page or two of the score I have not been listening critically to a note of the performance. I do not defend my conduct, present or past: I merely describe it so that my infirmities may be duly taken into account in weighing my critical verdicts. Boyhood takes its fun where it finds it, without looking beneath the surface; and, since society chose to dispose of its dead with a grotesque pageant out of which farcical incidents sprang naturally and inevitably at every turn, it is not to be wondered at that funerals made me laugh when I was a boy nearly as much as they disgust me now that

I am older, and have had glimpses from behind the scenes of the horrors of what a sentimental public likes to hear described as "God's acre."

BERNARD SHAW (1856-1950)
Music in London

DUBLIN FUNERAL—II

Here came the hearse, crawling along like a polished black beetle under the vivid blue sky, through the golden haze. He felt for coins in his pocket, and slid them through his fingers, counting; just enough to pay his cab-fare, tip the hearsemen and the grave-diggers. She'd soon be buried now out of the world's way. Heavy steps came up the stairs, and when he said, Come in, to a knock on the door, two hearsemen entered, clad in the blue-black suits of their kind, their heads furnished with high top-hats, their faces firmly set in seriousness. They were followed by some neighbours who came to help to carry the coffin down.

—We'll miss her, Sean, said one of them; and the kids will too—badly. A great oul' woman gone west —th' light o' heaven to her!

—There y'are, said the leading hearseman, handing an envelope to Sean; that's for you—th' bill.

—The bill? Oh, righto, said Sean carelessly, thrusting the envelope into his pocket. You can start to screw her down now.

—There'll be no screwin' down, nor no effin' funeral here till th' money's paid, said the hearseman harshly. Right, Bill? he added, turning to his mate.

—The bill'll be paid, said Sean, as soon as a cheque I have is cashed—your manager knows about it.

—I'm tellin' you no funeral'll leave here till th'

money's paid, repeated the hearseman fiercely; we want no thricks with cheques.

—Aw, murmured one of the neighbours, you couldn't leave th' poor woman sthranded like that; th' money'll be paid.

—Sthranded or no, said the hearseman, if th' money owed, four pound nineteen shillings, an' sixpence, isn't in them two hands—stretching them out—in ten minutes' time, we sail off, an' you can do what you like with th' stiff; an' them's th' last words!

Sean jumped down the stairs, rushed along the road, darted into a side street, and burst into Murphy's to splutter out the way things were, pleading for God's sake to let him have enough to pay the bill for coffin and hearse.

—Wait, now, said Murphy slowly; for it never does to rush money matthers. Cheque passed awright, couple o' days ago; so we're all serene. Had I known you were in a hurry, I'd a had things ready. I don't know there's as much as you want in the till—th' day's young yet. He stuck a hand into the till, raking forward some coins, and fingering gently a few pound notes. Wait till I see. One, two, three, four—there's four o' them, anyway for a start; an' five, ten, fifteen shillin's in half-crowns—for a funeral you should ha' warned me beforehand—sixteen, seventeen, eighteen—if I hadda known, I'd ha' had everything ready—nineteen; now which'll you have—two thrupenny bits, or six coppers?

—When'll I get the rest due to me? asked Sean, swiftly gathering up the notes and coins as they were handed out to him.

—Aw, sometime at th' end o' the week, when I've taken what's mine, an' when th' till's flush. If I hadda known you were in a hurry, I'd ha' had things ready; but Sean heard only the beginning of the sentence, for he was racing back, breathless, to where his mother patiently lay, waiting to be laid to rest. He handed the money to the hearseman who signed the receipt, the lid of the coffin was screwed down, and then the hearseman gestured to the neighbours to bear the box below.

—The burial docket? he asked of Sean, and carefully put it into a breast pocket. We'll have t'hurry, Bill, he said to his mate, if we're to get to th' cemetery in time to settle th' old lady properly.

Sean heard them hurrying down the stairs, heard the coffin bumping against the corners, and, with a bitter heart stood watching at the top, tense with shame at the scene about the money that had been played before the neighbours. He'd wait till the coffin had been rolled into the hearse, till the neighbours had climbed into their cabs, then he'd run down, and jump quietly into his own. Hearing a half-threatening, half-coaxing mutter of gee-up gee-up, there, he glanced from a window, and saw the funeral moving off at a quick trot without him, while the driver of his own cab, standing on the footboard, was trying to flick the window with his whip to draw Sean's attention to the departure. He rushed hither and thither looking for his cap, and finally tore down bareheaded, opened the door of the cab, and sprang headlong into it.

—Where'r all the others? came from the head of the driver which had suddenly thrust itself in at the window.

T'others? What others?

—What others! testily—why them's acomin' with you.

—There's no others coming with me, and Sean saw a look of dazed dismay spreading over the driver's face.

—Wha'—ne'er a one?

—No, ne'er a one. It doesn't matter.

—It matthers a helluva lot to me! he half shouted. A cab at a funeral with only a single one in it was never known before in th' world's histhory! If the cab carried you there on your own, I'd never be able to lift me head again in th' light o' day!

—Please go on, said Sean, plaintively, or I'll not be in time to take a part in the burial. I'll let you have five shillings for your pains.

—Five shillins, an' a funeral a gala occasion? With a load o' four, now, I'd look complete, an' be in ten shillins; with a full cab o' six, I'd look complete, an' feel complete, an' be fifteen shillins to th' good. Is there ne'er a one o' yous, he shouted to a sniggering group near by, ne'er a one o' yous man enough to lep into a cab beside a neighbour, near suicide with loneliness an' sorra, an' cheer him up with a glowin' pipe an' a warm word from t'other seat opposite? Ara, this is a poor place for a poor soul to set out on its last journey to meet its God.

Sean was about to jump from the cab, and overwhelm the driver with a burst of curses, but, thinking better of it, he sank back on the seat, and sighed. History was repeating itself; something like this had happened at his sister's funeral. What did it matter in the end? He had seen the last of her long ago. It was an empty world, an empty world for him.

SEAN O'CASEY (1880-1964)
Inishfallen, Fare Thee Well

TOMBSTONES

I have often heard the men long ago say that people are more contrary about their dead than about anything else, and I saw an instance of it myself a few years ago when I was sent up to a little graveyard outside Fethard. The job was a trefoil headstone with columns worked out of the solid. There was a base, a sub-base and a square of kerb, a damn nice little job.

Danny Melt was with me and when we arrived at the graveyard the people the job was for were there and I knew by the awkward way they were standing around that we were in for trouble. Most of them had their hands in their pockets and their eyes on the ground. There wasn't a word out of them, they just stood there, kicking up bits of sods. We introduced ourselves. Then the fun started. One quick-tempered devil said: "You are not going to put up any headstone here."

I knew better than to contradict him and waited for the other members to tackle the issue. The whole trouble boiled down to the fact that there were two sides to the family, brothers' sons, one of whom had been sent the money by an uncle in America to put up the headstone, and who had gone ahead with the job without consulting the others.

After an hour's bickering in which they nearly came to blows, I suggested to them that they get the Parish Priest to settle the matter. After a good deal of persuasion they agreed to try it and Danny Melt was sent off to explain to the Parish Priest. They said it would be better to send a strange man as he would not come for a local. After about a quarter of an hour he came along. He was the strangest sight I ever saw. Coming up through the headstones he looked like a large jam-wasp. He had a yellow and black jersey and no hat and his wisps of fair hair were flying in all directions. He had big rough boots on him and his socks were pulled up over the ends of his trousers. He was angry.

"What do ye mean by taking me away from me work? D'ye think I've nothing better to do than come up here and waste time on yer private squabbles? Who paid for the headstone?"

"It was paid for by an uncle in America," said one of them, "he sent the money to put up a headstone to his father and mother, and this crowd don't want it," said he, pointing to the other group, "because they weren't consulted. Me uncle knew that if he sent them the money they'd buy a mean job and blow the rest."

"Go down to the village and have a drink and square your differences," said the priest. "Strong farmers fighting over six foot of soil! There's room for the lot of ye in it, headstone and all."

They took his advice and down we all went and it wasn't one drink we had, but put in the whole evening at it and afterwards Danny and I sauntered back to the farmhouse where we were to be put up for the night. The next morning we were both craw-sick, so the good woman gave us a good tightener of the home-cured bacon and we went down to the village for a drink before starting for the graveyard. We had only the one, as we were anxious to get on with the work after the experience of the day before. We got up to the job and were all set to put in the foundation when we heard a shout of: "Drop that shovel," and over the wall came our friends of yesterday.

"Wasn't it all fixed up?" I asked. "Didn't ye agree that the job was to be put up?"

"We thought it over again," said the quick-tempered fellow, "and we're agin it now."

I lost my temper and called them a two-faced set of scoundrels and I'm sure they would have floored me but for the arrival of the crowd that paid for the job.

Then we had it all over again. Such eloquence! And in the end Danny suggested a drink and down with us all to the village. After a few rounds they softened and said: "What the hell are we fighting about? Sure there's only the loan of us all here." And it was agreed that the headstone could be erected the next day. And it was; all of them saying that there wasn't the like of it in any graveyard around.

SEUMAS MURPHY
Stone Mad

THE SCHOLAR AND HIS CAT

Each of us pursues his trade,
I and Pangur, my comrade;
His whole fancy on the hunt
And mine for learning ardent.

More than fame I love to be
Among my books, and study;
Pangur does not grudge me it,
Content with his own merit.

When—a heavenly time!—we are
In our small room together,
Each of us has his own sport
And asks no greater comfort.

While he sets his round sharp eye
On the wall of my study,
I turn mine—though lost its edge—
On the great wall of knowledge.

Now a mouse sticks in his net
After some mighty onset,
Then into my store I cram
Some difficult, darksome problem.

When a mouse comes to the kill
Pangur exults—a marvel!
I have, when some secret's won,
My hour of exultation.

Though we work for days or years
Neither the other hinders;
Each is competent and hence
Enjoys his skill in silence.

Master of the death of mice,
He keeps in daily practice;
I, too, making dark things clear,
Am of my trade a master.

ANONYMOUS (*c.* 850)
translated from the Irish by
FRANK O'CONNOR

LIADAIN

Gain without gladness
    Is in the bargain I have struck;
One that I loved I wrought to madness.

Mad beyond measure,
    But for God's fear that numbed her heart,
She that would not do his pleasure.

Was it so great,
    My treason? Was I not always kind?
Why should it turn his love to hate?

Liadain,
    That is my name; and Curithir
The man's I loved; you know my sin.

Too few, too fleet,
    The hours I rested at his side;
With him the passionate hours were sweet.

Woods woke
  About us for a lullaby,
And the blue waves in music spoke.

And now too late,
  More than for all my sins I grieve
That I turned his love to hate.

Why should I hide
  That he is still my heart's desire,
More than all the world beside?

A furnace blast
  Of love has melted down my heart;
Without his love it cannot last.

ANONYMOUS (9th cent.)
translated from the Irish by
FRANK O'CONNOR

THE OLD WOMAN OF BEARE

I the old woman of Beare
Once a shining shift would wear;
Now and since my beauty's fall
I have scarce a shift at all.

Plump no more I sigh for these
Bones bare beyond belief;
Ebbtide is all my grief;
I am ebbing like the seas.

It is pay
And not men ye love today,
But when we were young, ah, then,
We gave all our hearts to men.

Men most dear,
Horseman, huntsman, charioteer;
We gave them love with all our will,
But the measure did not fill.

Though today they ask so fine
Small the good they get of it;
They are worn-out in their prime
By the little that they get.

And long since the foaming steed
And the chariot with its speed
And the charioteer went by—
God be with them all, say I.

Luck has left me, I go late
To the dark house where they wait;
When the Son of God thinks fit
Let Him call me home to it.

For my hands as you may see
Are but bony wasted things,
Hands that once would grasp the hand,
Clasp the haughty neck of kings.

O my hands as may be seen
Are so scraggy and so thin
That a boy might start in dread
Feeling them about his head.

Girls are gay
When the year draws on to May,
But for me, so poor am I,
Sun will barely light the day.

Though I care
Nothing now to deck my hair;
I had headgear bright enough
When the kings for love went bare.

'Tis not age that makes my pain
But the eye that sees so plain
How when all it loves decays
Femon's ways are gold again.

Femon, Bregon, sacring stone,
Sacring stone and Ronan's throne,
Storms have sacked so long that now
Tomb and sacring stone are one.

Winter overwhelms the land,
Waves are noisy on the strand,
So I may not hope today
Prince or slave will come my way.

Where are they? Ah, well I know
Old and toiling bones that row
Alma's flood or by its deep
Sleep in cold that slept not so.

Welladay!
Every child outlives its play,
Year on year has worn my flesh
Since my fresh sweet strength went grey.

And O God,
Once again for ill or good
Spring will come and I shall see
Everything but me renewed.

Summer sun and autumn sun,
These I knew and they are gone,
And the winter time of men
Comes and they come not again.

And "Amen!" I cry and "Woe!"
That the boughs are shaken bare,
And that candlelight and feast
Leave me to the dark and prayer.

I who had my day with kings
And drank deep of mead and wine,
Drink whey-water with old hags
Sitting in their rags and pine.

"That my cups be cups of whey!"
"That Thy will be done!" I pray,
But the prayer, O Living God,
Stirs up madness in my blood.

And I cry "Your locks are grey"
At the mantle that I stroke;
Then I grieve and murmur, "Nay,
I am grey and not my cloak."

And of eyes that loved the sun
Age, my grief, has taken one,
And the other too will take
Soon for good proportion's sake.

Floodtide!
Flood or ebb upon the strand?
What the floodtide brings to you,
Ebbtide carries from your hand.

Floodtide
Ebbtide with the hurrying fall,
All have reached me, ebb and flow,
Until now I know them all.

Floodtide!
Not a man answers my call
Nor in darkness seeks my side;
A cold hand lies on them all.

Happy island of the main
To you the tide will come again,
Though to me it comes no more
Over the blank deserted shore.

Seeing it, I can scarcely say
"Here is such a place," today
What was water far and wide
Changes with the ebbing tide.

ANONYMOUS (10th cent.)
translated from the Irish by
FRANK O'CONNOR

THE SWEETNESS OF EARTH

Your voice to me is sweeter
  Than any churchbell's brawling,
Endlessly over the water,
  Cuckoos of the Bann, acalling.

I saw my people broken
  As flax is scutched by women
Over the field at Moyra
  Under the heels of foemen.

But the voice I hear by Derry
   Is not of men triumphant,
I hear their cry in the evening,
   Swans calm and exultant;

I hear the stag's belling
   Over the deep glen ringing;
Earth has no sweeter music,
   My heart pants at his singing.

Christ, Christ, hear me!
   Christ, Christ, of thy meekness!
Christ, Christ, love me!
   Sever me not from thy sweetness.

ANONYMOUS (12th cent.)
translated from the Irish by
FRANK O'CONNOR

WOODLORE

O man that for Fergus of the feasts dost kindle fire,
Whether afloat or ashore burn not the king of woods.

Monarch of Innisfail's forests the woodbine is, whom
   none may hold captive;
No feeble sovereign's effort is it to hug all tough trees in
   his embrace.

The pliant woodbine if thou burn, wailings for misfortune will abound,
Dire extremity at weapons' points or drowning in great
   waves will follow.

Burn not the precious apple-tree of spreading and low-
   sweeping bough;
Tree ever decked in bloom of white against whose fair
   head all men put forth the hand.

The surly blackthorn is a wanderer, a wood that the
    artificer burns not;
Throughout his body, though it be scanty, birds in their
    flocks warble.

The noble willow burn not, a tree sacred to poems;
Within his bloom bees are a-sucking, all love the little
    cage.

The graceful tree with the berries, the wizard's tree, the
    rowan, burn;
But spare the limber tree; burn not the slender hazel.

Dark is the colour of the ash; timber that makes the
    wheels to go;
Rods he furnishes for horsemen's hands, his form turns
    battle into flight.

Tenterhook among woods the spiteful briar is, burn
    him that is so keen and green;
He cuts, he flays the foot, him that would advance he
    forcibly drags backward.

Fiercest heat-giver of all timber is green oak, from him
    none may escape unhurt;
By partiality for him the head is set on aching, and by
    his acrid embers the eye is made sore.

Alder, very battle-witch of all woods, tree that is hottest
    in the fight—
Undoubtedly burn at thy discretion both the alder and
    white-thorn.

Holly, burn it green; holly, burn it dry;
Of all trees whatsoever the critically best is holly.

Elder that hath tough bark, tree that in truth hurts sore;
Him that furnishes horses to the armies from the sidh
    burn so that he be charred.

The birch as well, if he be laid low, promises abiding
    fortune;
Burn up most sure and certainly the stalks that bear the
    constant pods.

Suffer, if it so please thee, the russet aspen to come
    headlong down;
Burn, be it late or early, the tree with the palsied branch.

Patriarch of long-lasting woods is the yew, sacred to
    feasts, as is well-known;
Of him now build ye dark-red vats of goodly size.

Ferdedh, thou faithful one, wouldn't thou but do my
    behest:
To thy soul as to thy body, O man, 'twould work
    advantage.

ANONYMOUS (12th cent.)
translated from the Irish by
STANDISH HAYES O'GRADY (1832-1915)

SHE IS MY DEAR

She is my dear,
  Who makes me weep so many a tear,
And whom I love far more for it
  Than one that only brings good cheer.

She is my own,
  Day out, day in she hears me groan,
And does not care if I am sad,
  And would not grieve if I were gone.

She is my delight,
  She whose dear eyes are ever bright,
Whose hand will never prop my head,
  Who will not turn to me at night.

She is my all
    Who tells me nothing, great or small,
And does not see me when I pass
    And does not hear me when I call.

ANONYMOUS (16th cent.)
translated from the Irish by
FRANK O'CONNOR

I SHALL NOT DIE FOR THEE

O woman, shapely as the swan,
On your account I shall not die;
The men you've slain—a trivial clan—
Were less than I.

I ask me shall I die for these—
For blossom teeth and scarlet lips?
And shall that delicate swan-shape
Bring me eclipse?

Well-shaped the breasts and smooth the skin,
The cheeks are fair, the tresses free—
And yet I shall not suffer death,
God over me!

Those even brows, that hair like gold,
Those languorous tones, that virgin way,
The flowing limbs, the rounded heel
Slight men betray!

Thy spirit keen through radiant mien,
Thy shining throat and smiling eye,
Thy little palm, thy side like foam—
I cannot die!

O woman, shapely as the swan,
In a cunning house hard-reared was I:
O bosom white, O well-shaped palm,
I shall not die!

ANONYMOUS (16th cent.)
translated from the Irish by
PADRAIC COLUM (*b.* 1881)

DEAR DARK HEAD

Put your head, darling, darling, darling,
  Your darling black head my heart above;
Oh, mouth of honey with the thyme for fragrance,
  Who with heart in his breast could deny you love?

Oh, many and many a young girl for me is pining,
  Letting her locks of gold to the cold wind free,
For me, the foremost of our gay young fellows;
  But I'd leave a hundred, pure love, for thee!

Then put your head, darling, darling, darling,
  Your darling black head my heart above;
Oh, mouth of honey, with the thyme for fragrance,
  Who with heart in his breast could deny you love?

ANONYMOUS (16th-17th cent.)
translated from the Irish by
SIR SAMUEL FERGUSON (1810-1886)

RAFTERY THE POET

I am Raftery the poet,
Full of hope and love,
With eyes without light
And calm without torment.

Going west on my journey
By the light of my heart,
Weak and tired
To my road's end.

Look at me now,
My face to the wall,
Playing music
To empty pockets.

ANTHONY RAFTERY (1784-1835)
translated from the Irish by
FRANK O'CONNOR

THE ORPHAN

My father and my mother died and left me young and
    poor,
    But I would never mind bad luck if I had my good
    name;
What sort of comfort in this world or mercy at the end
    Can any hope for, having brought the likes of me to
    shame?

By the mountain's edge he lives who put my wits astray,
    The laughter in his cheek and his gold hair blown
        behind,
He promised he would wed me, said my mouth was
    like a rose—
    I cannot see the path for the tears that make me blind.

Meadow lands and ploughed lands lie in valleys far away
    Where apple trees and sloe bushes grow thickly as at
        home;
If my love say nothing what matter what all say?
    And if your mother slight me, her blood on the
        hearthstone.

ANONYMOUS (19th cent.)
translated from the Irish by
FRANK O'CONNOR

MY GRIEF ON THE SEA

My grief on the sea,
    How the waves of it roll!
For they heave between me
    And the love of my soul!

Abandoned, forsaken,
    To grief and to care,
Will the sea ever waken
    Relief from despair?

My grief and my trouble!
    Would he and I were
In the province of Leinster,
    Or County of Clare!

Were I and my darling—
  O heart-bitter wound!—
On board of the ship
  For America bound.

On a green bed of rushes
  All last night I lay,
And I flung it abroad
  With the heat of the day.

And my love came behind me,
  He came from the South;
His breast to my bosom,
  His mouth to my mouth.

ANONYMOUS (19th cent.)
translated from the Irish by
DOUGLAS HYDE (1860-1946)

RINGLETED YOUTH OF MY LOVE

Ringleted youth of my love,
  With thy locks bound loosely behind thee,
You passed by the road above,
  But you never came in to find me;
Where were the harm for you
  If you came for a little to see me;
Your kiss is a wakening dew
  Were I ever so ill or so dreamy.

If I had golden store
  I would make a nice little boreen
To lead straight up to his door,
  The door of the house of my storeen;

Hoping to God not to miss
   The sound of his footfall in it,
I have waited so long for his kiss
   That for days I have slept not a minute.

I thought, O my love! you were so—
   As the moon is, or sun on a fountain,
And I thought after that you were snow,
   The cold snow on top of the mountain;
And I thought after that you were more
   Like God's lamp shining to find me,
Or the bright star of knowledge before,
   And the star of knowledge behind me.

You promised me high-heeled shoes,
   And satin and silk, my storeen,
And to follow me, never to lose,
   Though the ocean were round us roaring;
Like a bush in a gap in a wall
   I am now left lonely without thee,
And this house, I grow dead of, is all
   That I see around or about me.

ANONYMOUS (19th cent.)
translated from the Irish by
DOUGLAS HYDE (1862-1946)

THE OUTLAW OF LOCH LENE

Oh many a day have I made good ale in the glen,
That came not of stream or malt, like the brewing of
   men;
My bed was the ground; my roof the green wood above,
And the wealth that I sought, one far kind glance from
   my love.

Alas on that night when the horses I drove from the
    field,
That I was not near my angel from terror to shield!
She stretched forth her arms, her mantle she flung to
    the wind,
And she swam o'er Loch Lene her outlawed lover to find.

Oh would that a freezing sleet-winged tempest did
    sweep,
And I and my love were alone far off on the deep;
I'd ask not a ship, nor a bark, nor pinnace to save,
With her arm round my neck I'd fear not the wind nor
    wave!

'Tis down by the lake where the wild tree fringes its
    sides,
The maid of my heart, my fair one of Heaven, resides;
I think as at eve she wanders its mazes along,
The birds go to sleep by the sweet, wild twist of her song.

ANONYMOUS (19th cent.)
translated from the Irish by
JAMES JOSEPH CALLANAN (1795-1829)

PEARL OF THE WHITE BREAST

There's a colleen fair as May,
For a year and for a day,
I've sought by every way
    Her heart to gain.
There's no art of tongue or eye
Fond youths with maidens try
But I've tried with ceaseless sigh,
    Yet tried in vain.

If to France or far-off Spain
She'd cross the watery main,
To see her face again
  The seas I'd brave.
And if 'tis Heaven's decree
That mine she may not be,
May the Son of Mary me
  In mercy save.

O thou blooming milk-white dove,
To whom I've given true love,
Do not ever thus reprove
  My constancy.
There are maidens would be mine,
With wealth in hand and kine,
If my heart would but incline
  To turn from thee.
But a kiss with welcome bland,
And a touch of thy dear hand
Are all that I demand—
  Wouldst thou not spurn;
For if not mine, dear girl,
O snowy-breasted Pearl!
May I never from the fair [1]
  With life return!

ANONYMOUS (18th cent.)
translated from the Irish by
GEORGE PETRIE (1789-1866)

[1] There is a slight mistranslation in Petrie's superb version of the
song. The Irish reads "May I never from Nenagh return."

THE POOR GIRL'S MEDITATION

I am sitting here,
Since the moon rose in the night;
Kindling a fire
And striving to keep it alight;
The folk of the house are lying
In slumber deep;
The cocks will be crowing soon:
The whole of the land is asleep.

May I never leave this world
Until my ill-luck is gone;
Till I have cows and sheep,
And the lad that I love for my own:
I would not think it long,
The night I would lie at his breast,
And the daughters of spite, after that,
Might say the thing they liked best.

Love covers up hate,
If a girl have beauty at all;
On a bed that was narrow and high,
A three-months I lie by the wall:
When I bethought on the lad
That I left on the brow of the hill,
I wept from dark until dark
And my cheeks have the tear-tracks still.

And, O young lad that I love,
I am no mark for your scorn:
All you can say of me
Is undowered I was born:

And if I've no fortune in hand,
Nor cattle nor sheep of my own,
This I can say, O my lad,
I am fitted to lie my lone.

ANONYMOUS
translated from the Irish by
PADRAIC COLUM (*b.* 1881)

THE LAMENT FOR
YELLOW-HAIRED DONOGH

Ye have seen a marvel in this town,
Yellow-haired Donogh and he put down;
In place of his hat a little white cap,
In place of his neckcloth a hempen rope.

I have come all night without my sleep
Like a little lamb in a drove of sheep,
With naked breast and hair awry
Over Yellow-haired Donogh to raise my cry.

I wept the first time by the lake-shore,
At the foot of your gallows I wept once more;
I wept again with an aching head
Among the English and you stretched dead.

If only I had you among your kin,
The Ballinrobe or the Sligomen,
They would break the gallows and cut you down,
And send you safe among your own.

It was not the gallows that was your due
But to go to the barn and thresh the straw,
To guide your plough-team up and down
Until you had made the green hill brown.

Yellow-haired Donogh, I know your case,
I know what brought you to this bad place:
The drink going round and the pipes alight
And the dew on the fields at the end of night.

Mullane that brought misfortune on,
My little brother was no stroller's son
But a handsome boy that was bold and quick
And would draw sweet sounds from a hurling stick.

Mullane, may a son not share your floor,
Nor a daughter ever leave your door;
The table is empty at foot and head,
And Yellow-haired Donogh is lying dead.

His marriage portion is in the house,
And it is not horses nor sheep nor cows,
But tobacco and pipes and candles lit—
Not grudging any his share of it.

ANONYMOUS (19th cent.)
translated from the Irish by
FRANK O'CONNOR

LET US BE MERRY BEFORE WE GO

If sadly thinking, with spirits sinking,
Could, more than drinking, my cares compose
A cure for sorrow from sighs I'd borrow,
And hope tomorrow would end my woes.
But as in wailing there's nought availing,
And Death unfailing will strike the blow,
Then for that reason, and for a season,
Let us be merry before we go.

To joy a stranger, a wayworn ranger,
In every danger my course I've run;
Now hope all ending, and death befriending,
His last aid lending, my cares are done.
No more a rover, or hapless lover,
My griefs are over—my glass runs low;
Then for that reason, and for a season,
Let us be merry before we go.

JOHN PHILPOT CURRAN (1750-1817)

AT THE MID HOUR OF NIGHT

At the mid hour of night, when stars are weeping, I fly
To the lone vale we loved, when life shone warm in
thine eye;
And I think oft, if spirits can steal from the regions
of air
To revisit past scenes of delight, thou wilt come to me
there,
And tell me our love is remembered even in the sky.

Then I sing the wild song it once was rapture to hear,
When our voices commingling breathed like one on the
ear;
And as Echo far off through the vale my sad orison
rolls,
I think O my love! 'tis thy voice from the Kingdom
of Souls
Faintly answering still the notes that once were so dear.

THOMAS MOORE (1779-1852)

THE NAMELESS ONE

Roll forth, my song, like the rushing river
   That sweeps along to the mighty sea;
God will inspire me while I deliver
      My soul to thee!

Tell thou the world, when my bones lie whitening
   Amid the last homes of youth and eld,
That there was once one whose veins ran lightning
      No eye beheld.

Tell how his boyhood was one drear night-hour,
   How shone for him, through his griefs and gloom,
No star of all heaven sends to light our
      Path to the tomb.

Roll on, my song, and to after-ages
   Tell how, disdaining all earth can give,
He would have taught men from wisdom's pages
      The way to live.

And tell how trampled, derided, hated,
   And worn by weakness, disease, and wrong,
He fled for shelter to God, who mated
      His soul with song—

With song which alway, sublime or vapid,
   Flowed like a rill in the morning beam,
Perchance not deep, but intense and rapid—
      A mountain stream.

Tell how this Nameless, condemned for years long
   To herd with demons from hell beneath,
Saw things that made him, with groans and tears, long
      For even death.

Go on to tell how, with genius wasted,
  Betrayed in friendship, befooled in love,
With spirit shipwrecked, and young hopes blasted
        He still, still strove.

Till spent with toil, dreeing death for others,
  And some whose hands should have wrought for him
(If children live not for sires and mothers),
        His mind grew dim.

And he fell far through that pit abysmal,
  The gulf and grave of Maginn and Burns,
And pawned his soul for the Devil's dismal
        Stock of returns.

But yet redeemed it in days of darkness,
  And shapes and signs of the final wrath,
When death, in hideous and ghastly starkness,
        Stood in his path.

And tell how now, amid wreck and sorrow,
  And want, and sickness, and houseless nights,
He bides in calmness the silent morrow
        That no ray lights.

And lives he still, then? Yes! Old and hoary
  At thirtynine, from despair and woe,
He lives, enduring what future story
        Will never know.

Him grant a grave to, ye pitying noble,
  Deep in your bosoms! There let him dwell!
He, too, had tears for all souls in trouble,
        Here and in Hell.
                    J. C. MANGAN (1803-1849)

TWENTY GOLDEN YEARS AGO

Oh, the rain, the weary, dreary rain,
  How it plashes on the window sill!
Night, I guess too, must be on the wane,
  Strass and *gass* around are grown so still.
Here I sit, with coffee in my cup—
  Ah, 'twas rarely I beheld it flow
In the tavern where I loved to sup
  Twenty golden years ago!

Twenty years ago, alas!—but stay—
  On my life, 'tis half-past twelve o'clock!
After all, the hours *do* slip away;
  Come, here goes to burn another block!
For the night, or morn, is wet and cold,
  And my fire is dwindling rather low:
I had fire enough when young and bold
  Twenty golden years ago.

Dear! I don't feel well at all somehow:
  Few in Weimar dream how bad I am;
Floods of tears grow common with me now—
  High-Dutch floods, that Reason cannot dam.
Doctors think I'll neither live nor thrive
  If I mope at home so. I don't know—
Am I living *now*? I *was* alive
  Twenty golden years ago!

Wifeless, friendless, flagonless, alone—
  Not quite bookless though, unless I choose—
Left with naught to do, except to groan,
  Not a soul to woo, except the Muse—

Oh, but this is hard for me to bear,
   Me, who whilom lived so much *en haut*,
Me who broke all hearts like China ware,
   Twenty golden years ago!

Perhaps, 'tis better-time's defacing waves
   Long have quenched the radiance of my brow—
They who curse me nightly from their graves
   Scarce could love me were they living now,
But my loneliness hath darker ills—
   Such dun duns as Conscience, Thought, and Co.,
Awful Gorgons! worse than tailors' bills
   Twenty golden years ago!

Did I paint a fifth of what I feel
   Oh, how plaintive you would ween I was!
But I won't, albeit I have a deal
   More to wail about than Kerner has!
Kerner's tears are wept for withered flowers,
   Mine for withered hopes—my scroll of woe
Dates, alas! from youth's deserted bowers,
   Twenty golden years ago!

Yet, may Deutschland's bardlings flourish long;
   Me, I tweak no beak among them—hawks
Must not pounce on hawks: besides, in song
   I could once beat all of them by chalks.
Though you find me, as I near my goal,
   Sentimentalizing like Rousseau,
Oh! I had a grand Byronian soul
   Twenty golden years ago!

Tick-tick, tick-tick!—not a sound save Time's,
   And the wind-gust as it drives the rain—
Tortured torturer of reluctant rhymes,
   Go to bed and rest thine aching brain!

Sleep! no more the dupe of hopes or schemes;
　　Soon thou sleepest where the thistles blow—
Curious anticlimax to thy dreams
　　Twenty golden years ago!

J. C. MANGAN (1803-1849)

THE SONG OF WANDERING AENGUS

I went out to the hazel wood,
Because a fire was in my head,
And cut and peeled a hazel wand,
And hooked a berry to a thread;
And when white moths were on the wing,
And moth-like stars were flickering out,
I dropped the berry in a stream
And caught a little silver trout.

When I had laid it on the floor
I went to blow the fire aflame,
But something rustled on the floor,
And some one called me by my name:
It had become a glimmering girl
With apple blossom in her hair
Who called me by my name and ran
And faded through the brightening air.

Though I am old with wandering
Through hollow lands and hilly lands,
I will find out where she has gone,
And kiss her lips and take her hands;

And walk among long dappled grass,
And pluck till time and times are done
The silver apples of the moon,
The golden apples of the sun.

W. B. YEATS (1865-1939)
Collected Poems of W. B. Yeats

A PRAYER FOR MY DAUGHTER

Once more the storm is howling, and half hid
Under this cradle-hood and coverlid
My child sleeps on.   There is no obstacle
But Gregory's wood and one bare hill
Whereby the haystack-and-roof-levelling wind,
Bred on the Atlantic, can be stayed;
And for an hour I have walked and prayed
Because of the great gloom that is in my mind.

I have walked and prayed for this young child an hour
And heard the sea-wind scream upon the tower,
And under the arches of the bridge, and scream
In the elms above the flooded stream;
Imagining in excited reverie
That the future years had come,
Dancing to a frenzied drum,
Out of the murderous innocence of the sea.

May she be granted beauty and yet not
Beauty to make a stranger's eye distraught,
Or hers before the looking-glass, for such,
Being made beautiful overmuch,
Consider beauty a sufficient end,
Lose natural kindness and maybe
The heart-revealing intimacy
That chooses right, and never find a friend.

Helen being chosen found life flat and dull
And later had much trouble from a fool,
While that great Queen, that rose out of the spray,
Being fatherless could have her way
Yet chose a bandy-legged smith for man.
It's certain that fine women eat
A crazy salad with their meat
Whereby the Horn of Plenty is undone.

In courtesy I'd have her chiefly learned;
Hearts are not had as a gift but hearts are earned
By those that are not entirely beautiful;
Yet many that have played the fool
For beauty's very self, has charm made wise,
And many a poor man that has roved,
Loved and thought himself beloved,
From a glad kindness cannot turn his eyes.

May she become a flourishing hidden tree
That all her thoughts may like the linnet be,
And have no business but dispensing round
Their magnanimities of sound,
Nor but in merriment begin a chase,
Nor but in merriment a quarrel.
O may she live like some green laurel
Rooted in one dear perpetual place.

My mind, because the minds that I have loved,
The sort of beauty that I have approved,
Prosper but little, has dried up of late,
Yet knows that to be choked with hate
May well be of all evil chances chief.
If there's no hatred in a mind
Assault and battery of the wind
Can never tear the linnet from the leaf.

An intellectual hatred is the worst,
So let her think opinions are accursed.

Have I not seen the loveliest woman born
Out of the mouth of Plenty's horn,
Because of her opinionated mind
Barter that horn and every good
By quiet natures understood
For an old bellows full of angry wind?

Considering that, all hatred driven hence,
The soul recovers radical innocence
And learns at last that it is self-delighting,
Self-appeasing, self-affrighting,
And that its own sweet will is heaven's will;
She can, though every face should scowl
And every windy quarter howl
Or every bellows burst, be happy still.

And may her bridegroom bring her to a house
Where all's accustomed, ceremonious;
For arrogance and hatred are the wares
Peddled in the thoroughfares.
How but in custom and in ceremony
Are innocence and beauty born?
Ceremony's a name for the rich horn,
And custom for the spreading laurel tree.

W. B. YEATS (1865-1939)
Collected Poems of W. B. Yeats

ON BEHALF OF SOME IRISHMEN
NOT FOLLOWERS OF TRADITION

They call us aliens, we are told,
Because our wayward visions stray
From that dim banner they unfold,
The dreams of worn-out yesterday.

The sum of all the past is theirs,
The creeds, the deeds, the fame, the name,
Whose death-created glory flares
And dims the spark of living flame.
They weave the necromancer's spell,
And burst the graves where martyrs slept,
Their ancient story to retell,
Renewing tears the dead have wept.
And they would have us join their dirge,
This worship of an extinct fire
In which they drift beyond the verge
Where races all outworn expire.
The worship of the dead is not
A worship that our hearts allow,
Though every famous shade were wrought
With woven thorns above the brow.
We fling our answer back in scorn:
"We are less children of this clime
Than of some nation yet unborn
Or empire in the womb of time.
We hold the Ireland in the heart
More than the land our eyes have seen,
And love the goal for which we start
More than the tale of what has been."
The generations as they rise
May live the life men lived before,
Still hold the thought once held as wise,
Go in and out by the same door.
We leave the easy peace it brings:
The few we are shall still unite
In fealty to unseen kings
Or unimaginable light.
We would no Irish sign efface,
But yet our lips would gladlier hail
The firstborn of the Coming Race
Than the last splendour of the Gael.

No blazoned banner we unfold—
One charge alone we give to youth,
Against the sceptred myth to hold
The golden heresy of truth.

GEORGE RUSSELL ("A. E.") (1867-1935)
Selected Poems

NON DOLET

Our friends go with us as we go
Down the long path where Beauty wends,
Where all we love foregathers, so
Why should we fear to join our friends?

Who would survive them to outlast
His children; to outwear his fame—
Left when the Triumph has gone past—
To win from Age not Time a name?

Then do not shudder at the knife
That death's indifferent hand drives home;
But with the Strivers leave the Strife,
Nor, after Cæsar, skulk in Rome.

OLIVER ST. JOHN GOGARTY (1878-1957)
Collected Poems

JOHN-JOHN

I dreamt last night of you, John-John,
And thought you called to me;
And when I woke this morning, John,
Yourself I hoped to see;

But I was all alone, John-John,
Though still I heard your call;
I put my boots and bonnet on,
And took my Sunday shawl,
And went full sure to find you, John,
          At Nenagh fair.

The fair was just the same as then,
Five years ago to-day,
When first you left the thimble-men,
And came with me away;
For there again were thimble-men
And shooting galleries,
And card-trick men and maggie-men,
Of all sorts and degrees;
But not a sight of you, John-John,
          Was anywhere.

I turned my face to home again,
And called myself a fool
To think you'd leave the thimble-men
And live again by rule,
To go to mass and keep the fast
And till the little patch;
My wish to have you home was past
Before I raised the latch
And pushed the door and saw you, John,
          Sitting down there.

How cool you came in here, begad,
As if you owned the place!
But rest yourself there now, my lad,
'Tis good to see your face;
My dream is out, and now by it
I think I know my mind:
At six o'clock this house you'll quit,
And leave no grief behind;—

But until six o'clock, John-John,
        My bit you'll share.

The neighbours' shame of me began
When first I brought you in;
To wed and keep a tinker man
They thought a kind of sin;
But now this three years since you've gone
'Tis pity me they do,
And that I'd rather have, John-John,
Than that they'd pity you,
Pity for me and you, John-John
        I could not bear.

Oh, you're my husband right enough,
But what's the good of that?
You know you never were the stuff
To be the cottage cat,
To watch the fire and hear me lock
The door and put out Shep—
But there, now, it is six o'clock
And time for you to step.
God bless and keep you far, John-John
        And that's my prayer.

THOMAS MACDONAGH (1878-1916)
Poems

LAST LINES—1916

Written the night before his execution

The beauty of the world hath made me sad,
This beauty that will pass;
Sometimes my heart hath shaken with great joy
To see a leaping squirrel in a tree,

Or a red ladybird upon a stalk,
Or little rabbits in a field at evening,
Lit by a slanting sun
On some green hill where shadows drifted by,
Some quiet hill where mountainy man hath sown
And soon would reap; near to the gate of Heaven;
Or children with bare feet upon the sands
Of some ebbed sea, or playing on the streets
Of little towns in Connacht,
Things young and happy.
And then my heart hath told me:
These will pass,
Will pass and change, will die and be no more,
Things bright and green, things young and happy;
And I have gone upon my way
Sorrowful.

                            PADRAIC PEARSE (1879-1916)

PADRAIC O'CONAIRE,
GAELIC STORYTELLER

They've paid the last respects in sad tobacco
And silent is this wakehouse in its haze;
They've paid the last respects; and now their whiskey
Flings laughing words on mouths of prayer and praise;
And so young couples huddle by the gables,
O let them grope home through the hedgy night—
Alone I'll mourn my old friend, while the cold dawn
Thins out the holy candlelight.

Respects are paid to one loved by the people;
Ah, was he not—among our mighty poor—
The sudden wealth cast on those pools of darkness,
Those bearing, just, a star's faint signature;

And so he was to me, close friend, near brother,
Dear Padraic of the wide and sea-cold eyes—
So lovable, so courteous and noble,
The very West was in his soft replies.

They'll miss his heavy stick and stride in Wicklow—
His story-talking down Winetavern Street,
Where old men sitting in the wizen daylight
Have kept an edge upon his gentle wit;
While women on the grassy streets of Galway,
Who hearken for his passing—but in vain,
Shall hardly tell his step as shadows vanish
Through archways of forgotten Spain.

Ah, they'll say: Padraic's gone again exploring
But now down glens of brightness, O he'll find
An alehouse overflowing with wise Gaelic
That's braced in vigour by the bardic mind,
And there his thoughts shall find their own fore-fathers—
In minds to whom our heights of race belong,
In crafty men, who ribbed a ship or turned
The secret joinery of song.

Alas, death mars the parchment of his forehead;
And yet, for him, I know, the earth is mild—
The windy fidgets of September grasses
Can never tease a mind that loved the wild;
So drink his peace—this grey juice of the barley
Runs with a light that ever pleased his eye—
While old flames nod and gossip on the hearthstone
And only the young winds cry.

F. R. HIGGINS (1896-1941)
The Gap of Brightness

MEMORY OF BROTHER MICHAEL

It would never be morning, always evening,
Golden sunset, golden age—
When Shakespeare, Marlowe and Jonson were writing
The future of England page by page
A nettle-wild grave was Ireland's stage.

It would never be spring, always autumn
After a harvest always lost—
When Drake was winning seas for England
We sailed in puddles of the past
Pursuing the ghost of Brendan's mast.

The seeds among the dust were less than dust,
Dust we sought, decay,
The young sprout rising smothered in it
Cursed for being in the way—
And the same is true to-day.

Culture is always something that was,
Something pedants can measure:
Skull of bard, thigh of chief,
Depth of dried-up river.
Shall we be thus forever?
Shall we be thus forever?

PATRICK KAVANAGH (b. 1905)
A Soul for Sale

SHE MOVED THROUGH THE FAIR

My young love said to me, "My brothers won't mind,
And my parents won't slight you for your lack of kind."
Then she stepped away from me, and this she did say
"It will not be long, love, till our wedding day."

She stepped away from me and she moved through the
    fair,
And fondly I watched her go here and go there,
Then she went her way homeward with one star awake,
As the swan in the evening moves over the lake.

The people were saying no two were e'er wed
But one had a sorrow that never was said,
And I smiled as she passed with her goods and her gear,
And that was the last that I saw of my dear.

I dreamt it last night that my young love came in,
So softly she entered, her feet made no din;
She came close beside me, and this she did say
"It will not be long, love, till our wedding day."

PADRAIC COLUM (*b.* 1881)

THE MAID OF THE
SWEET BROWN KNOWE

Come all ye lads and lasses and hear my mournful tale,
Ye tender hearts that weep for love to sigh you will not
    fail,

'Tis all about a young man and my song will tell you
     how
He lately came a-courting of the Maid of the Sweet
     Brown Knowe.

Said he, "My pretty fair maid, could you and I agree,
To join our hands in wedlock bands, and married we
     will be;
We'll join our hands in wedlock bands, and you'll have
     my plighted vow,
That I'll do my whole endeavours for the Maid of the
     Sweet Brown Knowe."

Now this young and pretty fickle thing, she knew not
     what to say,
Her eyes did shine like silver bright and merrily did
     play;
Says she, "Young man, your love subdue, I am not ready
     now,
And I'll spend another season at the foot of the Sweet
     Brown Knowe."

"Oh," says he, "My pretty fair maid, now why do you
     say so?
Look down in yonder valley where my verdant crops do
     grow
Look down in yonder valley at my horses and my plough
All at their daily labour for the Maid of the Sweet
     Brown Knowe."

"If they're at their daily labour, kind sir, 'tis not for me,
I've heard of your behaviour, I have, indeed," says she;
"There is an inn where you drop in, I've heard the
     people say,
Where you rap and you call and you pay for all, and go
     home at the dawn of day."

"If I rap and I call and I pay for all, my money is all
  my own,
I'll never spend your fortune, for I hear that you've got
  none.
You thought you had my poor heart broke in talking to
  me now,
But I'll leave you where I found you, at the foot of the
  Sweet Brown Knowe."

ANONYMOUS (18th cent.)

BALLINDERRY

'Tis pretty to be in Ballinderry,
'Tis pretty to be in Aghalee
'Tis prettier to be in bonny Rams Island
Sitting under an ivy tree.
        Och hone! Och hone! Och hone! Och hone!

Oh, that I was in little Rams Island
Oh, that I was with Phelimy Diamond!
He would whistle, and I would sing,
Till we would make the whole Island ring.
        Och hone! Och hone! Och hone! Och hone!

ANONYMOUS

I KNOW WHERE I'M GOING

I know where I'm going,
   I know who's going with me,
I know who I love,
   But the dear knows who I'll marry.

I'll have stockings of silk,
   Shoes of fine green leather,
Combs to buckle my hair
   And a ring for every finger.

Feather beds are soft,
   Painted rooms are bonny;
But I'd leave them all
   To go with my love Johnny.

Some say he's dark,
   I say he's bonny,
He's the flower of them all
   My handsome, coaxing Johnny.

I know where I'm going,
   I know who's going with me,
I know who I love,
   But the dear knows who I'll marry.
                              ANONYMOUS (19th cent.)

JOHNNY, I HARDLY KNEW YE

While going the road to sweet Athy,
            Hurroo! hurroo!
While going the road to sweet Athy,
            Hurroo! hurroo!
While going the road to sweet Athy,
A stick in my hand and a drop in my eye,
A doleful damsel I heard cry:
      "Och, Johnny, I hardly knew ye!
      With drums and guns, and guns and drums
      The enemy nearly slew ye;
      My darling dear, you look so queer,
      Och, Johnny, I hardly knew ye!

"Where are your eyes that looked so mild?
      Hurroo! hurroo!
Where are your eyes that looked so mild?
      Hurroo! hurroo!
Where are your eyes that looked so mild,
When my poor heart you first beguiled?
Why did you run from me and the child?
      Och, Johnny, I hardly knew ye!
             With drums, etc.

"Where are the legs with which you run?
      Hurroo! hurroo!
Where are the legs with which you run?
      Hurroo! hurroo!
Where are the legs with which you run
When you went to carry a gun?
Indeed, your dancing days are done!
      Och, Johnny, I hardly knew ye!
             With drums, etc.

"It grieved my heart to see you sail,
      Hurroo! hurroo!
It grieved my heart to see you sail,
      Hurroo! hurroo!
It grieved my heart to see you sail,
Though from my heart you took leg-bail;
Like a cod you're doubled up head and tail.
      Och, Johnny, I hardly knew ye!
             With drums, etc.

"You haven't an arm and you haven't a leg,
      Hurroo! hurroo!
You haven't an arm and you haven't a leg,
      Hurroo! hurroo!
You haven't an arm and you haven't a leg,
You're an eyeless, noseless, chickenless egg;

You'll have to be put with a bowl to beg:
      Och, Johnny, I hardly knew ye!
                With drums, etc.

"I'm happy for to see you home,
      Hurroo! hurroo!
I'm happy for to see you home,
      Hurroo! hurroo!
I'm happy for to see you home,
All from the island of Sulloon,
So low in flesh, so high in bone;
      Och, Johnny, I hardly knew ye!
                With drums, etc.

"But sad as it is to see you so,
      Hurroo! hurroo!
But sad as it is to see you so,
      Hurroo! hurroo!
But sad as it is to see you so,
And to think of you now as an object of woe,
Your Peggy'll still keep ye on as her beau;
      Och, Johnny, I hardly knew ye!
      With drums and guns, and guns and drums
      The enemy nearly slew ye;
      My darling dear, you look so queer,
      Och, Johnny, I hardly knew ye!"
                ANONYMOUS (18th cent.)

SHULE AROON

I would I were on yonder hill,
'Tis there I'd sit and cry my fill,
And every tear would turn a mill,
Is go d-teidh tu, a mhurnin, slan!

Siubhail, siubhail, siubhail, a ruin!
Siubhail go socair, agus siubhail go ciuin,
Siubhail go d-ti an doras agus eulaigh liom,
Is go d-teidh tu, a mhurnin, slan! [1]

I'll sell my rock, I'll sell my reel,
I'll sell my only spinning-wheel,
To buy for my love a sword of steel,
Is go d-teidh tu, a mhurnin, slan!
    Siubhail etc.

I'll dye my petticoats, I'll dye them red,
And round the world I'll beg my bread,
Until my parents shall wish me dead,
Is go d-teidh tu, a mhurnin, slan!
    Siubhail etc.

I wish, I wish, I wish in vain,
I wish I had my heart again,
And vainly think I'd not complain,
Is go d-teidh tu, a mhurnin, slan!
    Siubhail etc.

But now my love has gone to France,
To try his fortune to advance;
If he e'er come back, 'tis but a chance,
Is go d-teidh tu, a mhurnin, slan!
    Siubhail etc.

ANONYMOUS
(18th cent.)

[1] Come, come, come, O Love!
Quickly come to me, softly move;
Come to the door, and away we'll flee,
And safe for aye may my darling be!

THE BRIDGE OF GLASS

A little while after that they saw an island and a fort in
it. There was a glass bridge before the door. Whenever
they went up on the bridge, they would slide backwards.
They saw a woman coming out of the fort with a pail
in her hand. She lifted a glass plank from the bottom
of the bridge and filled her pail from the spring under
the plank. Then she went into the fort. "Tell the
steward to come and meet Mael Duin," said German.
"Mael Duin, indeed," said the woman as she shut the
door after her, and with that she made the brass fur-
nishings and the bronze net on them shake, and the
noise they made was a soft stringed gentle music and
it made them sleep until the next morning. When
they woke in the morning they saw the same woman
come out of the fort with her pail in her hand and fill
it from the same well that was under the plank. "Ah
tell the steward come and meet Mael Duin," said German.
"A lot I care about Mael Duin," said she as she shut the
door. The same music weakened them and again threw
them into sleep until the following day. They were
three days and three nights in that condition. The
fourth day after that the woman came to them and she
looked beautiful. She had a bright cloak and a gold
circlet in her mane of hair. She had golden hair. She
had two silver sandals on her rosy feet. She had a silver
brooch with bosses of gold in her cloak and a silver
shift on her white body. "Welcome, Mael Duin," said
she and she named each man especially with his own
proper name. "It is a long time since your coming is

known and waited for." After that she brought them into a big house that was near the sea and had their boat brought ashore. After that they saw in the house a bed for Mael Duin alone and a bed for each three of his people. She brought food to them in a basket and it was like cheese or curds. She gave each three a share. Any taste that a man would like he would find on it. She served Mael Duin separately. Then she filled her pail under the same plank and poured out for them. She gave a share to each three. Then she recognized when they had enough. She ceased serving them. "This woman would be a right wife for Mael Duin," said the men of the company. Then she went away from them with her basket and her pail. His company said to Mael Duin, "Will we ask her if she'll sleep with you?" "What harm would it do you to ask her?" he answered. She came next day at the same time to serve them, as she had done before. They said to the girl, "Will you be be friendly with Mael Duin and sleep with him? And why don't you stay here tonight?" She said she didn't know or understand what sin was. After that she went into her house and she came back next morning at the same time to serve them. And when they were filled and merry they said the same words to her. "Tomorrow," she said, "you'll get your answer about that." Then she went to her house, and they slept on their beds. When they woke they were in their boat on a rock and they never again saw the island or the fort or the woman or the place in which they had been.

ANONYMOUS
Voyage of Maelduin
translated from the Irish by
FRANK O'CONNOR

THE FAIRIES—I

The chief of these powers is usually called the "fairies." The country-people have many other names for them which they prefer. But, most often, they feel no need of distinguishing them by particular names. They call them simply "them." In the pronoun they summarize both their nameless power and their immanence. No greater specification is necessary where such powers crowd so closely in upon one's life. The acts and rituals which spring out of this belief are similarly broad in scope. They range from minor doings and turns of speech of daily life to the most hidden practices of rare and deadly black magic.

Perhaps the native name gives the best definition. The whole fairy-cult is under attack these days. The forces of the Church and school are pitted against it. It is nothing more than "pisherogues," the countryman will tell you. The word is usually translated as "superstition," but the English word contains too great a bias for us to use it. The "pisherogues" are much more than ignorant superstitions. In the light of an acquaintance with the practices of the world's peoples, they are easily understandable in much broader terms. They form a symbolic order overlying the values of social life and clothing them in emotional terms in much the same way as do unofficial dogmas and unofficial, non-logical cosmologies among all peoples, not excepting those of our own urban civilization of today. In that, they respond to recognizable sociological and psychological necessities. In its own way, Yankee New England is as fertile of such non-logical beliefs as is rural Ireland. Rural Ireland is different only in that she has preserved an older and more ancient terminology in which to build her particular symbolism. She has her own genius in the matter which expresses the age-long continuities of her culture. . . . . . .

For the good people are not entirely fearsome. I have often heard countrymen, steeped in the old lore, say, "They'll leave you alone if you don't be in their way." One makes a great mistake to think of any holder of popular belief as a person ridden with superstitious fear, unable to make his way through ordinary life. As one countryman told another collector, Lady Gregory, in the days before the war: "If we knew how to be neighbourly with them, they would be neighbourly and friendly with us."

It is a question, then, of giving "them" their due. Where older custom survives, certain precautions must be taken. You are probably all familiar with many of them. Food and water must be left for them at night. Dirty water must not be thrown out at night. For the night is a "lonely time"; "you wouldn't like to be out in it." The fairies are abroad. Were the water thrown out, there is danger that it might dirty them as they pass along a fairy path or make a nocturnal visit. Then they will be angry, and disaster will follow. A hen, a pig, a cow, even a child may sicken and die.

But this anger of theirs, you see, results from direct affront. And that affront lies, really, in improper conduct. In the case of dirty water, it lies directly in improper conduct of the household. Throwing out dirty water is slovenly and bad management. The community condemns it as much as do the fairies who might be wetted.

Consequently, one can begin to see the existence of a projection of values into the world of belief. Dangerous as "they" are, they bring good luck and prosperity as well, if they receive their proper due. Their favour follows proper conduct of the household and good household management in daily life. Thus one finds such statements possible as the following, in which an old fellow of North Clare, an authority on such matters, speaks of "their" nocturnal visits:

"They very often put up at a house in the night. They would come to certain houses, and if they liked the house and it was good and clean and everything swept for them, they would come often to the same house, and that house would be prosperous. If it was dirty and they found no comfort in it they would not stop. They'd go to strong houses like the Careys" (he named a comfortable, neat family of small farmers in the neighbourhood). "You often see a little old woman going along the road and stopping in asking for a bite to eat, and you might give it to her, and she looking to see was it a good house for them to stop in it."

Thus many tales told of the good people point a moral. In this light such a common tale as that of the herdsman's house is readily understandable. The herdsman, as a landless man, is regarded by the small farmers as being a "cut" below themselves; consequently, his untidiness is a byword among them. One version of the story goes, in synopsis, as follows:

"Many families moved into a herdsman's place, but they were all chased out of it. Finally, one family moved in, cleaned up the house, and a 'paving path' around it. A little old woman visits the wife, borrows a cooking-pot and is similarly well treated. In gratitude she explains that the woman of the house and her husband will always prosper and never be molested, because they alone of all the families had cleaned up the place where 'they' walk."

CONRAD ARENSBERG
The Irish Countryman

THE FAIRIES—II

Up the airy mountain,
  Down the rushy glen,
We daren't go a-hunting
  For fear of little men;
Wee folk, good folk,
  Trooping all together;
Green jacket, red cap,
  And white owl's feather!

Down along the rocky shore
  Some make their home—
They live on crispy pancakes
  Of yellow tide-foam;
Some in the reeds
  Of the black mountain lake,
With frogs for their watch-dogs
  All night awake.

High on the hill-top
  The old King sits;
He is now so old and gray
  He's nigh lost his wits.
With a bridge of white mist,
  Columbkill he crosses,
On his stately journeys
  From Slieveleague to Rosses;
Or going up with music
  On cold starry nights,
To sup with the Queen
  Of the gay Northern Lights.

They stole little Bridget
  For seven years long;
When she came down again
  Her friends were all gone.
They took her lightly back,
  Between the night and morrow;
They thought that she was fast asleep,
  But she was dead with sorrow.
They have kept her ever since
  Deep within the lakes,
On a bed of flag-leaves,
  Watching till she wakes.

By the craggy hill-side
  Through the mosses bare,
They have planted thorn-trees
  For pleasure here and there.
Is any man so daring
  As dig one up in spite,
He shall find their sharpest thorns
  In his bed at night.

Up the airy mountain,
  Down the rushy glen,
We daren't go a-hunting
  For fear of little men;
Wee folk, good folk,
  Trooping all together;
Green jacket, red cap,
  And white owl's feather!

WILLIAM ALLINGHAM (1824-1889)

THE STOLEN CHILD

Where dips the rocky highland
Of Sleuth Wood in the lake,
There lies a leafy island
Where flapping herons wake
The drowsy water-rats;
There we've hid our faery vats,
Full of berries
And of reddest stolen cherries.
Come away, O human child!
To the waters and the wild
With a faery, hand in hand,
For the world's more full of weeping than you can understand.

Where the wave of moonlight glosses
The dim grey sands with light,
Far off by furthest Rosses,
We foot it all the night,
Weaving olden dances,
Mingling hands and mingling glances
Till the moon has taken flight;
To and fro we leap
And chase the frothy bubbles,
While the world is full of troubles
And is anxious in its sleep.
Come away, O human child!
To the waters and the wild
With a faery, hand in hand,
For the world's more full of weeping than you can understand.

Where the wandering water gushes
From the hills above Glen-Car,
In pools among the rushes
That scarce could bathe a star,

We seek for slumbering trout
And whispering in their ears
Give them unquiet dreams;
Leaning softly out
From ferns that drop their tears
Over the young streams.
Come away, O human child!
To the waters and the wild
With a faery, hand in hand,
For the world's more full of weeping than you can understand.

Away with us he's going,
The solemn-eyed;
He'll hear no more the lowing
Of the calves on the warm hillside,
Or the kettle on the hob
Sing peace into his breast,
Or see the brown mice bob
Round and round the oatmeal-chest.
For he comes, the human child,
To the waters and the wild
With a faery, hand in hand,
From a world more full of weeping than he can understand.

W. B. YEATS (1865-1939)
Collected Poems of W. B. Yeats

TO THE LEANAN SIDHE

Where is thy lovely perilous abode?
    In what strange phantom-land
Glimmer the fairy turrets whereto rode
    The ill-starred poet band?

Say, in the Isle of Youth hast thou thy home,
  The sweetest singer there,
Stealing on winged steed across the foam
  Thorough the moonlit air?

Or, where the mists of bluebell float beneath
  The red stems of the pine,
And sunbeams strike thro' shadow, dost thou breathe
  The word that makes him thine?

Or by the gloomy peaks of Errigal,
  Haunted by storm and cloud,
Wing past, and to thy lover there let fall
  His singing-robe and shroud?

Or is thy palace entered thro' some cliff
  When radiant tides are full,
And round thy lover's wandering, starlit skiff,
  Coil in luxurious lull?

And would he, entering on the brimming flood,
  See caverns vast in height,
And diamond columns, crowned with leaf and bud,
  Glow in long lanes of light.

And there, the pearl of that great glittering shell
  Trembling, behold thee lone,
Now weaving in slow dance an awful spell,
  Now still upon thy throne?

Thy beauty! ah, the eyes that pierce him thro'
  Then melt as in a dream;
The voice that sings the mysteries of the blue
  And all that Be and seem!

Thy lovely motions answering to the rhyme
  That ancient Nature sings,
That keeps the stars in cadence for all time,
  And echoes thro' all things!

Whether he sees thee thus, or in his dreams,
  Thy light makes all lights dim;
An aching solitude from henceforth seems
  The world of men to him.

Thy luring song, above the sensuous roar,
  He follows with delight,
Shutting behind him Life's last gloomy door,
  And fades into the Night.

THOMAS BOYD (1867-1927)

THE WARRIOR

Patrick, you chatter too loud
  And lift your crozier too high;
Your stick would be kindling soon
  If my son Osgar stood by.

If my son Osgar and God
  Wrestled it out on the hill,
And I saw Osgar go down
  I would say your God fought well.

But how could the Lord you praise
  Or his mild priests singing a tune
Be better than Fionn the swordsman,
  Generous, faultless Fionn?

GLENIFF HORSESHOE, COUNTY SLIGO
(Bord Fáilte)

SPERRIN MOUNTAINS, COUNTY TYRONE
(Northern Ireland Tourist Board)

DUN AENGUS, INISHMORE, ARAN ISLANDS
(Bord Fáilte)

LOUGH KEY FOREST PARK, COUNTY ROSCOMMON
(Bord Fáilte)

By the strength of their hands alone
  The Fenians' battles were fought,
With never a spoken lie,
  Never a lie in thought.

There never sat priest in church,
  A tuneful psalm to raise
Better-spoken than they,
  Scarred by a hundred frays.

Whatever your monks have called
  The law of the King of Grace,
That was the Fenians' law;
  His home is their dwelling place.

If happier house than Heaven
  There be, above or below,
'Tis there my master Fionn
  And his fighting men will go.

Ah, priest, if you saw the Fenians,
  Filling the strand beneath,
Or gathered in streamy Naas,
  You would praise them with every breath.

Patrick, ask of your God
  Does he remember their might,
Or has he seen east or west
  Better men in a fight?

Or known in his own land,
  Above the stars and the moon,
For wisdom, courage, and strength
  A man the like of Fionn?

ANONYMOUS (14th cent.?)
translated from the Irish by
FRANK O'CONNOR

GENEROSITY

If only the brown leaf were gold
The tree sheds when the year is old!
Silver, the foam upon the bay,
Fionn would give it all away.

ANONYMOUS (12th cent.)
translated from the Irish by
FRANK O'CONNOR

GAELIC COMES TO ENGLAND

On the arrival of the bishop, the king appointed him his
episcopal see in the island of Lindisfarne, as he desired.
Which place, as the tide ebbs and flows, is twice a day
enclosed by the waves of the sea like an island; and again,
twice, when the beach is left dry, becomes contiguous
with the land. The king also humbly and willingly in
all things giving ear to his admonitions, industriously
applied himself to build up and extend the Church of
Christ in his kingdom; wherein, when the bishop, who
was not perfectly skilled in the English tongue, preached
the Gospel, it was a fair sight to see the king himself
interpreting the Word of God to his ealdormen and
thegns, for he had thoroughly learned the language of
the Scots during his long banishment. . . .

It is said, that when King Oswald had asked a bishop
of the Scots to administer the Word of faith to him and
his nation, there was first sent to him another man of
more harsh disposition, who, after preaching for some
time to the English and meeting with no success, not
being gladly heard by the people, returned home, and

in an assembly of the elders reported, that he had not
been able to do any good by his teaching to the nation
to whom he had been sent, because they were intractable
men, and of a stubborn and barbarous disposition.

BEDE (673-735)
translated (1907) from the Latin by
A. M. SELLAR

IRELAND v. ROME—I

To go to Rome—
  Is little profit, endless pain;
The Master that you seek in Rome,
  You find at home, or seek in vain.

ANONYMOUS (9th cent.)
translated from the Irish by
FRANK O'CONNOR

IRELAND v. ROME—II

WHITBY 664

KING Oswy first made an opening speech, in which he
said that it behoved those who served one God to observe
one rule of life; and as they all expected the same kingdom in heaven, so they ought not to differ in the celebration of the heavenly mysteries; but rather to inquire
which was the truer tradition, that it might be followed
by all in common; he then commanded his bishop,
Colman, first to declare what the custom was which he
observed, and whence it derived its origin. Then Colman
said, "The Easter which I keep, I received from my elders,
who sent me hither as bishop; all our forefathers, men

beloved of God, are known to have celebrated it after the same manner; and that it may not seem to any contemptible and worthy to be rejected, it is the same which the blessed John the Evangelist, the disciple specially beloved of our Lord, with all the churches over which he presided, is recorded to have celebrated." When he had said thus much, and more to the like effect, the king commanded Agilbert to make known the manner of his observance and to show whence it was derived, and on what authority he followed it. Agilbert answered, "I beseech you, let my disciple, the priest Wilfrid, speak in my stead; because we both concur with the other followers of the ecclesiastical tradition that are here present, and he can better and more clearly explain our opinion in the English language, than I can by an interpreter."

Then Wilfrid, being ordered by the king to speak, began thus:—"The Easter which we keep, we saw celebrated by all at Rome, where the blessed Apostles, Peter and Paul, lived, taught, suffered, and were buried; we saw the same done by all in Italy and in Gaul, when we travelled through those countries for the purpose of study and prayer. We found it observed in Africa, Asia, Egypt, Greece, and all the world, wherever the Church of Christ is spread abroad, among divers nations and tongues, at one and the same time; save only among these and their accomplices in obstinacy, I mean the Picts and the Britons, who foolishly, in these two remote islands of the ocean, and only in part even of them, strive to oppose all the rest of the world." When he had so said, Colman answered, "It is strange that you choose to call our efforts foolish, wherein we follow the example of so great an apostle, who was thought worthy to lean on our Lord's bosom, when all the world knows him to have lived most wisely." Wilfrid replied, "Far be it from us to charge John with folly, for he literally observed the precepts of the Mosaic Law, whilst the Church was still

Jewish in many points, and the Apostles, lest they should give cause of offence to the Jews who were among the Gentiles, were not able at once to cast off all the observances of the Law which had been instituted by God, in the same way as it is necessary that all who come to the faith should forsake the idols which were invented by devils. For this reason it was, that Paul circumcised Timothy, that he offered sacrifice in the temple, that he shaved his head with Aquila and Priscilla at Corinth; for no other advantage than to avoid giving offence to the Jews. Hence it was, that James said to the same Paul, "Thou seest, brother, how many thousands of Jews there are which believe; and they are all zealous of the Law." And yet, at this time, when the light of the Gospel is spreading throughout the world, it is needless, nay, it is not lawful, for the faithful either to be circumcised, or to offer up to God sacrifices of flesh. So John, according to the custom of the Law, began the celebration of the feast of Easter, on the fourteenth day of the first month, in the evening, not regarding whether the same happened on a Saturday, or any other week-day. But when Peter preached at Rome, being mindful that our Lord arose from the dead, and gave to the world the hope of resurrection, on the first day of the week, he perceived that Easter ought to be kept after this manner: he always awaited the rising of the moon on the fourteenth day of the first month in the evening, according to the custom and precepts of the Law, even as John did. And when that came, if the Lord's day, then called the first day of the week, was the next day, he began that very evening to celebrate Easter, as we all do at the present time. But if the Lord's day did not fall the next morning after the fourteenth moon, but on the sixteenth, or the seventeenth, or any other moon till the twenty-first, he waited for that, and on the Saturday before, in the evening, began to observe the holy solemnity of Easter. Thus it came to pass, that Easter Sunday was only kept from the fifteenth moon to the twenty-first. Nor does this evangelical and apostolic tradition abolish the Law, but rather fulfil it; the command being to keep the passover from the fourteenth moon of the first month in the evening to the twenty-first moon of the same month in the evening; which observance all the successors of the blessed John in Asia, since his death, and all the Church throughout the world, have since followed; and that this is the true Easter, and the only one to be celebrated by the faithful, was not newly decreed by the council of Nicaea, but only confirmed afresh; as the history of the Church informs us.

"Thus it is plain, that you, Colman, neither follow the example of John, as you imagine, nor that of Peter, whose tradition you oppose with full knowledge, and that you neither agree with the Law nor the Gospel in the keeping of your Easter. For John, keeping the Paschal time according to the decree of the Mosaic Law, had no regard to the first day of the week, which you do not practise, seeing that you celebrate Easter only on the first day after the Sabbath. Peter celebrated Easter Sunday between the fifteenth and the twenty-first moon which you do not practise, seeing that you observe Easter Sunday from the fourteenth to the twentieth moon; so that you often begin Easter on the thirteenth moon in the evening, whereof neither the Law made any mention, nor did our Lord, the Author and Giver of the Gospel, on that day either eat the old passover in the evening, or deliver the Sacraments of the New Testament, to be celebrated by the Church, in memory of His Passion, but on the fourteenth. Besides, in your celebration of Easter, you utterly exclude the twenty-first moon, which the Law ordered to be specially observed. Thus, as I have said before, you agree neither with John nor Peter, nor with the Law, nor the Gospel, in the celebration of the greatest festival."

To this Colman rejoined: "Did the holy Anatolius,

much commended in the history of the Church, judge contrary to the Law and the Gospel, when he wrote, that Easter was to be celebrated from the fourteenth to the twentieth moon? Is it to be believed that our most reverend Father Columba and his successors, men beloved by God, who kept Easter after the same manner, judged or acted contrary to the Divine writings? Whereas there were many among them, whose sanctity was attested by heavenly signs and miracles which they wrought; whom I, for my part, doubt not to be saints, and whose life, customs, and discipline I never cease to follow."

"It is evident," said Wilfrid, "that Anatolius was a most holy, learned, and commendable man; but what have you to do with him, since you do not observe his decrees? For he undoubtedly, followed the rule of truth in his Easter, appointed a cycle of nineteen years, which either you are ignorant of, or if you know it, though it is kept by the whole Church of Christ, yet you despise it as a thing of naught. He so computed the fourteenth moon in our Lord's Paschal Feast, that according to the custom of the Egyptians, he acknowledged it to be the fifteenth moon on that same day in the evening; so in like manner he assigned the twentieth to Easter Sunday, as believing that to be the twenty-first moon, when the sun had set. That you are ignorant of the rule of this distinction is proved by this, that you sometimes manifestly keep Easter before the full moon, that is, on the thirteenth day. Concerning your Father Columba and his followers, whose sanctity you say you imitate, and whose rule and precepts confirmed by signs from Heaven you say that you follow, I might answer, then when many, in the day of judgment, shall say to our Lord, that in His name they have prophesied, and have cast out devils, and done many wonderful works, our Lord will reply, that He never knew them. But far be it from me to speak thus of your fathers, for it is much more just to believe good than evil of those whom we know not. Wherefore I do not deny those also to have been God's servants, and beloved of God, who with rude simplicity, but pious intentions, have themselves loved Him. Nor do I think that such observance of Easter did them much harm, as long as none come to show them a more perfect rule to follow; for assuredly I believe that, if any teacher, reckoning after the Catholic manner, had come among them, they would have as readily followed his admonitions, as they are known to have kept those commandments of God, which they had learned and knew.

"But as for you and your companions, you certainly sin, if, having heard the decrees of the Apostolic see, nay, of the universal Church, confirmed, as they are, by Holy Scripture, you scorn to follow them; for, though your fathers were holy, do you think that those few men, in a corner of the remotest island, are to be preferred before the universal Church of Christ throughout the world? And if that Columba of yours, (and, I may say, ours also, if he was Christ's servant) was a holy man and powerful in miracles, yet could he be preferred before the most blessed chief of the Apostles, to whom our Lord said, 'Thou art Peter, and upon this rock I will build my Church, and the gates of hell shall not prevail against it, and I will give unto thee the keys of the kingdom of Heaven?'"

When Wilfrid had ended thus, the king said, "Is it true, Colman, that these words were spoken to Peter by our Lord?" He answered, "It is true, O king!" Then said he, "Can you show any such power given to your Columba?" Colman answered, "None." Then again the king asked, "Do you both agree in this, without any controversy, that these words were said above all to Peter, and that the keys of the kingdom of Heaven were given to him by our Lord?" They both answered, "Yes." Then the king concluded, "And I also say unto you, that he is the door-keeper, and I will not gainsay him, but I desire, as far as I know and am able, in all things to obey his laws, lest haply when I come to the gates of the kingdom of Heaven, there should be none to open them, he being my adversary who is proved to have the keys."

BEDE (673-735)
translated (1907) from the Latin by
A. M. SELLAR

MO CHUA AND HIS THREE TREASURES

Mo Chua and Colm Cille were contemporaries, and when Mo Chua . . . was in a hermitage in the wilderness he had no wordly possession but a cock, a mouse and a fly. The cock used to keep midnight matins for him. The mouse would only let him sleep five hours in a day and night, and whenever he wanted to sleep longer, being exhausted from overmuch cross-vigil and prostration, the mouse would lick his ear and wake him. The fly's task was to walk along each line he read in his psalter, and when he was tired from singing psalms the fly would halt on the line he had left till he returned for further psalmody.

Soon afterwards the three treasures died, and Mo Chua wrote a letter to Colm Cille when he was in Scotland, and bemoaned the loss of his flock.

Colm Cille wrote to him and said:—

"Brother," said he, "you need scarcely be surprised at the death of the flock you have lost, for there is no misfortune except where wealth is."

I think by this joking of real saints that they were not much interested in worldly goods, unlike most of the people of our time.

GEOFFREY KEATING (1570-1646)
History of Ireland
translated from the Irish by
FRANK O'CONNOR

IRISH MISSIONARIES

SEVENTH CENTURY

The place which they governed shows how frugal and temperate he and his predecessors were, for there were very few houses besides the church found at their departure; indeed, no more than were barely sufficient to make civilized life possible; they had also no money, but only cattle; for if they received any money from rich persons, they immediately gave it to the poor; there being no need to gather money, or provide houses for the entertainment of the great men of the world; for such never resorted to the church, except to pray and hear the Word of God. The king himself, when occasion required, came only with five or six servants, and having performed his devotions in the church, departed. But if they happened to take a repast there, they were satisfied with the plain, daily food of the brethren, and required no more. For the whole care of those teachers was to serve God, not the world—to feed the soul, and not the belly.

For this reason the religious habit was at that time held in great veneration; so that wheresoever any clerk or monk went, he was joyfully received by all men, as God's servant; and even if they chanced to meet him upon the way, they ran to him, and with bowed head, were glad to be signed with the cross by his hand, or blessed by his lips. Great attention was also paid to their exhortations; and on Sundays they flocked eagerly to the church, or the monasteries, not to feed their bodies, but to hear the Word of God; and if any priest happened to come into a village, the inhabitants came together and asked of him the Word of life; for the priests and clerks went to the villages for no other reason than to preach, baptize, visit the sick, and, in a word, to take care of

their souls; and they were so purified from all taint of
avarice, that none of them received lands and possessions
for building monasteries, unless they were compelled to
do so by the temporal authorities; which custom was
for some time after universally observed in the churches
of the Northumbrians.

BEDE (673-735)
translated (1907) from the Latin by
A. M. SELLAR

THE PRIEST

Grant me, sweet Christ, the grace to find—
  Son of the Living God!—
A small hut in a lonesome spot
  To make it my abode.

A little pool but very clear
  To stand beside the place,
Where all men's sins are washed away
  By sanctifying grace.

A pleasant woodland all about,
  To shield it from the wind,
And make a home for singing birds
  Before it and behind.

A southern aspect for the heat,
  A stream along its foot,
A smooth green lawn with rich top soil
  Propitious to all fruit.

My choice of men to live with me
  And pray to God as well;
Quiet men of humble mind—
  Their number I shall tell.

Four files of three or three of four;
   To give the psalter forth;
Six to pray by the south church wall
   And six along the north.

Two by two my dozen friends—
   To tell the number right—
Praying with me to move the King
   Who gives the sun its light.

A lovely church, fit home for God,
   Bedecked with linen fine,
Where over the white Gospel page
   The Gospel candles shine.

A little house where all may dwell
   And body's care be sought
Where none shows lust or arrogance,
   None thinks an evil thought.

And all I ask of housekeeping
   I get and pay no fees;
Leeks from the garden, poultry, game,
   Salmon and trout and bees.

My share of clothing and of food,
   From the King of fairest face,
And I to sit at times alone
   And pray in every place.

ANONYMOUS (9th cent.)
translated from the Irish by
FRANK O'CONNOR

THOUGHTS

How my thoughts betray me!
　How they flit and stray!
Well they may appal me
　On the Judgment Day.

Through the psalms they wander
　Roads that are not right,
Mitching, noising, squabbling
　In God's very sight.

Through august assemblies,
　Groups of gamesome girls,
Then through woods, through cities,
　Like the wind in whirls.

First down lordly highways
　Boisterously they stride,
Then through desert byways
　Secretly they glide.

In their whims, unferried,
　Oversea they fly,
Or in one swift motion
　Spin from earth to sky.

Lost to recollection,
　Near and far they roam;
From some monstrous errand
　Slyly they slink home.

Who has ropes to bind them?
　Where are fetters fit?
Those who lack all patience,
　Cannot stand or sit.

No sharp sword appals them,
  Nor any lifted whip;
Like an eel's tail, greasy,
  From my grasp they slip.

Lock nor frowning dungeon,
  Nor sentinelled frontier,
Town-wall, sea, nor fortress
  Halts their mad career.

Christ the chaste, the cherished,
  Searcher of the soul,
Grant the seven-fold spirit
  Keep them in control.

Rule my thoughts and feelings,
  You who brook no ill;
Make me yours forever,
  Bend me to your will.

Grant me, Christ, to reach you;
  With you let me be
Who are not frail nor fickle
  Nor feeble-willed like me.

ANONYMOUS (10th cent.)
translated from the Irish by
FRANK O'CONNOR

AN OLD FLAME

The Monk to his Psalter

How good to hear your voice again,
  Old love, no longer young but true
As when in Ulster we grew up,
  And slept together, I and you.

Though when at first we went to bed,
  Sweet girl whose wisdom comes from Heaven,
I was a boy with no bad thoughts,
  A modest lad, and barely seven.

We wandered Ireland over then,
  Our souls and bodies free of shame;
My goose-face lit with love of you,
  An idiot with no fear of blame.

You always had the good advice
  Wherever we went wandering;
Better I thought your pointed wit
  Than idle converse with some king.

You slept with four men after that,
  Yet did not sin in leaving me,
And now a virgin you come back—
  I see the thing that all men see.

For safe within my arms again,
  Weary with wandering many ways,
The face I love is shadowed now,
  Though lust attends not its last days.

Faultless, my old love seeks me out!
  I greet you with a joyous heart;
You will not let me drown in Hell;
  With you I'll learn that holy art.

Since all the world your praises sings,
  And all men praise your wanderings past,
If I can keep your counsel sweet
  I shall come safe to God at last.

You are a token and a sign
   To men of what all men must heed;
Each day you make your lovers know
   God's praise is all the work they need.

So may He grant me, by your grace,
   A quiet end, an easy mind,
And light my pathway with His face
   When the dead flesh is left behind.

ANONYMOUS (10th cent.)
translated from the Irish by
FRANK O'CONNOR

THE PENAL LAWS

There are, however, grievous faults on both sides: and
as there are a set of men, who, not content with re-
taliating upon Protestants, deny the persecuting spirit
of the Catholics, I would ask them what they think of
the following code, drawn up by the French Catholics,
against the French Protestants, and carried into execution for one hundred years, and as late as the year 1765,
and not repealed till 1782.

"Any Protestant clergyman remaining in France
three days, without coming to the Catholic worship, to
be punished with death. If a Protestant sends his son
to a Protestant schoolmaster for education, he is to
forfeit 250 livres a month, and the schoolmaster who
receives him, 50 livres. If they send their children to
any seminary abroad, they were to forfeit 2000 livres,
and the child so sent became incapable of possessing
property in France. To celebrate Protestant worship,
exposed the clergyman to a fine of 2800 livres. The fine
for a Protestant hearing it, was 1300 livres. If any
Protestant denied the authority of the Pope in France,

his goods were seized for the first offence, and he was hanged for the second. If any Common Prayer-book, or book of Protestant worship, be found in the possession of any Protestant, he shall forfeit 20 livres for the first offence, 40 livres for the second, and shall be imprisoned at pleasure for the third. Any person bringing from beyond sea, or selling, any Protestant book of worship, to forfeit 100 livres. Any magistrate may search Protestant houses for such articles. Any person, required by a magistrate to take an oath against the Protestant religion, and refusing, to be committed to prison, and if he afterwards refuse again, to suffer forfeiture of goods. Any person sending money over sea to the support of a Protestant seminary, to forfeit his goods, and be imprisoned at the king's pleasure. Any person going over sea, for Protestant education, to forfeit goods and lands for life. The vessel to be forfeited which conveyed any Protestant woman or child over sea, without the king's licence. Any person converting another to the Protestant religion, to be put to death. Death to any Protestant priest to come into France; death to the person who receives him; forfeiture of goods and imprisonment to send money for the relief of any Protestant clergyman: large rewards for discovering a Protestant parson. Every Protestant shall cause his child, within one month after birth, to be baptized by a Catholic priest, under a penalty of 2000 livres. Protestants were fined 4000 livres a month for being absent from Catholic worship, were disabled from holding offices and employments, from keeping arms in their houses, from maintaining suits at law, from being guardians, from practising in law or physic, and from holding offices, civil or military. They were forbidden (bravo, Louis XIV!) to travel more than five miles from home without licence, under pain of forfeiting all their goods, and they might not come to court under pain of 2000 livres. A married Protestant woman, when convicted of being of that persuasion, was liable to forfeit two-thirds of her jointure; she could not be executrix to her husband, nor have any part of his goods; and during her marriage she might be kept in prison unless her husband redeemed her at the rate of 200 livres a month, or the third part of his lands. Protestants, convicted of being such, were, within three months after their conviction, either to submit, and renounce their religion, or, if required by four magistrates, to abjure the realm, and, if they did not depart, or departing returned, were to suffer death. All Protestants were required, under the most tremendous penalties, to swear that they considered the Pope as the head of the Church. If they refused to take this oath, which might be tendered at pleasure by any two magistrates, they could not act as advocates, procureurs, or notaries public. Any Protestant taking any office, civil or military, was compelled to abjure the Protestant religion; to declare his belief in the doctrine of transubstantiation, and to take the Roman Catholic sacrament within six months, under the penalty of 10,000 livres. Any person professing the Protestant religion, and educated in the same, was required, in six months after the age of sixteen, to declare the Pope to be the head of the Church; to declare his belief in transubstantiation, and that the invocation of saints was according to the doctrine of the Christian religion; failing this, he could not hold, possess, or inherit landed property; his lands were given to the nearest Catholic relation. Many taxes were doubled upon Protestants. Protestants keeping schools were imprisoned for life, and all Protestants were forbidden to come within ten miles of Paris or Versailles. If any Protestant had a horse worth more than 100 livres, any Catholic magistrate might take it away, and search the house of the said Protestant for arms."

Is not this a monstrous code of persecution? Is it any wonder, after reading such a spirit of tyranny as is here exhibited, that the tendencies of the Catholic religion should be suspected, and that the cry of No Popery should be a rallying sign to every Protestant nation in Europe? . . . Forgive, gentle reader, and gentle elector, the trifling deception I have practised upon you. This code is not a code made by French Catholics against French Protestants, but by English and Irish Protestants against English and Irish Catholics: I have given it to you, for the most part, as it is set forth in Burn's "Justice" of 1780: it was acted upon in the beginning of the last king's reign, and it was notorious through the whole of Europe, as the most cruel and atrocious system of persecution ever instituted by one religious persuasion against another. Of this code, Mr. Burke says, that "it is a truly barbarous system; where all the arts are an outrage on the laws of humanity and the rights of nature; it is a system of elaborate contrivance, as well fitted for the oppression, imprisonment and degradation of a people, and the debasement of human nature itself, as ever proceeded from the perverted ingenuity of man."

SYDNEY SMITH (1771-1845)
*Selections from the writings of
the Rev. Sydney Smith*

AND MORE LAW

Perceval, at whom the following is aimed, was author of the bill to prevent medicines reaching France during a plague.

I cannot describe the horror and disgust which I felt at hearing Mr. Perceval call upon the then ministry for measures of vigour in Ireland. If I lived at Hampstead upon stewed meats and claret; if I walked to church every Sunday before eleven young gentlemen, with their faces washed, and their hair pleasingly combed; if the Almighty had blessed me with every earthly

comfort—how awfully would I pause before I sent forth
the flame and the sword over the cabins of the poor,
brave, generous, open-hearted peasants of Ireland! How
easy it is to shed human blood—how easy it is to persuade
ourselves that it is our duty to do so—and that the
decision has cost us a severe struggle—how much, in all
ages, have wounds and shrieks and tears been the cheap
vulgar resources of the rulers of mankind—how difficult
and how noble it is to govern in kindness, and to found
an empire upon the everlasting basis of justice and
affection!—But what do men call vigour? To let loose
hussars and to bring up artillery, to govern with lighted
matches, and to cut, and push, and prime—I call this,
not vigour, but the *sloth of cruelty and ignorance*. The
vigour I love consists in finding out wherein subjects are
aggrieved, in relieving them, in studying the temper
and genius of a people, in consulting their prejudices,
in selecting proper persons to lead and manage them,
in the laborious, watchful, and difficult task of increasing
public happiness by allaying each particular discontent.
In this way Hoche pacified La Vendée—and in this way
only will Ireland ever be subdued. But this, in the eyes
of Mr. Perceval, is imbecility and meanness; houses are
not broken up—women are not insulted—the people
seem all to be happy; they are not rode over by horses,
and cut by whips. Do you call this vigour?—Is this
government? . . .

What is it possible to say to such a man as the gentleman of Hampstead, who really believes it feasible to
convert the four million Irish Catholics to the Protestant
religion, and considers this as the best remedy for the
disturbed state of Ireland? It is not possible to answer
such a man with arguments; we must come out against
him with beads, and a cowl, and push him into a hermitage. It is really such trash, that it is an abuse of the
privilege of reasoning to reply to it. Such a project is
well worthy the statesman who would bring the French

to reason by keeping them without rhubarb, and exhibit to mankind the awful spectacle of a nation deprived of neutral salts. This is not the dream of a wild apothecary indulging in his own opium; this is not the distempered fancy of a pounder of drugs, delirious from smallness of profits; but it is the sober, deliberate, and systematic scheme of a man to whom the public safety is entrusted, and whose appointment is considered by many as a masterpiece of political sagacity. What a sublime thought, that no purge can now be taken between the Weser and the Garonne; that the bustling pestle is still, the canorous mortar mute, and the bowels of mankind locked up for fourteen degrees of latitude! When, I should be curious to know, were all the powers of crudity and flatulence fully explained to his majesty's ministers? At what period was this great plan of conquest and con- stipation fully developed? On whose mind was the idea of destroying the pride and the plasters of France first engendered? Without castor oil they might, for some months, to be sure, have carried on a lingering war; but can they do without bark? Will the people live under a government where antimonial powders cannot be procured? Will they bear the loss of mercury? "There's the rub." Depend upon it, the absence of the materia medica will soon bring them to their senses, and the cry of *Bourbon and bolus* burst forth from the Baltic to the Mediterranean.

SYDNEY SMITH (1771-1845)
*Selections from the writings of
the Rev. Sydney Smith*

TO A BOY

Do not waste your time
   But serve some noble end;
The basketmaker breaks
   The spray that will not bend.

In youth open your mind,
   And let all learning in;
Words the head does not shape
   Are worthless, out and in.

Words wit has not salted,
   No nearer the heart than the lip
Are nothing more than wind,
   A puppy's insolent yelp.

So let all learning in;
   Be pure in mind and breast,
For the voice that speaks to the heart
   Pleases the Master best.

ANONYMOUS (16th cent.)
translated from the Irish by
FRANK O'CONNOR

PRAYER AT DAWN

I was taught prayer as a child, to bend the knee
And beat the breast, asking his peace of Christ,
To wake with delight at the first sweet call of the bird
In praise of the Lord God punished and crucified.

Woe for this sleep on me now and my bed not readied
    at dawn,
And I no longer in haste to praise the might of the King,
Beating my breast and bowing my knees with grief
When the first wind wakes the first bird to sing.

When the cock starts suddenly up with a cry,
And from deep sands the fish rise to the waters' height,
And buried sparks ascend in the morning fire—
Woe, woe for this slumber of yours, you senseless soul!

Ah, senseless soul!   Great is the folly of sleep
When sparks rise from the hoarded flame at dawn,
And boughs are stirred and leaves are stirred in the wind,
And even the birds are singing the Lord God's praise.
                         DIARMUID O'SHEA (18th cent.)

EPILOGUE

Joy Be With Us

Joy be with us, and honour close the tale;
Now do we dip the prow, and shake the sail,
And take the wind, and bid adieu to rest.

With glad endeavour we begin the quest
That destiny commands, though where we go,
Or guided by what star, no man doth know.

Uncharted is our course, our hearts untried,
And we may weary ere we take the tide,
Or make fair haven from the moaning sea.

Be ye propitious, winds of destiny,
On us at first blow not too boisterous bold;
All Ireland hath is packed into this hold,
Her hope flies at the peak.   Now it is dawn,
And we away.   Be with us Mananaun.

JAMES STEPHENS (1881-1950)
Collected Poems

PRINCIPAL DATES IN
IRISH HISTORY

432 St. Patrick's mission to Ireland.
563 Colm Cille's Mission to Iona.
590 Columbanus' Mission to Burgundy.
597 Death of Colm Cille, Augustine arrives in England.
664 Synod of Whitby.
795 Beginning of the Danish raids.
968 Brian defeats Danes at Sulcoit.
1014 Battle of Clontarf and death of Brian.
1166 Flight of Dermot MacMurrough.
1170 Strongbow lands.
1171 Henry II lands.
1172 The Pope "grants" Ireland to Henry II.
1175 Death of Rory O'Connor, last native king.
1315 Invasion of Edward Bruce.
1367 Statutes of Kilkenny.
1394 Richard II visits Ireland.
1399 Second visit of Richard II.
1534 Rebellion of Silken Thomas.
1536 First Reformation parliament.
1537 Silken Thomas executed.
1548 Sean the Proud becomes O'Neill.
1556 Plantation of Leix and Offaly.
1567 Sean the Proud assassinated.
1569 First Desmond revolt.
1579 Second Desmond revolt.
1586 Plantation of Munster.
1587 Kidnapping of Red Hugh O'Donnell.
1592 Trinity College, Dublin, founded.
1598 Victory of O'Neill and O'Donnell at the Yellow Ford.
1601 Defeat of O'Neill and O'Donnell at Kinsale.
1603 O'Neill surrenders.
1607 O'Neill and O'Donnell leave Ireland.
1608 Plantation of Ulster.
1613 Chichester's parliament.
1632 Strafford becomes viceroy.
1641 Irish rebellion begins.
1642 Owen Roe O'Neill arrives. Catholic Confederacy.
1645 Papal Nuncio, Rinuccini, arrives.
1646 O'Neill wins battle of Benburb.
1649 O'Neill dies. Cromwell arrives. Massacres at Drogheda and
      Wexford.

1660 Restoration of Charles II.
1685 Accession of James II.
1687 Tyrconnell Lord Lieutenant.
1689 Siege of Derry.
1690 Battle of the Boyne.
1691 Battle of Aughrim. Treaty of Limerick signed—
1692 And broken. Catholics excluded from office.
1695 Beginning of penal laws against Catholics.
1724 Swift's *Drapier's Letters.*
1729 Swift's *A Modest Proposal.*
1745 Death of Swift.
1778 Irish Volunteers formed.
1782 Irish parliamentary independence proclaimed—
1783 And recognised by England.
1791 Foundation of the United Irishmen.
1796 Tone's attempted invasion.
1798 The French land.
1800 Act of Union with England.
1803 Emmett's rebellion.
1828 O'Connell wins the Clare Election—
1829 And forces Catholic Emancipation.
1842 "The Nation" founded.
1845 Famine.
1848 Smith O'Brien's rebellion.
1867 The Fenian rising.
1877 Parnell assumes leadership.
1879 Davitt founds the Land League.
1881 Gladstone's Land Act.
1886 Gladstone's First Home Rule Bill.
1890 Parnell divorce case. Deposed from leadership.
1891 Death of Parnell.
1892 Gladstone's Second Home Rule Bill defeated.
1893 Hyde founds the Gaelic League.
1899 Arthur Griffith founds The United Irishman.
1902 Yeats founds the National Theatre Society.
1905 Arthur Griffith founds the "Sinn Féin" Party.
1907 The "Playboy" riots.
1912 Third Home Rule Bill.
1916 Easter Week rebellion. Irish Republic proclaimed.
1919 Dail Eireann founded.
1921 Treaty between Great Britain and Ireland.
1922 Treaty ratified. Civil War. *Ulysses* published.
1924 O'Casey's *Juno and the Paycock* performed.
1927 Kevin O'Higgins assassinated.
1939 Death of Yeats.
1949 Ireland declared an independent republic.

INDEX OF AUTHORS, SOURCES, FIRST LINES

"A.E." (GEORGE RUSSELL), 327
Adieu to Belashanny, where I was bred and born, 55
ALLINGHAM, WILLIAM, 55, 139, 347
Aran Islands, The, 287
ARENSBERG, CONRAD, 259, 344
ARNOLD, MATTHEW, 275
At the mid hour of night, when stars are weeping, 319
Autobiography, (Trollope), 177, 178

Ballinderry, 337
BARRINGTON, SIR JONAH, 139, 183, 262, 278
BAX, SIR ARNOLD, ("Dermot O'Byrne"), 123
BEDE, THE VENERABLE, 354, 355, 362
Bell, The, 168, 172
Bells are booming down the bohreens, 27
Bells of Shandon, The, 29
BERKELEY, GEORGE, BISHOP, 95
BETJEMAN, JOHN, 27
Bible in Ireland, The, 38, 129, 136
Big Fellow, The, 125
BLUNT, WILFRID SCAWEN, 118, 161
BORROW, GEORGE, 47, 186
Boswell's Life of Johnson, 176
BOYD, THOMAS, 350
Boyne Water, The, 89

Call My Brother Back, 35
CALLANAN, J. J. 37, 313
Canon of Aughrim, The, 161
CARLYLE, THOMAS, 269, 271

Cast a cold eye, 221
Castle Rackrent, 144, 265
Charwoman's Daughter, The, 196, 201
CLARKE, J. I. C., 65
Clear as air, the western waters, 51
Cockles and Mussels, 167
COLUM, PADRAIC, 131, 137, 335
COLUM, PADRAIC (translator), 308, 316
Come all ye lads and lasses, 335
COPPARD, A. E., 237
County of Mayo, The, 52
County Mayo, 54
CROSS, ERIC, 233, 235
CURRAN, JOHN PHILPOT, 318

Dark Rosaleen, 82
Dead at Clonmacnoise, The, 50
Dear Dark Head, 309
DE LA TOCNAYE, LE CHEVALIER, 128
Deserted Village, The, 159
Do not waste your time, 374
Dramatis Personae, 210, 221
Drapier's Fourth Letter, The, 94, 232
Dreaming of the Bones, The, 81
Drover, A, 137
Dublin Ballad: 1916, A, 123
Dublin Days, 222

Each of us pursues his trade, 298
Easter 1916, 121
EDGEWORTH, MARIA, 144, 193, 265
EMMET, ROBERT, 110

English Humorists, 182
Englishman in Ireland, The, 118
Epitaphs, 221
Examination of Certain Abuses, An, 165
Experiences of an Irish R. M., 148, 150

Fairies, The, 347
Farewell, Patrick Sarsfield, wherever you may roam, 87
FERGUSON, SIR SAMUEL (translator), 309
Fishmonger's Fiddle, 237
FLOWER, ROBIN, 43
Four ducks on a pond, 139
FOX, GEORGE, (translator), 52

Gain without gladness, 299
GALLEGHER, PATRICK, 132, 134
Gaol Gate, The, 252
Gap of Brightness, The, 332
GIBBINGS, ROBERT, 220
GOGARTY, O. ST. JOHN, 329
Going Into Exile, 284
GOLDSMITH, OLIVER, 159, 180
Gougane Barra, 37
Grant me, sweet Christ, the grace to find, 363
Grave of Rury, The, 51
GREGORY, LADY, 212, 215, 252

Hail and Farewell, 199
HALL, MR. AND MRS. S. C., 40
Have I a wife? Bedam I have! 222
HAYES, RICHARD, 108
HEAD, RICHARD, 164
HEALY, MAURICE, 192, 249, 272, 273
Here's pretty conduct, Hugh O'Rourke! 242
HIGGINS, F. R., 332
History of Ireland (Keating), 74, 76, 361

Honoured I lived e'erwhile with honoured men, 118
How good to hear your voice again, 366
How my thoughts betray me! 365
Hugh Maguire, 85
Humorous Tales, 97
HYDE, DOUGLAS, (translator), 311, 312

I am of Ireland, 25
I am Raftery the poet, 310
I am sitting here, 316
I dreamt last night of you, John-John, 329
I have met them at close of day, 121
I know where I'm going, 337
I the old woman of Beare, 300
I shall not call for help until they coffin me, 91
I Shall Not Die For Thee, 308
I was taught prayer as a child, 374
I went out to the hazel wood, 324
I will arise and go now, 53
I would I were on yonder hill, 340
If only the brown leaf were gold, 354
If sadly thinking, with spirits sinking, 318
In a quiet water'd land, a land of roses, 50
In Dublin's fair city, 167
In the County Tyrone, in the town of Dungannon, 230
In Wicklow and West Kerry, 63, 188
Inishfallen, Fare Thee Well, 61, 214, 216, 292
Inniskeen Road: July Evening, 59
Ireland: Its Scenery, Character, etc., 40
Irish Countryman, The, 259, 344
Irish Dancer, The, 25

Irish Journey, An, 31, 33, 34
Irish Law Reports, 1907, 154
Irish Miles, 42, 59
Irish Sketch Book, 176
Irish Writing, 223
It is my sorrow that this day's troubles, 107
It was not the famine killed them, 161
It would never be morning, always evening, 334

John-John, 329
Johnny, I Hardly Knew Ye, 338
JOHNSON, SAMUEL, 176
Journal (Wolfe Tone), 100
Journals, The, (Lady Gregory), 212, 215
Joy Be With Us, 376
Joy be with us, and honour close the tale, 376
JOYCE, JAMES, 115
July the First, of a morning clear 89

KAVANAGH, PATRICK, 59, 334
KEATING, GEOFFREY, 74, 76, 361
KENNY, EDWARD, 203, 205, 281
Kilcash, 45
Kincora, 79
KIPLING, RUDYARD, 97

Lake Isle of Innisfree, The, 53
Lament for Yellow-Haired Donogh, The, 317
Land Leaguers, The, 155, 192
Last Invasion of Ireland, The, 108
Last Lines, 91
Last Lines—1916, 331
LAVELLE, THOMAS, 52
Lavengro, 47, 186
Leinster, Munster and Connacht, 216
Let Us Be Merry Before We Go, 318
Letter to Thomas Moore, 186

Letters to Florence Farr, 257, 258
Liadain, 299
Life has conquered, 91
Life of Charles Stewart Parnell, The, 114
Love like heat and cold, 241
Lovely is the Lee, 220

MAC LIAG, 79
MACDONAGH, THOMAS, 329
MACDONAGH, THOMAS, (translator), 171
MACELGUN, CATHAL BUIDHE, 171
McLAVERTY, MICHAEL, 35
MAHONY, FRANCIS SYLVESTER ("Father Prout"), 29
Maid of The Sweet Brown Knowe, The, 335
MANGAN, J. C., 320, 322
MANGAN, J. C. (translator), 79, 82
Memory of Brother Michael, 334
MITCHEL, JOHN, 113
Modest Proposal, A, 92
MOORE, GEORGE, 199
MOORE, THOMAS, 111, 112, 319
MURPHY, SEUMAS, 295
Music in London, 289
My father and my mother died, 310
My Grief on the Sea, 311
My sorrow that I am not by the little dun, 53
My young love said to me, 335

Nameless One, The, 320
NICHOLSON, ASENATH, 38, 129, 136
NIC SHIUBHLAIGH, MAIRE, 203, 205, 281
Non Dolet, 329
Now with the springtime the days will grow longer, 54

O man that for Fergus of the

feasts dost kindle fire, 305

O my dark Rosaleen, 82

O Paddy dear, and did ye hear, 96

O woman, shapely as the swan, 308

O write it up above your hearth, 123

O'BRIEN, FLANN (Brian O'Nolan), 168, 172

O'BRIEN, R. BARRY, 114

O'BRIEN OF KILFENORA, LORD, 154

O'BYRNE, DERMOT, (Sir Arnold Bax), 123

O'CASEY, SEAN, 61, 214, 216, 292

O'CONNOR, FRANK, 42, 59, 125, 216

O'CONNOR, FRANK (translator), 44, 45, 54, 67, 69, 71, 74, 85, 87, 91, 107, 241, 242, 245, 246, 250, 252, 257, 276, 277, 298, 299, 300, 304, 307, 310, 317, 342, 352, 354, 355, 361, 363, 365, 366, 374

O'FAOLAIN, SEAN, 31, 33, 34

O'FLAHERTY, LIAM, 284

O'GRADY, STANDISH HAYES (translator), 305

Oh many a day have I made good ale in the glen, 313

Oh! the French are on the sea, 99

Oh, the rain, the weary, dreary rain, 322

Oh, to have a little house! 131

Oh, where, Kincora! is Brian the great? 79

O'HUSSEY, EOCHY, 85

Old Ireland, 189

Old Munster Circuit, The, 192, 249, 272, 273

Old Woman of Beare, The, 300

Old Woman of the Roads, An, 131

On Behalf of Some Irishmen Not Followers of Tradition, 327

O'NOLAN, BRIAN ("Flann O'Brien"), 168, 172

On the deck of Patrick Lynch's boat I sit in woeful plight, 52

Once more the storm is howling, 325

O'RAHILLY, EGAN, 91

Orphan, The, 310

O'SHEA, DIARMUID, 374

O'SULLIVAN, SEUMAS, 53

Our friends go with us as we go, 329

Outlaw of Loch Lene, The, 313

Paddy the Cope, 132, 134

Padraic O'Conaire, Gaelic Story-teller, 332

Parnell, 118

Patrick Sarsfield, 87

Patrick, you chatter too loud, 352

Pearl of the White Breast, 314

PEARSE, PADRAIC, 331

Personal Sketches, 139, 183, 262, 278

PETRIE, GEORGE, (translator), 314

Playboy of the Western World, The, 246

Ploughman and Other Poems, 59

Poor Girl's Meditation, The, 316

Portrait Of The Artist As A Young Man, 115

Prayer at Dawn, 374

Prayer for My Daughter, A, 325

Prelude, 62

Priest, The, 363

Princess, The, 41

PROUT, FATHER, 29

Put your head, darling, darling, darling, 309

RAFTERY ANTHONY, 54, 310

"Read out the names!" and Burke sat back, 65

Reminiscences of My Irish Journey,

269, 271
Righteous Anger, 222
Ringleted youth of my love, 312
RINUCINNI, 176
Roll forth, my song, like the rushing river, 320
ROLLESTON, T. W., 50, 51
ROSS, MARTIN, 148, 150
RUSSELL, GEORGE, ("A.E."), 327

Scholar and His Cat, The, 298
Scholars, regrettably, must yell, 276
Selections from the Writings of the Rev. Sydney Smith, 368, 371
SELLAR, A. M. (translator), 354, 355, 362
Shan Van Vocht, The, 99
SHAW, G. B., 257, 289
She Is Far From The Land, 112
She is far from the land where her young hero sleeps, 112
She Is My Dear, 307
She Moved Through The Fair, 335
Shule Aroon, 340
Siege of Howth, The, 69
Since to-night the wind is high, 74
Slievenamon, 107
SMITH, SYDNEY, 186, 368, 371
SOMERVILLE, E. Œ., 148, 150
Song of Wandering Aengus, The, 324
Soul For Sale, A, 334
Splendid Years, The, 203, 205, 281
Starling Lake, The, 53
STEPHENS, JAMES, 196, 201, 206, 222, 223, 376
Still south I went and west, 62
Stolen Child, The, 349
Stone Mad, 295
STRONG, L. A. G., 222
Student, The, 277
Study of Celtic Literature, The, 275

SULLIVAN, A. M., 189
Sunday in Ireland, 27
Sweet Auburn! loveliest village of the plain, 159
Sweetness of Earth, The, 304
SWIFT, JONATHAN, 92, 94, 165, 221, 232
SYNGE, J. M., 62, 63, 188, 246, 287

Tailor and Ansty, The, 233, 235
Tell him the thing is a lie! 241
TENNYSON, ALFRED LORD, 41
THACKERAY, WILLIAM MAKE-PEACE, 176, 182
The beauty of the world hath made me sad, 331
The bicycles go by in twos and threes, 59
The dark cliff towered up to the stars that flickered, 43
The lanky hank of a she in the inn over there, 222
The night before Larry was stretched, 228
The rest I pass, one sentence I unsay, 118
The splendour falls on castle walls, 41
The student's life is pleasant, 277
The yellow bittern that never broke out, 171
There is a green island in lone Gougane Barra, 37
There's a colleen fair as May, 314
They call us aliens, we are told, 327
They've paid the last respects in sad tobacco, 332
'Tis pretty to be in Ballinderry, 337
To A Boy, 374
To go to Rome, 355
To Meath of the pastures, 137
To The Leanan Sidhe, 350
TONE, THEOBOLD WOLFE, 100

Too cold this night for Hugh Maguire, 85
Tour in Connemara, 193
Tour in Ireland, 264
TROLLOPE, ANTHONY, 155, 177, 178, 192
Twenty Golden Years Ago, 322

Under Ben Bulben, 221
Up the airy mountain, 347

Voyage of Maelduin, 342

Wearing of the Green, The, 96
Western Island, The, 43
What better fortune can we find, 246
What shall we do for timber? 45

When he who adores thee has left but the name, 111
When once I rose at morning, 44
Where dips the rocky highland, 349
Where is thy lovely perilous abode? 350
While going the road to sweet Athy, 338
Winding Banks of Erne, The, 55
With deep affection, 29

Ye have seen a marvel in this town, 317
YEATS, W. B., 53, 81, 118, 121, 210, 221, 258, 324, 325, 349
Yellow Bittern, The, 171
YOUNG, ARTHUR, 264
Your voice to me is sweeter, 304